Hit My Smoke!

Forward Air Controllers in Southeast Asia

Hit My Smoke!

Forward Air Controllers in Southeast Asia

by
Jan Churchill

Sunflower University Press®

1531 Yuma • P. O. Box 1009 • Manhattan, Kansas 66505-1009 USA

Other Books by Jan Churchill

On Wings to War

The New Labrador Retriever

COVER: Painting by Keith Ferris. (From author's collection).

The Miracle at Kham Duc, an original painting by Keith Ferris, depicts the evacuation of the Kham Duc Special Forces Camp on 11 May 1968, in which FACs played a key role. Without the coordinated work of the FACs and fighters, the evacuation would not have been successful. The final three men are shown being rescued by a C-123 piloted by Joe Jackson who received the Medal of Honor when he landed during heavy fire. Providentially, the rocket shot at the front of the airplane did not explode.

Keith Ferris is one of aviation's most honored artists. He is a major contributor to the Air Force Art Program. Ferris has flown in almost every aircraft in the Air Force inventory. His 25 x 75 foot mural, *Fortresses Under Fire*, covers the entire back wall of the World War II Gallery of the National Air and Space Museum in Washington, D.C. His major work, *Force for Freedom*, depicting 75 aircraft to celebrate the 50th anniversary of the Air Force, was featured on the April 16, 1997, issue of *Aviation Week and Space Technology*. The O-1 and O-2 are in the lower right-hand corner; the F-100 is centered under the B-2A. In addition to his art, Ferris is a lecturer, historian, model builder, and inventor.

ISBN 0-89745-215-1 pbk
ISBN 0-89745-216-X hdbk

Edited by Sonie Liebler
Layout by Lori L. Daniel

*Dedicated to Those Who
Did Not Come Back*

Contents

Foreword

FORWARD AIR CONTROLLERS *were developed by both the Allies and the Germans in World War II to provide accurate, low-level spotting of the enemy, which fighter-bombers and others could not provide. Even in earlier wars, men were aloft for aerial observation. The aerial observer had the ability to see over the hill, to note accurately, and to mark enemy positions. Some could communicate with their counterpart on the ground. Flying light aircraft, they could land in almost any field or on roads to report enemy positions verbally.*

In the Korean conflict, the FAC's airborne role became better defined as he controlled the fighters launching from far-away bases. Instead of the very light aircraft used in World War II, FACs in Korea flew the rugged North American AT-6 Texan.

In the Vietnam War of 1963-1973, the two-seat Cessna O-1 Bird Dog was the first aircraft available for FACing.

This was followed by the twin-engine Cessna O-2, a sort of interim aircraft while the North American Rockwell OV-10A Bronco was being developed. When the enemy started to use better antiaircraft weapons, these FAC aircraft flying low and slow were at great risk.

The Fast FAC, using jet aircraft, then played an important role. No matter what aircraft the FAC flew, what might have seemed like an undesirable job turned out to be one of great responsibility. The slow FACs had a key role in South Vietnam. No pilot could make a single airstrike without the FAC who rolled in to select and mark targets with no gunsight. The FAC ran the air war and had a great sense of satisfaction when finding a cleverly camouflaged target.

The guys in Laos, however, were FACing a war that wasn't happening. The *Ravens* were an extraordinary group, usually too warrior-like and aggressive for the South Vietnam scene. Their work took courage, day in and day out, with a high casualty list for their dangerous missions.

The FACs in South Vietnam and Laos did their job in spite of the politics of the war, and they were loyal to each other. This book helps you to understand the lengths to which they would go, with no regard for their own safety, to help their comrades on the ground. Supported by their ground crews, the FACs were especially brave and cool pilots, who flew constantly at low levels, and who with aplomb searched out the enemy, called up strike forces and marked the targets for them with rockets or flares, and then guided them in and out. They also searched for downed fliers and helped direct their rescue.

There are not enough medals to capture the true dedication, sacrifice, and bravery of these selfless fighters. According to veteran Harry Riley,

Southeast Asia. From Lieutenant Colonel John J. Lane, Jr., *Command and Control Communication Structures in Southeast Asia* (Maxwell AFB, AL: Air War College, Air University, 1981), p. 38.

> I can testify, because had it not been for a few specific FACs at the Battle of Bu Prang, Vietnam, in 1969, risking their lives for us "grunts" in the foxhole, it's chilling to think what may have been in store for me. This is not to say there was not other support . . . there was . . . but our FACs are a breed, a motivator, a force multiplier without measure. I wish I could explain the bond that developed in my heart for these professionals, but I can't. Only a combat veteran can fully understand the heartfelt gratitude one warfighter has for another . . . no greater love has he.

Jan Churchill has paid a fine, long-overdue tribute to these valiant men and thus deserves our thanks.

Colonel George E. "Bud" Day
Fast FAC and Medal of Honor Recipient, Vietnam

Acknowledgments

Q UITE A FEW PEOPLE have made contributions to this book. Special thanks to those who reviewed the manuscript, wholly or in part: Colonel Darrel Whitcomb (USAF), Lieutenant Colonel Mark Berent (USAF, Ret.), Colonel Carl D. Goembel, Sergeant James J. Stanford (USAF, Ret.), and Major Doug Call (USAF, Ret.).

To those who provided pictures, manuals, and interviews, I am very grateful: Robert H. Jacobson, James F. McMurray, Jim Oliver, James W. Swanson, Ben Owen, Stuart E. Kane, Roy Dalton, James L. Champlin, Richard L. Griffin, Sid Johnson, Allen R. Groth, Jay Mengel, Jack C. Cummings, Paul Burrows, Robert C. Mikesh, Robert Monroe, John Heimburger, George R. Partridge, Tom Yarborough, Mary Ann Harrison, Kent W. Owen, Pete Conforti, Anthony P. Ford, Garry G. Cooper, Duane Aasted, John Rogers, Ron Schuh, Richard A. Slowik, Richard Gary Mucho, Gary Pavlu, David L. Helms,

Jim McDevitt, Robert C. Miller, Jr., Doug Jones, Douglas B. Aitken, Bob Berry, Michael E. Jackson, Fred W. Mc-
Neil, Tom Milligan, Joe Hillner, Flick Guerrina, Richard C. Lawrence, Byron R. Tetrick, Harold Icke, Grove Nor-
wood, Ralph D. Kunce, Frank M. Kricker, Ron O. Rinehart, Craig William Duehring, H. Ownby, Jim Stanford,
Karl Polifka, William H. Rees, Marvin Curtis Patton, David L. Shields, Dale C. Kingsbury, Joseph Potter, Fred R.
Wilkie, Gerald A. White, Robert W. Viegel, and Forward Air Controllers and the members of the CASBAR, an in-
ternet source for combat aviators of all stripe, rank, and nationality.

The author is indebted to Professor Robin Higham and Carol A. Williams, of Sunflower University Press, for
their interest in this manuscript. Thanks also to the many FACs whom I have met at air shows who have shared
their Vietnam flying experiences with me.

——————— ⌇⌇ ———————

Preface

Many Forward Air Controllers (FACs) were interviewed as I worked on this book. We discussed their training, what they flew, where they lived, their most interesting missions, and their impressions of the FAC assignment. Each man told me what happened during his tour. Their experiences varied, depending on the area where they were based, the year, the aircraft they were flying, and the duties they were asked to perform. To a man, all the pilots I interviewed declared it was the best assignment in their military career.

Facing the responsibility of command at a very young age, some FACs flew low and slow in unarmed aircraft in dangerous terrain and horrible weather with enemy guns trained on them, while others were "Fast" FACs in jet aircraft, facing bigger guns. They were all dedicated to flying their aircraft to accomplish a mission. They were supported by equally dedicated maintenance and ground crews.

An OV-10A, 1967.

Jack Cummings Collection

It is impossible to tell every FAC's story, and indeed, this is not a complete history of FACing, but it is a genuine attempt to tell the reader what it was like to be a Forward Air Controller. This book is intended as a sincere tribute to these men, and an epitaph to those who were killed in action. The FACs performed above and beyond the call of duty in their pivotal role in the Vietnam War.

As you read, think of the monstrous thunderstorms, the monsoon rains, the poor visibility due to smoke, thick haze, and low clouds, the thick jungle canopy, and the green mountains and deep valleys. Remember the oppressive heat, a searing sun, sweat-drenched men, dark gray clouds, and low ceilings below which the pilots had to work.

The interviews quoted in this book are available in their entirety from Sunflower University Press in the MA/AH Publishing Series.

Introduction

FACS — The Forward Air Controller

*T*HE FORWARD AIR CONTROLLER, *better known as the FAC, came into his own during the air war in Southeast Asia (SEA) in the 1960s and 1970s. The concept of aerial control was not new. In Vietnam, the FACs were the key to the employment of tactical air power, and a vital and indispensable part of the tactical air war, serving as the flying link between forces on the ground and strike aircraft. They were also essential for the interdiction campaign in Laos and Cambodia. Lieutenant Kent W. Owen explained, "The FAC is the link between the ground and air forces and, in reality, is the hub around which the delivery of all in-country ordnance is dependent."*

In World War II (1941-1945), Korea (1950-1953), and Vietnam (1963-1973), the FAC, a USAAF/USAF pilot, had started out in the mud attached to U.S. Army units with the GIs, but ended up performing the mission in aircraft. It was not a job that could be done well from ground vantage points in most instances. However, there were times when a FAC was shot down and then continued to work airstrikes from wherever he fell. The World War II FACs, limited in number, were called *Horsefly*. The Korean War FACs were called *Mosquito*. Vietnam, with an abundance of FACs, had a variety of call signs.

In Vietnam, the FAC's many duties included control of close air support for troops and Special Forces teams, Search and Rescue (SAR), Visual Reconnaissance (VR), control of strike aircraft against interdiction targets, escort and cover missions for convoys, clandestine operations, instructing Vietnamese Air Force (VNAF) pilots on FAC procedures, and advising ground commanders on close air support and the Army of the Republic of Vietnam (ARVN) and VNAF on overall Forward Air Control matters. The FAC's secondary role as an advisor to ground commanders gave a young officer his first real chance to fill a staff position. Lieutenant Owen notes, "He is part of the actual planning team for the ground operations. Without his advice, the commander cannot know the availability or capabilities of the Air Force to support a given position."

FACs also adjusted Army and Navy artillery fire, did Bomb Damage Assessment (BDA), directed clearing operations for landing zones (LZ) , and supported day and night interdiction in Laos and Cambodia. In South Vietnam, the FACs ran the air war from their small, unarmed Cessna-built O-1 Bird Dogs and O-2As, and later the better-equipped North American Rockwell OV-10 Broncos. FACing was also done from larger aircraft such as the Lockheed C-130 Hercules, Fairchild C-123 Provider, Fairchild C-119 Flying Boxcar, and Douglas C-47 Skytrain (Gooney Bird), as well as from jets flown by Fast FACs.

While the uniformed services had their FACs in Vietnam, the Central Intelligence Agency had the use of the civilian-clad, but actually USAF, FACs — *Ravens* — to fight the secret war in Laos.

What began in 1961 as a small U.S. assistance program to train the South Vietnamese to protect themselves grew into a massive military effort by all the U.S. military services, as well as those of other countries. The conflict took place in several major areas: North Vietnam, South Vietnam, the northern part of Laos known as the Plain of Jars (PDJ), and the southern Laotian panhandle. The Plain of Jars was a critical military objective, and gets its name from huge stone jars, perhaps used as funeral urns centuries ago, on this 40-mile-wide, 500-square-mile plateau. Later, the action spread into Cambodia and lasted until 1975.

Because of the nature of the terrain of the battle, the Forward Air Controller became a necessity in Southeast Asia.

Chapter 1

The Origins of Forward Air Control

O N A HOT, sunny day in 1794 in Belgium, the first airborne military observer directed strikes for ground commanders. A French officer, fighting in the Battle of Fleurus, spent ten hours aloft in a balloon observing Austrian and Dutch troop movements. He dropped instructions to the ground commanders in small ballasted bags, helping the French win the battle and launching the world's first air force, the Aerostatic Corps.

During the years 1861-1863 of the American Civil War, the Balloon Corps of the Army of the Potomac sent aerial observers aloft to spy on enemy troops and direct artillery fire. In 1898, aerial observers were also airborne in balloons to direct artillery fire in the Spanish-American War.

Military tacticians in World War I were cognizant of the advantages of using airborne observers. Both sides employed aircraft for reconnaissance, aerial bombing, and artillery observation.

U.S. Marine Corps air units were the first to organize close air support of ground forces in the so-called small wars in Haiti, Santo Domingo, and Nicaragua during the 1920s and early 1930s. The guerrilla warfare encountered in Central America necessitated small patrol columns that had to penetrate far into rough, heavily forested mountains and the remote jungles of the back country. Air liaison was the only way for the commanders to maintain contact with these patrols.

One of the first U.S. uses of Forward Air Control techniques came in Nicaragua on 27 October 1927 when a Marine patrol used cloth ground panels to signal the direction and range to the opposing enemy forces for its fighter-bombers. The Marines also employed observation planes (Curtiss F8C Falcons and Vought O2U Corsairs) equipped with Navy radio spotting sets, powered by a wind-driven generator, and with a range of about 50 miles.

For communications, aircraft zoomed in to pick up messages hung on a line stretched between two poles. Bombing and strafing, as a result of these messages, often saved the patrols.

In December 1940, the U.S. War Department directed the Air Corps to conduct tests aimed at developing techniques and methods for directing and controlling combat aviation during combined air-ground operations. Tests were carried out in Louisiana and North Carolina. When the U.S. Army Air Forces (USAAF) was established on 20 June 1941, it published a regulation establishing Air-Ground Cooperation Parties (AGCP, later Air-Ground Control Party). USAAF personnel were assigned to Army, corps, and division headquarters to advise ground commanders on tactical air employment. They were tasked to give clearance for striking preplanned targets, directing artillery fire, controlling attacks against enemy forces extremely close to friendly troops, and assessing bomb damage.

During World War II, Forward Air Control played an important part in the brutal Aleutian campaign of 1942-1943 — the Thousand Mile War. On 16 May 1943, during the invasion of the Attu Islands, General Eugene M. Landrum ordered Colonel William O. Eareckson, of the U.S. Army Air Corps (USAAC), to coordinate airstrikes with ground operations. Eareckson commandeered a Navy Vought Kingfisher, a two-place single-engine observation seaplane from the seaplane tender *Casco*. He flew this maneuverable aircraft beneath low cloud decks and through mountainous terrain in search of enemy targets, thus pioneering a technique that would in the future be known as "Forward Air Controller." When he found a target, he would spiral up through the clouds, rendezvous with the strike aircraft, and lead them to the target. On some missions, Eareckson would pick out targets and relay their positions to the bombers circling above.

The mission was dangerous because there were long periods of intense ground fire from the Japanese. And because the Kingfisher was vulnerable to enemy fire, Eareckson carried a "bullet-hole kit" of rubber plugs and patching material in his cockpit. When necessary, he would beach his aircraft to repair battle damage, and then take off to continue his mission.

During the assault against the enemy at Bougainville, in the Pacific, in November 1943, the first formally trained Marine Forward Air Controllers guided the Navy aircraft that were attacking the Japanese strongholds. They were so accurate that the ordnance was dropped within 75 yards of friendly positions.

In the European theater, campaigns lasted for months and covered huge areas, involving large armies and air forces. A somewhat different technique of air support evolved. Originally, the Forward Air Controller was a radio-equipped grounded pilot who traveled up front with the foot soldiers. This provided a vital communications link with supporting aircraft. One Forward Air Controller was assigned to each Tactical Air Cooperation Party — later Tactical Air Control Party (TACP) — and brigade, and at a battalion, an additional controller — the Air Liaison Officer (ALO) — was added. The control system permitted the battalion commander to request emergency air support, bringing aircraft over the target area in a matter of minutes. To direct these aircraft, the Forward Air Controller had to be located where he could see the friendly frontlines, the attacking aircraft, and the target. This took skill because the close air support was executed near the frontlines.

Experienced U.S. fighter-bomber pilots — often squadron leaders nicknamed "Rover Joes" during World War II — directed aerial control between 1939 and 1945. In the air, they picked out targets and directed the bombers to them. Their British counterparts were "Rover David" and "Rover Patty." The Rover Joes were a great success as they put bombs on targets within 1,000 yards of the Allied troops.

Initially in World War II, the Army had been reluctant to use air power in case it would hit its own

During World War II, a "Rover Joe" L-5 Sentinel guides weary 324th Fighter Group P-40L Warhawks to a mountain target in Italy on 1 December 1944. The Mediterranean Allied Air Force used former fighter pilots as ground observers with Rover Joes to locate targets as fighters circled overhead, then radioed their position so that the fighter-bombers could take them out. Rover Joes coordinated fighter-bomber and infantry action in mountain approaches.   USAF photo, Jeff Ethell Collection

troops; and USAAF pilots were also concerned about strikes on friendly troops. Eventually, however, the fighters led the bombers in, directed by air support parties on the ground. In the Pacific, the Army Air Forces Air Support Parties worked with the Navy to direct their planes and guns. Thus ground air support parties became a key element of Army doctrine — precursors to the Forward Air Controller.

In addition, by 1943, the new commander of the Allied Northwest African Air Force, British Air Marshal Arthur "Maori" Coningham, was practicing this close union between air and ground forces. Because of limited air resources, control had to be centralized at division and headquarters and missions assigned by a commander who was fully conversant with their capabilities. In contrast, later on in Vietnam, young lieutenants — not just commanders — would have the same authority.

During OPERATION SUPERCHARGE II, the Western Desert Air Force solved the difficulties in coordinating air with ground action by using colored smoke as well as grenades, flares, or flashing lamps for marking the area to be attacked. The prevailing

methods of tactical bombing support required that the troops remain at least a mile away from the target rather than marking the forward line by smoke or panels, or using radio communications directly to the airplanes.

At the Battle of El Hamma in North Africa, in March 1943, massive air support was used to help the British Eighth Army push across the Mareth Line. During the heaviest part of the battle, an air controller, located in a forward tank, communicated with the aircraft, guiding them to targets in his view. He directed 412 aircraft sorties against German defensive positions. This new control method worked so well that a forward controller was again employed in the Salerno operations of the Fifth U.S. Army in May 1943. The potential of Forward Air Control was becoming apparent.

Later in 1943, the Twelfth Air Force Tactical Air Command, operating from North Africa, prepared to invade Sicily and Italy. Colonel Earl T. Reichert (U.S. Army, now Ret.), then a captain, and Bill Davidson, assigned to the Combat Operations Section of the Tactical Air Command (TAC), wrote plans for the invasion using lessons learned in North Africa that included air control. Early in 1943, as the Sicilian campaign was underway, the frontline troops would run into a target — a nest of enemy opposition of troops, tanks, or a mixture of both. Reichert recalled the events:

WE HAD AIR SUPERIORITY after we got past Rome. So, now we could devote attention to the support of General [Mark] Clark's army. The targets were there, but they disappeared by the time the fighter-bombers arrived. It took too much time for the information to get back to Army headquarters, and then to the Army Air Force.

—————— ✠ ——————

And thus the AAF started using a squadron of 12 aircraft — 4 loaded with napalm, 4 with 1,000 pounders, and 4 with 500 pounders. The 12th Tactical Air Command used pre-fragged (pre-determined) targets for their fighter-bombers, but it was the squadron leader who decided what to attack. The 12-aircraft squadrons went out on a regular basis, giving coverage all day.

Dick Hudson, a U.S. Navy crewman on an LST (Landing Ship, Tank; Navy landing craft), remembers seeing the aircraft directed to strike the 88mm field artillery tank guns hidden in caves. The L-4 aircraft (the Army version of the Piper J-3 Cub) could find them and call in the fighter-bombers. The L-4s also adjusted Navy artillery.

But there was still the problem of targets disappearing. Although the Fifth Army had liaison aircraft, they were not equipped with radios that could contact the fighter-bombers. However, their presence did speed up identifying the targets and getting the information back to headquarters. Another problem was that the artillery spotter was restricted to flying over friendly held territory; he could not fly behind the enemy lines to see many lucrative targets.

Unhappy with this restriction, then-Captain Reichert went to General Gordon P. Seville, commander of the 12th TAC, and asked if he could borrow a couple of liaison aircraft from General Mark Clark, for he felt that it would be a good idea to get his own pilots up in these VHF — Very High Frequency — radio-equipped aircraft so that they could talk to the fighter-bomber pilots. In this way, information could be passed on in short order. At first, General Clark didn't like this plan, but about a week later he gave

General Seville two Stinson L-5 Sentinels. Volunteers were requested from the fighter-bomber pilots who were skeptical at first, but soon became intrigued with the idea of flying the L-5s.

With SCR-522 VHF radios, directives went to all the fighter-bomber units explaining that the armed reconnaissance (recce) missions would have first priority. When *Horsefly*, the L-5 airborne controller, contacted them, the fighter-bombers were to follow his instructions and hit the targets indicated.

It wasn't long before the Army felt the positive impact on its own frontlines from Army Air Forces strikes on these targets immediately behind the enemy's frontlines — just far enough away so that artillery spotters couldn't see them. To accomplish this objective, the *Horsefly* had to fly 10 to 15 miles behind the enemy lines, at 4,000 feet Above Ground Level (AGL), to be out of the range of rifle fire. This altitude was effective for picking out tank concentrations, troops, tank depots, and other targets.

On 28 June 1944, a group of fighter aircraft worked with four FACs to support the 1st Armored Division. The top of the wings of the Forward Air Control planes were painted one of four different colors so that the fighters overhead rather than the enemy could easily identify them. The FAC call signs were *Horsefly Blue, Horsefly Red, Horsefly Green,* and *Horsefly Yellow.* They led the fighter aircraft to targets in the path of advancing ground troops. Colonel Mike Strok (U.S. Army, Ret.) recalled that in World War II, "the Germans knew we painted the *Horseflies* silver, so they only shot at the olive drab aircraft. So, [*then*] we painted the *Horseflies* olive drab. The Germans stopped firing at the artillery adjusting aircraft, thinking they might be *Horseflies.*"

From February 1944 to the end of the war in August 1945, the 12th TAC went to Italy, southern France, and southern Germany. They never lost a *Horsefly* to enemy ground fire or to enemy air. Reichert recalled, "We did lose one when the pilot landed in a small field near the frontlines. It had a ditch the pilot didn't see that wiped out the landing gear."

Horsefly had started out as a questionable operation. However, the L-4s and later the L-5s were very effective as they maintained a dawn-to-dusk patrol along the frontline area. The Germans learned to make little or no movement of troops or vehicles because by so doing they would give away their positions and artillery fire would rain down on them.

Captain George R. Partridge, 523rd Tactical Fighter Squadron, a USAF FAC with the 2nd Battalion, 2nd Infantry, 3rd Brigade, First Infantry Division, at Lai Khe Air Strip, Ben Cat, Vietnam, 16 October 1965. Partridge landed an O-1 Bird Dog at Lai Khe during FAC orientation to check the work progress on the strip.

Colonel Strok explained why the L-4 Cub was so feared:

WE COINED a phrase that one L-4 Cub sometimes had more firepower than a whole squadron of B-17 Flying Fortresses dropping bombs. Some of the airborne pilots fired as many as 100 artillery guns of various calibers. That much firepower is awesome and devastating. From this evolved the idea that when the fighter-bombers came in for strikes, we provided a form of cover for them, which will never be found in official Army manuals. The Germans learned not to fire at the Cubs for fear of retribution, which was usually swift and quite effective.

After Rome was captured in June 1944, the action was in the mountainous area of the Apennines. The L-4s were underpowered at altitude, and thus the L-5s were used. The Italian landscape was quite confusing from the fighter-bombers' vantage point, so they were glad to have the airborne controllers.

These efforts finalized the concept of the Forward Air Controller. Colonel Strok concluded, "It turned out to be a Jim-dandy application of tactical air. It used close air support to great advantage."

Another form of World War II forward air control were the British *Pathfinders* who located and marked targets in Germany by dropping guidance flares for bombers. One pilot flew to the target area and circled

aloft for two hours while radioing instructions to four Royal Air Force *Pathfinder* planes as to where to drop flares. The American bombers also had *Pathfinder* guidance for the lead bombardier in the attacking force.

War Department Field Manual 31-35 of 1942 made no mention of a "Forward Air Controller." Thus, when the airborne FAC concept evolved in 1944, there was no official doctrinal name. The most commonly used term for the airborne FAC during World War II was "forward controller." In 1946, however, the War Department published a revised Field Manual 31-35, which incorporated the lessons of World War II and clearly defined both the role of the FAC (*i.e.*, ground FAC) and the role of the Tactical Air Coordinator Airborne (TACA) (*i.e.*, airborne FAC).

By 1950, these were also the doctrinal names included in the Army Field Forces/Tactical Air Command Training Directive, *Joint Training Directive for Air-Ground Operations*, which governed air-ground cooperation during the Korean War.

Korea, 1950-1953

The Korean War Forward Air Controller, known as the *Mosquito*, played a much greater role in tactical air control than did the World War II *Horsefly* FAC. The limited nature of the Korean War, combined with U.S. control of the air, all contributed to the *Mosquito* FAC becoming a symbol of excellence in close air support.

Even though the airborne controller was an important enough innovation to be included in U.S. Army doctrine (Field Manual 31-35) following the end of World War II, no airborne FAC was maintained in peacetime, between 1945 and 1950 in part because the U.S. Air Force became an independent service in September 1947. The Field Manual specified Tactical Air Control Parties, each composed of a FAC and enlisted radio personnel, to be stationed near the frontlines to direct airstrikes. An Air Liaison Officer (ALO) would advise the ground commander on the use of air power.

As the Korean War got underway, confusion reigned. Operations officers frequently were unable to post the location of friendly troops, and thus Army liaison pilots refused to fly near uncertain targets. The communications circuit back to the fighter bases in Japan was out of order 75 percent of the time. Accordingly, General Edward J. Timberlake, acting commander of the Fifth Air Force, scheduled Lockheed F-80 Shooting Star jet flights from Itazuke and Ashiya, Japan, at 20-minute intervals during daylight hours. The fighters would check in over the Taejon, Korea, *Angelo* Ground Control Station. If *Angelo* had no assigned targets, the fighter pilots proceeded up the roads between Osan and Seoul looking for targets of opportunity.

General Timberlake had TACPs operating from jeeps. The Canadians had the equivalent, called Air Contact Teams. The weather was usually awful, ground communications were unreliable, and the mountainous terrain hindered operations. The jeeps had no equipment that would allow the Forward Air Controller to leave the vehicle in a sheltered spot while he proceeded on foot to a vantage point from which he could see the target.

On 9 July 1950, 14 days after the Communists crossed the 38th Parallel, Lieutenant Colonel Stanley P. Latiolas, Fifth Air Force Operations Officer, suggested having a slower aircraft spot, and then call in a jet and direct it to the target. The U.S. fighter-bombers were based in Japan, and with their tremendous thirst for fuel, there wasn't much time for them to search around for targets; at low altitude, they consumed fuel at a great rate, and their blinding speed hindered their ability to find the enemy. At Taejon, Colonel John R. Murphy, remembering the success of the *Horsefly* in World War II, asked Major General Earl Partridge, Fifth Air Force, for an operations officer and five pilots who could fly reconnaissance.

The first pilots to fly the airborne FAC mission in Korea were Lieutenants James A. Bryant and Frank G. Mitchell, operating from a desolate strip at Taejon known as K-5. They first flew in with two Stinson L-5G Sentinel liaison aircraft, modified with four-channel VHF radios that turned out to be inoperative. They then borrowed two of the 24th Division Air Section's Cessna U-17 Skywagons and flew three-hour flights over the target area using the call signs *Angelo Fox* and *Angelo George*. From these tiny aircraft they worked ten flights of Lockheed F-80 Shooting Stars against the enemy lines in spite of some confusion, as the fighters had not been briefed to expect airborne controllers.

The Bomb Damage Assessment (BDA) for the day included many tanks and vehicles destroyed or damaged. In addition to directing the jets to targets, the airborne controllers also plotted frontline positions, which proved invaluable in later actions. In spite of the confusion caused by the lack of briefings, it was an outstanding day.

Continued efforts were made to use the liaison aircraft, but they lacked enough speed to evade the enemy. Several were shot down by North Korean Russian-built Yak fighter planes.

Lieutenant Harold E. Morris (USAF) thought the old World War II trainer, the North American T-6 Texan, would do the job, and thus on 10 July 1950, at Taejon, he made some flights to prove his point. His unit flew three missions that day in the T-6 equipped with an ARC-3 radio set. Lieutenant Morris found tanks moving along the Chonju-Unsan Road. He was working a flight of Royal Australian Air Force (RAAF) F-51 Mustangs (until 1948, called P-51s) when his radio went out, but he continued to direct the fighters by dipping his wings sharply over the targets.

In their first experience with airborne controllers, the RAAF pilots were very accurate, and throughout the war the FAC *Mosquitos* routinely conducted bombing strikes without benefit of radio contact because many of the United Nations bombers operated on different frequencies.

———— ⚙ ————

On the day that Lieutenants Bryant and Mitchell had located a lucrative target of 42 tanks moving along a main road, a first-class Forward Air Control unit — the 6147th Tactical Control Group — saw its beginnings. From a T-6 Texan, Bryant and Mitchell directed the knocking out of the 17 tanks near Chonui by F-80s.

The 6147th was known as the *Mosquito* Group, and because there was no definite system for airborne forward controllers, the pilots improvised according to conditions. Their effectiveness was immediately apparent, and more T-6s were acquired. A Fifth Air Force fragmentary operations order gave the airborne controllers radio call signs, *Mosquito Able, Mosquito Baker,* and so on to *Mosquito How.* A fragmentation operations order was the daily supplement to the standard operations order governing the conduct of the air war. It contained mission number and function, type of ordnance, time on target, and other instructions.

In addition to controlling fighters, the FACs had minor roles: guiding supply and mail drops to the frontline troops, occasionally directing field artillery, adjusting Navy gunfire on coastal targets, providing night direction to Douglas B-26 Invaders, assisting with helicopter pickups, and voice and psychological warfare. For missions, the T-6s were heavily loaded with smoke grenades and an extra P-51 Mustang belly tank, holding an additional 40 gallons of fuel. Later, a dozen smoke rockets were hung from the wings. Both pilot and his backseat observer were fully equipped with seat-pack 28-foot nylon parachutes, .45-caliber pistols, flare guns, Mae Wests, flashlights, and occasionally binoculars. All this added 1,000 pounds extra weight, cutting the top speed to 100 mph and the climb rate to 85 mph. The service ceiling was so low that the T-6 was always vulnerable to enemy fire.

The *Mosquito* pilots had to fly down on the deck to find targets, often between the muzzles of devastating enemy artillery. They would pull up, gaining altitude, jinking in all directions to avoid being hit as they flew out to where they could begin a marking run while they were briefing the fighters. This accomplished, they would dive toward the target, trading altitude for airspeed as they snapped up in a wingover, then dropped out half-stalled until they were in a position to fire a smoke rocket. After the fighters attacked, the T-6s would go back down low for a BDA. They kept constant radio contact with the fighter-bombers and *Mosquito Shirley*, the airborne communications center.

The T-6s were equipped with an outmoded gun-sight. The pilots learned to line up their aircraft by sighting down the row of rivets along the nose of the airplane, and then, when the last rivet was four inches below the target, they triggered off the rockets. Sometimes the T-6 pilot had to stand the aircraft on one wing so that he and the observer could get a good look at the target under the aircraft. At first, the T-6s had .50-caliber guns, but too many pilots took on whole Antiaircraft Artillery (AAA) batteries, or tried to knock out T-34 tanks, instead of waiting for the fighters, and thus the guns were ordered removed.

For communications, the T-6 had three radio sets: the VHF 522 and ARC-3 were combined to give the aircraft 12 channels at either the front or the back seat; the SCR 300 (31) allowed the *Mosquitos* to talk directly to the tank columns and forward ground patrols. These sets were always netted in at Channel 20 for ground-air liaison, and could only be operated from the T-6 backseat and had limited range. However, they often saved the day as the *Mosquitos* flew above the ground columns as they moved ahead, covering their fronts and flanks. All TACPs on the ground had the same radios.

Initially, all FAC training was conducted in the Korean theater. Training in the U.S. began in May 1953 at the Combat Crew Training Center (CCTC), 3600th Flying Training Group (Fighter) at Luke Air Force Base, Arizona. When the cease-fire was signed on 26 July 1953, the T-6 Airborne Controller Course at Luke AFB was terminated at a time when it was the only air controller school in the world. The last class graduated on 15 August 1953, making a total of 51 men who had completed the course since its inception. However, the first Luke graduates arrived in Korea after the armistice was signed.

U.S. Navy and U.S. Marine Corps Aircraft

The *Mosquitos* worked with U.S. Navy and U.S. Marine Corps aircraft in addition to those of the Air Force. The Navy planes would launch off their carriers and check in with *Mosquito Mellow*, a Douglas C-47 airborne communications aircraft. The Navy operated two carriers together for mutual protection, and thus there was a tremendous fighter force stacked up over *Mellow Control*. To solve the problem, the Navy furnished airborne controllers to work with the *Mosquitos* in front of the 2nd Division, the area for which it was agreed the carrier aircraft would provide close air support.

The C-47 Forward Air Control aircraft *Mosquito Shirley* and *Mosquito Phyllis Anne* also covered a lot of area and both waterfronts in east and west Korea. These aircraft that directed both air and artillery strikes were known as the "Buffer Zone Airlines."

The USMC had a different doctrine. Its infantry forces were lightly gunned, so that aviation made up for the lack of artillery. Each Marine battalion was accompanied by a forward air observer who would call down supporting aircraft from a flight that the Marine Air Wing (MAW) normally had airborne over its Marines. Support of its ground troops was a primary mission of Marine air. In Korea, Marine Observation Squadron VMO-6 flew the OY-1 Sentinel, a two-seat light observation aircraft built by the Stinson Aircraft Division of Consolidated Vultee Aircraft Corporation. This small airplane had an aluminum and wood framework covered by fabric and was powered by a 185 hp Lycoming 0-435-1 6-cylinder, horizontally opposed, air-cooled engine. Its maximum speed was 129 mph.

VMO-6 flew the OY-1 until May 1951 when the squadron started receiving the O1-E Cessna Bird Dog, another tandem two-seat, tailwheel aircraft. This ship was all metal, powered by a 213 hp Continental 6-cylinder 0-470-11, air-cooled engine. The O1-E had gyroscopic instruments and a superior rate of climb compared to the OY-1. The Marines used the O-1E (L-19) with a pilot and a tactical air observer in the backseat to direct airstrikes.

U.S. Army Corps Areas

Mosquito aircraft were on station in each U.S. Army corps area during daylight hours. When the enemy was detected, they would radio the Joint Operations Center, usually located in Seoul. JOC would vector fighter-bombers to the target areas. To get closer to the frontlines, the 6147th moved northward from Taegu, first to Kimpo on 5 October and then to Seoul Municipal Airfield (K-16) on 18 October. By November 1950, the frontlines were well into North Korea.

The T-6s started using belly tanks for an extra two hours of cruising time, often penetrating 50 miles in advance of friendly lines. When they got so far away that their radios wouldn't reach the JOC, they contacted either *Mosquito Mellow* or *Mosquito Godfrey*, the C-47B radio relay aircraft orbiting high overhead, usually at 10,000 feet on station, 20 miles behind enemy lines. Pilots of the relay aircraft were assigned to the 6148th Tactical Control Squadron.

By 1951, the Communists put up enough ground fire to keep the *Mosquitos* from ranging way out ahead of friendly forces. The T-6s were seldom permitted to penetrate more than two miles into enemy territory. During the last year and a half of the war, the northern operating area was restricted by a bomb line about eight miles north of the frontline. Airstrikes were only allowed south of the bomb line if they were controlled by the *Mosquitos* or radar.

The Fifth Air Force also used faster aircraft for Forward Air Control. The 45th Tactical Recce Squadron of RF-51s sought targets to the rear of enemy lines. Relays of North American F-51 Mustangs and Chance Vought F4U Corsairs were assigned to certain areas to search for and destroy targets of opportunity. They were to become familiar with their routes so that they would recognize changes in camouflaged objects. This new truck-hunting plan had great success. Sometimes north of the bomb line, fighter-bomber strikes were directed by airborne controllers (not from the *Mosquito* Squadron) in F-51 or F-80 aircraft. The bomb line fluctuated day by day. Anything north of it was fair game.

The T-6 Texan was too "hot" — too fast — an aircraft to operate from the average ground division's light aviation airstrip, which was the same problem encountered by the heavy observation aircraft in World War II. At the Eighth Army's suggestion, the 6147th Tactical Control Group tested the L-19 aircraft as a FAC airplane in July 1951, but rejected them as too vulnerable to ground fire. Little did they know that the L-19, the Army version of the Cessna O-1 Bird Dog, would be considered by many pilots as the best Forward Air Control aircraft in Vietnam.

The greatest danger to the FAC in Korea was heavy, small-arms fire, being hit by artillery or mortar, and cables. Because the controller flew below treetop level, the enemy began stringing heavy cables from one hilltop to another in hopes of catching the wing of an unwary pilot. Unfortunately, this worked all too often. Sometimes the *Mosquitos* followed rivers home at very low altitude when the ceiling was low. The mountaintops on each side of the river would be obscured by the clouds. Enemy guerrillas, familiar with the *Mosquito's* route, would sneak over the river valley, on the Allied side, to string cables.

A Distinguished Flying Cross was awarded to First Lieutenant Chester L. Brown, who flew the last FAC mission of the Korean War on 15 June 1953. Brown was later an O-1 FAC in Vietnam, supporting the Seventh ARVN Division in the Mekong Delta, attached to the military group in the city of Ben Tre, Kien Hoa Province. On that last mission in Korea, flying his T-6 near Anchor Hill, he directed 14 fighters against a powerful enemy offensive. Disregarding his own personal safety, he remained over enemy territory for long periods of time without the benefit of flak suppression. He dove repeatedly to dangerously low altitudes through intense ground fire to mark the targets with his smoke rockets. He supervised each fighter pass so that he might best utilize the available ordnance. Brown's efforts destroyed supply depots, enemy mortars, personnel shelters, trenches, and automatic weapon positions.

By the end of the Korean War, the *Mosquitos* had flown 40,354 missions. The 6147th received two Presidential Unit Citations and one Korean Presidential Unit Citation. Because of a job well done, there was talk about designing a new aircraft for the airborne controller. Instead, the *Mosquito* FACs were disbanded three years after the fighting ceased. The 6147th was redesignated the 6148th Air Base Group.

In 1954, the USAF did initiate a Forward Air Con-

Theater Indoctrination School at Phan Rang Air Base, March 1968. Front row, far r.: Captain John Heimburger, behind him Captain John Knight; front center, l. of can, Lieutenant Colonel Lane; back row, Captain Goldsmith, Major Lennie Smith, Captain Vega, Captain Hill, Herb Netheray, Captain Bob Kellock, and Captain Hough.

trol course in conjunction with the Army at the Air-Ground Operations School at Southern Pines, North Carolina, but there was little updating of concepts. This school was later transferred to Keesler AFB, Biloxi, Mississippi.

After 1956, the USAF was without a forward airborne control organization. The *Mosquito* FAC was looked on as a battlefield expedient with no permanent place in Air Force doctrine. The *STRICOM (U.S. Strike Command) Manual* was later revised to acknowledge that a "Tactical Air Controller" could be used when Tactical Air Control Parties were not capable of directing operations.

In 1957, the U.S. Continental Army Command and the USAF Tactical Air Command published air-ground doctrine in a document entitled *Joint Air-Ground Operations* (1957), in which the term "FAC" referred to the ground FAC. There was no reference at all to an airborne FAC. At the same time, the U.S. Strike Command continued to address the forward airborne controller role, which retained its old name, Tactical Air Coordinator (Airborne).

Between 1956 and 1962, no one was trained for the airborne FAC mission, and there were no specific aircraft designated for the job. The USAF completely disregarded the effectiveness of an airborne FAC when reviewing "lessons learned" from the Korean War. The Air Force was primarily interested in strategic forces, maximized manpower, and nuclear warfare, and therefore had no interest in light aircraft.

The Army exerted primary influence on the Forward Air Control function, emphasizing a ground control team (later redesignated the Tactical Air Control Party), while the Air Force gave its first priority to building up its strategic forces, including intercontinental ballistic missiles. The U.S. involvement in Southeast Asia resurrected the FAC concept.

Chapter 2

FACs in Southeast Asia

French Forward Air Controllers

URING THE INDOCHINA WAR (1946-1954), the French Colonial Army fought against the Communist Vietminh who wanted to liberate Vietnam from French rule. The French flew as Forward Air Controllers in Morane-Saulnier M.S. 500 Criquets (French-built Fieseler Fi 156s), providing air control for the American-built P-63 Kingcobras. The Criquets, equipped with sets of radios for communicating with the ground troops and the fighters, frequently saved hard-pressed ground units by directing the fighters in attacks.

In 1949, American P-63 Kingcobras, built by Bell Aircraft and Company, were shipped to Saigon for use by the French. Grumman F5 Hellcats and F8F-1/F8F-1B Bearcats, which seemed better suited to the short runways used by the French, arrived in 1951. The French used the Bearcat (called "Beercats") primarily for ground attack. B-26 Douglas Invaders (designation changed to A-26 during the Vietnam War) were sent to Tan Son Nhut Air Base on 4 November 1950. Douglas C-47 transports were also used by the French forces.

The first USAF advisors arrived in Saigon on 8 November 1950. Initially, they were assigned to the Air Force section of the Military Assistance Advisory Group (MAAG), Indochina. At the end of the Korean War, the Americans had begun supplying the French with the brand new L-19A Bird Dog, to replace the older M.S. 500 Criquets. The U.S. supplied the French with a tremendous amount of military aid, and underwrote a large portion of the war's cost. The situation became very serious by 1953 when, in April, General Giap's troops began an invasion of northern Laos.

In 1954, following the defeat of the French garrison at Dien Bien Phu, a conference at Geneva provided for a temporary division of Vietnam, pending general elections in the summer of 1956. Laos was supposed to be neutral. President Dwight D. Eisenhower felt that if Laos fell to the Communist Bloc, the free world would lose the rest of Southeast Asia and Indonesia, and like a domino effect, open the gateway for the Communists in India, Burma, and Thailand. However, Eisenhower would not agree to any outright presence of U.S. military troops in Southeast Asia.

The U.S. developed a secret American military aid program for Laos, and, in 1955, underwrote the entire Laotian defense budget. The CIA was heavily involved. Its proprietary airline, Air America Inc. (formerly Civil Air Transport), was the China-based airline co-founded by famed Flying Tiger Claire Chennault. Established at Udorn Royal Thai Air Force Base (RTAFB) in Thailand, Air America performed a number of dangerous missions including resupply, troop movements, and search and rescue operations.

In August 1956, President Eisenhower made the fateful decision to aid South Vietnam while it built up its forces against a North Vietnamese attack. From 1957 to 1959, the U.S. advisory group in Vietnam was relatively small. The advisors could not speak the Vietnamese language and knew nothing of their customs. Before 1962, the advisors returning from Vietnam were under a "Seal of Secrecy," having to sign a certificate binding them to secrecy on their operations while there. Until 1965, the advisors were the main source of information for the American military.

By 1958, the U.S. had military advisors in Laos,

and U.S. Army Brigadier General John A. Heintges was sent there to study the situation. The Special Forces Field Training Teams (FTTs) from the 7th Special Forces Group at Fort Bragg, North Carolina, were sent to Laos in July 1959. That same year, the U.S. State Department set up a disguised military mission, Program Evaluation Office (PEO), in Vientiane. It was staffed by infantry officers called "technicians" wearing civilian clothes, including a general to train the Laotian army. In 1960, Major (later Brigadier General) Harry "Heinie" Aderholt was assigned to support CIA operations in the Far East. He flew around Laos with Laotian General Vang Pao, picking out sites for landing strips known as Lima Sites (LS). Sergeant James J. Stanford, a *Butterfly* FAC, recalled, "Most of these were unbelievable, 300 to 400 feet long, not in a straight line, with all sorts of inclines. Some were shaved off mountain tops and some followed curved ridge lines."

In 1961, the CIA hired Kuomintang (KMT) mercenaries for the secret war in neutral Laos. At the same time, the Soviet Union increased its support of the Pathet Lao, the Laotian Communist guerrillas. By 1962, North Vietnam, later aided by China, made a deal with Laos to build all-weather roads over the Annamite Mountains, and through strategic mountain passes on the Vietnamese border into the Laotian panhandle, one from Nape Pass to Kam Keut and another from Mu Gia Pass to Nhommarath. They also constructed roads in northern Laos from Dien Bien Phu to the southwest and another from North Vietnam to Sam Neua, the Pathet Lao capital. The North Vietnamese used extensive measures to mask their use of what became to be known as the Ho Chi Minh Trail.

The Ho Chi Minh Trail developed into a complex trail and road system that ran through Laos, thereby avoiding the demilitarized zone (DMZ). Covering between 3,000 and 4,000 miles, the trail consisted of an intricate maze of tunnels, switchbacks, truck parks, and maintenance parks.

Ambassador William H. Sullivan, in charge of the military operations for the CIA, was posted to Laos in late 1964. He ran the war there, much to the chagrin of Army and USAF generals and high-ranking officers. Sullivan obtained A-26 Invaders, A-1 Skyraiders, and T-28 Trojans from the Air Commando Wing. He understood how to fight the war — not with ineffective high-speed jets, but rather with the slow, prop-driven aircraft — at the time when the USAF favored jets and General Curtis

A T-28 Trojan with napalm containers, 1967.   Jack Cummings Collection

as a training mission to Bien Hoa AB in October 1961. Five FACs went to Vietnam on 2 February 1962. The first combat-ready unit to be stationed in Vietnam was Detachment 2 Alpha of the 4400th Combat Crew Training Squadron (CCTS) dispatched to Vietnam (under the code name JUNGLE JIM) from Eglin AFB, Florida, to train Vietnamese personnel in offensive operations including Forward Air Control tactics and techniques. The Detachment of 16 aircraft (4 SC-47 airlift planes used as flareships, 8 T-28 Trojans, and 4 B-26 Invaders) arrived at Bien Hoa Air Base on 16 November 1961. Vietnamese markings (a five-pointed white star in a blue circle, with one red and two orange-yellow horizontal bars on each side, all outlined in red) were painted on the USAF planes for political and diplomatic reasons. In December 1961, the code name was changed to FARM GATE.

As part of the FARM GATE operation, the Tactical Air Control System (TACS) was established to train the South Vietnamese in offensive air operations that included FAC techniques and tactics. Vietnamese Air Force pilots and observers were trained in the O-1F Bird Dog. The USAF and VNAF flew together, but only the VNAF could direct airstrikes by direction of the Saigon government. The Vietnamese believed that the pilot should fly the aircraft and the observer direct the airstrikes. This rule persisted until 1965. However, as the war expanded, a shortage of VNAF pilots resulted as their observers went into pilot training. The VNAF pilots were junior officers with neither the rank nor the experience to be air commanders. Lacking authority, they were hesitant to put in airstrikes.

On 13 January 1962, FARM GATE T-28s flew with a Vietnamese FAC directing missions in support of a Republic of Vietnam outpost that was under Viet Cong attack. The following week, T-28s and RB-26s struck targets from Saigon north to Quang Tri Province near the DMZ. By the end of January, FARM GATE crews had flown 229 sorties.

LeMay, USAF Chief of Staff, believed in strategic bombing.

In 1962, unmarked T-28s were given to Laos in a program called "Class A." CIA pilots delivered them out of Udorn, Thailand, which was only 45 miles from Vientiane, Laos. Two years later, the CIA used the U.S. Agency for International Development (USAID) as a cover to give secret support to the air operations in Laos. "Water Pump" (a part of Project 404) was the code name for training Lao and Thai pilots at Udorn, Thailand, by the Air Commando Training Detachment 1, 56th Special Operations Wing. It was set up by Major Harry Aderholt in March 1964 for the secret purpose of rescuing American pilots shot down over the Ho Chi Minh Trail. Civilian (CIA) helicopters flew those missions. The training for the Laotian pilots in the T-28s was to allow them to accompany the helicopters for protection. Native Hmong pilots (Laotian hill tribesmen) were also trained, but it took longer — three years — before they were ready to work with Forward Air Controllers.

That same year, the North Vietnamese installed 16 AAA guns around the Plain of Jars capable of firing up to 15,000 feet. However, the bombing of North Vietnam overshadowed the murky events in Laos. As the situation in Vietnam heated up, the conflict in Laos was pushed into the background.

U.S. Air Force FACs to Vietnam
The USAF was authorized to send a detachment

Roy Dalton volunteered for an assignment that he couldn't discuss with his family. In November 1964, he was the first rated officer sent to the "Water Pump" detachment at Vientiane, Laos. His assignment was Lima Site 36 (Na Khang, elevation 4,400 feet). Only a few other Americans were there from another agency. Dalton had no aircraft and flew around via Air America helicopters. From mountaintops he directed airstrikes, either in close air support of friendlies, or to destroy enemy trucks. Air America pilots were not keen on flying over a hot combat zone, even though they got extra pay for doing it. Dalton said, "Most of their pilots gave me the runaround when I would ask, could I use you for a FAC and go out there?" Air controller Dalton directed the Royal Laotian Air Force (RLAF) and the "Thai B" pilots who flew Laos-marked aircraft.

The 19th Tactical Air Support Squadron (TASS)

The USAF 19th TASS was activated at Bien Hoa AB on 17 June 1963, under Lieutenant Colonel John J. Wilfong, with 4 O-1s and 22 crew. In August, 18 more planes arrived on the *USS Card*. Because the USAF pilots were not authorized to put in airstrikes, 11 experienced Vietnamese observers joined the squadron. In August, 25 officers and 69 airmen underwent factory training to gain proficiency in the U.S. Army L-19 Bird Dog. By September, they had opened a training center at Nha Trang. There were 44 pilots for the 22 L-19s, as well as the Vietnamese observers. Training for the pilots included a month of preflight instruction, and three months of primary flight training that included 80 hours of flying. Early in 1964, the squadron was combat ready. According to the Rules of Engagement (ROE), the airstrikes had to be handled by a Vietnamese Air Force FAC. If this controller directed an attack on friendly people, he was subject to prosecution. In many instances, the VNAF failed to capitalize on strike-aircraft firepower because of this rule.

The Rules of Engagement

USAF airmen in Vietnam instructing the Vietnamese Air Force in combat air support tactics and techniques in 1962 needed guidance on the rules governing airstrikes. The VNAF had very few rules other than the restriction not to cross into Laos or Cambodia and certain limitations on the use of ordnance. A VNAF pilot was free to strike a target once the Air Operational Center (AOC) or higher authority approved.

Commander-in-Chief Pacific Command (CINCPAC) directed the Military Assistance Advisory Group to offer the VNAF assistance, if they desired it, in developing an updated set of Rules of Engagement. The new ROE were approved in April 1962. On 24 November 1962, Military Assistance Command Vietnam (MACV) established operational restrictions for U.S. aircraft flying combat support missions. The FARM GATE aircrews were ordered not to fly combat missions without a Vietnamese crew member on board, and their aircraft were to bear Vietnamese markings. The USAF crews, under normal conditions, could not fly closer than three miles to the Cambodian border. All targets had to be approved by the Vietnamese and marked by a VNAF FAC. The USAF airplanes were strictly defensive. Before they could do anything, they had to be fired on first.

The Special Forces working with the USAF Air Commandos were exempt from the requirement to have a VNAF FAC on board on all airstrikes. In lieu of a Forward Air Controller, they tried to have a hand-picked government person on board who could approve a target for a strike and contact the Air Operations Center for support aircraft through the Special Forces net. Under these conditions, FARM GATE aircraft could strike a target without the presence of a VNAF FAC.

The Rules of Engagement were basically unchanged through 1964. The U.S. was technically at peace despite its involvement in Southeast Asia. However, some exceptions were made. On 25 January 1963, CINCPAC authorized Commander U.S. Military Assistance Vietnam (COMUSMACV) to waive certain rules under especially grave conditions, specifically the requirement that a Vietnamese be on board all USAF strike aircraft. The 2nd Air Division was authorized to permit USAF pilots to launch airstrikes without a VNAF FAC under two conditions:

1. In direct support of outposts attacked at night, provided they were directed by a C-47 flareship, which could maintain continuous contact with the ground and the strike crew; and
2. When dropping ordnance in a free-fire zone (2nd Air Division Regulation 54-4, 22 January 1963).

While this made some of the ROE more flexible, there were still too many rules that hampered the pilots. Restrictions of 1964 precluding reconnaissance by VNAF and USAF liaison planes below 500 feet were unrealistic. Colonel David S. Mellish, III Corps Air Liaison Officer, recommended a search altitude of 150 feet above the trees to find concealed Viet Cong (VC). Colonel Mellish pointed out that Army liaison pilots were doing a better job at finding and photographing the enemy because they were permitted to fly as low as 50 to 100 feet. This did cause losses, however. As the war went on, the enemy obtained better weapons that resulted in more changes of the minimum altitudes.

U.S. Army aircraft flew under different rules. They were not required to have Vietnamese markings, they could fire back when fired on, and they did not have to have a Vietnamese pilot on board to do so.

In 1966, a major revision to the Rules of Engagement specified that all targets selected for attack had to be approved by the Vietnamese province chief or higher authority. The exceptions were areas declared to be free of friendly forces and civilians. The ROE stated that USAF FACs alone would control airstrikes in support of U.S. Army forces. If none were available, a VNAF FAC or "Skyspot" MSQ-77 and TPQ-10 ground control radar could be called upon.

Fred McNeil (*Covey 502*), call sign of the 20th Tactical Air Support Squadron explained that the ROE were taken seriously:

IN FAC WORK, one of the ROE in Laos, Cambodia, and Vietnam, was that with certain exceptions, no U.S. military aircraft could put any ordnance on the ground unless they were under the direct control of a FAC. That was ROE everywhere. If there was a short-round incident, which meant a friendly guy hurt or killed, the FAC bore primary responsibility.

That was brought home to me very vividly when I was doing in-country training with the 504th when I first arrived in-country. There was a regular FAC outfit based there with us. One day, while we were still in training, one of the FAC O-2 pilots was out on a mission in central Cambodia at a rubber plantation supporting one of the big operations over there. Apparently there was a short-round incident where a South Vietnamese soldier was working on the ground and was injured by USAF TAC air. The FAC was immediately called off the area and ordered back to the base. When he landed, the entire group staff, headed by a full colonel, was waiting for this young captain. As he taxied up, he knew he was in trouble. Later, in the middle of the night, he received a telephone call.

The voice at the other end said, "This is General O'Brien, Chief of Staff of the USAF. Tell me what happened, son. I've got to go in and brief the President [*Nixon*] in a few moments. This kid was almost speechless, but that's how seriously they took short rounds. They had warned us all through in-country training. 'You had better make sure you FACs know what you are doing.' We were the umpires in the whole game. We knew the ROE and had to be experts in everything. When a question came up in combat out in the field, it was always given to the FACs. We were the arbitrators.

As a consequence, we were tested on the ROE in our area every 30 days. We had to take a written exam. It was like being a traffic cop or a baseball umpire. When a strike was made — and I found this to be kind of wild when I first did it — the fighter pilots didn't decide what direction to attack or make the run in on, they didn't decide in which direction they would break off in. The FAC briefed them on what to do.

———— ✧ ————

Even though the Rules of Engagement were classified Top Secret until 1985, the enemy had ways of learning them and using that knowledge to advantage. The FAC needed to be able to make a judgment about the best way to perform a mission based on his knowledge of the immediate situation, and thus undoubtedly there were times when the inappropriate rule caused a great deal of frustration. There were various rules for different locations and activity, and they were constantly changing. FACs had to take written "Romeo" (nickname for ROE) exams frequently for each of the political areas that they worked. The ROE were unbelievably complex, and were different for each branch (Army, USAF, Marines, and Navy) of the service, and even were changed at will by the politicians in Washington.

Not only were the FACs hindered by the complicated Rules of Engagement, they also had to deal with the REMFs (Rear-Echelon Mother Fuckers). There were many "types" in Vietnam who flew a desk and just wanted to get a "combat tour" on their records. Chris Robbins wrote, in a definitive article, in *Sport Aviation* ("The Ravens," July 1996, p. 44):

The REMFs and Romeos fed off one another in a deadly symbiosis that destroyed the spirit of the warrior. Disgruntled pilots longed to go

Bill McAllister, "Mac the FAC."   Robert H. Jacobson Collection

somewhere they would be allowed to fight the war to the maximum, held back by a minimum of rules and rear echelon types.

Some squadron commanders were more concerned about their careers than the concerns of their pilots. The pilots did not have much admiration for these officers. When some career majors and lieutenant colonels realized that this was a war that could not be won, they aimed for promotions by filling in squares in career development.

Locating the Enemy

The Forward Air Controller spent about 60 percent of his time doing aerial reconnaissance to find the enemy. It was hard to tell the difference between friendly people and the enemy unless they wore uniforms, carried arms, and fired on the aircraft. As the war went on, the enemy improved its methods for camouflage. When troops moved by day they wore foliage-covered backpacks. But if they didn't keep the foliage fresh, it was a dead giveaway from the air.

William W. MacAllister, an O-1 FAC known as "Mac the FAC," related one of his most interesting experiences in the April 23, 1965, *Time* magazine article, "Who's Fighting in Vietnam." He describes a tree "walking" down a hill in the midst of Viet Cong territory. He followed the tree, and found *more* walking trees. When he dove down in his O-1, however, "they became stationary trees real fast." MacAllister called in an airstrike and, he says, "We had ourselves a forest fire."

The FACs learned to spot hedgerows where none grew before. The enemy used religious temples to stash ammo and sometimes wore orange monks' robes when they walked down a road. They dressed

in women's clothing and carried children in their arms. False bottoms were built in sampans to hide supplies. One USAF FAC noted grass floating and trailing mud on a canal. On closer observation, he saw Viet Cong walking on the bottom of the stream holding the grass over their heads. The mud gave them away.

The Daily Intelligence Summary (DISUM), which supported the FAC operation, received ground-sensor truck information each morning, which was passed on to the Forward Air Controller. By analyzing the movement pattern, the Intelligence personnel would determine the general location of the areas where the trucks were hidden during the day. This information was combined with the Seventh Air Force intelligence information, previous FAC reports, photo reconnaissance inputs, and covert Intelligence reports. The information was briefed to the FAC prior to each mission. The controller would combine this data with his intimate knowledge of his sector. He would look for dust in the trees, splash marks on stream banks, ruts in mud puddles, and discolored river water near a fording point — all indicators of truck traffic.

Clandestine monitoring of the Ho Chi Minh Trail was essential to the interdiction effort. Fields of "Spikebuoy" and "Adsid" acoustical sensors, which buried themselves two and a half feet into the ground and "listened" for seismic disturbances along the Trail, were dropped by air from Navy OP-2E highly modified Lockheed Neptunes of Squadron VO-67. The "Igloo White" electronic sensor system was activated in Laos in 1967. Lockheed RC-121 Constellation aircraft of the 533rd Reconnaissance Wing flew orbits over Laos to relay the signals from the sensors to the infiltration surveillance center that collected and analyzed the signals at Nakhon Phanom, Thailand.

The enemy would construct false camps to fool the FACs and keep their attention away from another location. They would hide their cooking fires by scooping out a hole in the ground just big enough for a small pot to sit in over burning coals. Smoke was diffused by angling hollow bamboo flutes away from the fire for several feet and siphoning off the smoke in small amounts. During his early morning and dusk flights, the FAC would look for smoke clustering above the trees.

The North Vietnamese Army (NVA) had garden plots to supplement their rice diets, in sharp contrast to the "slash and burn" farming techniques of the

Laotians, and thus the presence of garden plots and a source of water indicated that NVA troops were near. The relationship to the route structure told whether the encampment supported the logistics network or was used as a stopover point for infiltrating troops.

FACs would try to entice the enemy out of hiding and encourage his movement by flying past a suspicious area and then looking back through binoculars to catch the movement. But once a target was found, the FAC stayed clear of the area until the strike aircraft arrived.

Fred McNeil (*Covey* 502) tells of the time he made a wonderful discovery of a hidden cache:

ONE DAY I SPOTTED a raft on the San River. Then it disappeared near Virachei, an old French logging camp in Cambodia. The only way I could find this 40-foot raft that was hugging the bank was to fly down very low (in an O-2) over the river and look under the trees. The river was fairly wide. I knew there wasn't any antiaircraft around there and not much small arms, so it wasn't that big a deal. I flew down this river real low, about 50 feet above the water. I saw a spot that looked like a little stream going off the river. That's where the raft had gone. It was hiding back there.

That day I was lucky enough to get some TAC Air to go after this raft full of supplies. I had nothing else to go on, so I told the fighters all I want is some Mk-82s [*bombs*]. I told the fighters where to set their fuzes and I put them in where I had mentally put the entrance to this stream. From up in the air there was nothing to see. So I memorized a certain bush across from the stream entrance and put a Willie Pete [*white phosphorous smoke rocket*] in. The bombs blew some trees down and opened up things in there. All the way back this stream bed was filled with 40- and 50-foot rafts. Hundreds of them all brand new!

I went back the next day and they gave me all the TAC Air I needed after they saw the photos I took. I must have gotten 20 airstrikes on this target. Intelligence found out that nearby had been an old French sawmill, and this was a raft factory. Just dumb luck. I found that raft factory with monstrous rafts.

To avoid detection, the enemy wouldn't fire on the Forward Air Controller as this would bring on an airstrike. Thus, the enemy gun positions were the most difficult targets for the FACs to detect. Gun crews rarely fired at a FAC in the daytime unless he had, or was about to, find a target in the immediate vicinity. The gun crews knew that once they had given their position away, they were subject to airstrikes. Once cornered, however, the enemy made every effort to shoot down the aircraft.

If the pilot flew with windows open (easy to do in a O-1), he could figure out the size and intensity of the weapons. Normal ground fire resembled yellow strobes; tracers had red streaks. Small-arms fire sounded like the click or pop of a dry stick snapping, popcorn popping, or an engine backfiring. Weapons of 20mm or more gave out a distinct deep-throated "pom." If the FAC could determine the direction of the enemy ground fire, he had a better chance of avoiding it. From 1968 on, intensive USAF visual reconnaissance forced the enemy to nearly cease all daytime operations except in areas hidden from the air. Even then, he would be detected by the surveillance activity of Army patrols and Special Forces units.

The USAF had to extend its FAC activities to the hours of darkness, and the ground fire that greeted the FAC at night could be seen for miles. The tracers from the 37mm guns terminated with seven distinct bursts one right after the other, while the 23mm fired a stream of red balls that looked like they came from a fire hose.

The O-1 was of little practical value at night reconnaissance except for harassment. Later, the combination of the O-2A, OV-10, and FAC-carrying flareships did an excellent job.

The FACs knew their Area of Operations (AO) very well. Any deviation from normal activity was considered suspicious. The province Forward Air Control plan was initiated in Vinh Binh Province. FACs were assigned to specific areas with the same observers flying over the same area daily in a well-ordered pattern to spot unusual enemy activity more easily. Upon discovering the enemy, they became controllers for the airstrikes.

Two FACs who compiled a great record, with their ability to ferret out gun positions, were First Lieutenants Leonard J. "Thunderchicken" Funderburk and Donal W. Payne. When "Thunderchicken" left the 23rd TASS he had accounted for the destruction of more than 220 AAA weapons, and Payne was not too far behind.

Marking Targets
One of the most important jobs of the airborne

Major Fred "Mac" McNeil, *Covey* 502, 20th Tactical Air Support Squadron, Detachment 1, Pleiku Air Base in Military Region II, stands by a Cessna O-2A with rocket launchers.

controller was to verify and mark a target conspicuously so that strike aircraft could drop ordnance with telling effect. In 1962, the VNAF FAC's most common method of marking was to drop a smoke grenade out of the window of the O-1, or to request a smoke round from ARVN guns. However, hand-dropped smoke grenades were not accurate unless dropped from low altitude from an aircraft flying on the deck at about 50 feet AGL. Early in 1962, Captains Douglas K. Evans and Thomas N. Cairney, the first American FACs in Southeast Asia, suggested using rifle-launched smoke grenades or installing a rocket-type launcher on liaison aircraft to mark targets with greater accuracy. The VNAF didn't like these methods. Sometimes the smoke of the rockets was trapped under the trees, or the rockets would be buried in mud. Mk-6 parachute flares were determined to be the most effective in the South Vietnamese jungles.

As the Viet Cong antiaircraft fire improved, the O-1 Bird Dog was forced to fly higher in order to survive, making a rocket-powered marker a necessity. The O-1 could fire high-explosive marking rockets accurately from 1,500 feet with minimum

exposure to enemy fire. The best firing altitude was at 800 feet, but this exposed the O-1 to enemy fire. The USAF decided to use the 2.75-inch rocket motor to carry three different types of warheads. White phosphorus (WP) or high-explosive (HE) rockets were most commonly used. In late 1964, the 3.5-inch white phosphorus rocket head was fitted to the 2.75-inch rocket motor.

Marking at night was a tricky operation under the best of conditions, but decidedly worse in bad weather and over jungle or mountainous terrain. Crews could experience vertigo and spatial disorientation. Rendezvous was difficult. However, the most critical problem was marking targets accurately in order to separate friendly from enemy troops. During the Ia Drang Valley operation in 1965, one FAC suggested the ground commander fill empty 105mm howitzer casings with sand soaked with JP-4 (jet fuel). Then when the enemy attacked, they were to light these torches, which were placed at the corners of the camp perimeter. These torches were an excellent reference, enabling the fighters to drop ordnance as close as 50 meters to the perimeter. Another method was to mark with 50-gallon drums cut in half and filled with jellied gasoline. Trip flares would be attached so that approaching enemy soldiers would set them off. The troops also used the Vietnamese trick of a flaming arrow pointing toward enemy positions. These arrows could be made of many materials.

Controlling Airstrikes

Strike control was a FAC art. Airstrikes were either preplanned or immediate because of the tactical situation. When the Forward Air Controller took off, he notified his TACP he was en route to the target area and his Time Over Target (TOT). After talking to the requesting commander and any other commanders of friendly units within two or three kilometers of the target, he furnished the brigade and division headquarters with exact target coordinates and then secured clearance for the strike.

The fighters would arrive at a specified rendezvous point. On UHF (Ultra High Frequency) radio, the FAC would then brief them with a thorough rundown on the target, location of friendly troops and their relation to the target and enemy troops, points of probable enemy ground fire, bombing tactics, sequence of ordnance delivery, and a safe, or best, bailout direction.

Night rendezvous methods matched day operations, except that the FAC and the strike pilots had a harder time finding each other. The O-2A/OV-10 controller normally furnished fighters with a Tactical Air Control Navigational Aid (TACAN) distance and radial to the rendezvous point, while the O-1 pilots, having no TACAN, channeled rendezvous coordinates to the strike aircraft by way of the Tactical Air Control Party and Direct Air Support Center (DASC). In the rendezvous area, the fighters held above the FAC's altitude. Join-up usually entailed a showing of wing lights or rotating beacons upon the order, "Go Christmas Tree!" When the FAC spotted the fighters, he would complete the join-up with a clock-code statement, such as, "I'm in your three o'clock position, low."

Night attacks were difficult. The smoke from the flares would spread out, forming a ceiling and causing confusing reflections. The fighters, under ROEs, turned off their position lights as soon as they started their run-in, so that it was hard to see them. Tracers at night were sometimes confusing, too. The enemy used green tracers. The red, used by U.S. guns, were captured by the enemy and used to confuse the Americans.

The target would be marked by the FAC using

Willie Petes, or by the ground troops. The FAC then used the smoke as a reference point to direct the fighters. When they were cleared in "hot," indicating they were to fire their ordnance, the FAC would say, "Hit my smoke!"

When the FAC had to mark in swampy areas, he would release his rocket in a shallow dive to prevent the rocket from burying itself in the mud. As a last resort, to counter these conditions, the FAC could mark with tracers. But because the tracer flashes vanished almost instantly, the strike aircraft had to be very alert.

Friendly troops near a target area might mark with their prearranged smoke grenades, colored signal panels, tracer crossfire, or artillery/mortar rounds. The enemy tried to confuse the issue by using similar signals, especially colored smoke. Sometimes the enemy used a stolen radio to give false commands to deceive the FACs.

Throughout the marking run, the FAC kept an eye on the strike aircraft, making sure they observed the marker impact and knew its distance from the target. Every second counted, as any delay allowed the enemy to pack up and move away, and thus when possible, the run-in heading for marking corresponded to, or was the reciprocal of, the strike aircraft's attack heading. Each fighter had to "tally" the smoke. If the situation was too dangerous for more than one pass, or if the fighter was low on fuel, it was "one pass, haul ass."

The FAC set up the strike so that ordnance fell toward the enemy to avoid injuring friendly ground troops should bombs skip across the terrain. If the landscape dictated, ordnance might have to be dropped parallel to friendly troops. Only an extreme emergency justified a drop toward the friendly troops. The FAC's judgment was crucial under such circumstances. If the target and marker fell within the minimum safe distance, the ground commander had to decide whether or not the strike would go on. Two markers were generally used when striking close to friendlies, bracketing the strike zone if possible. In extreme, desperate battles, the ground commanders would ask for strikes right on top of their positions.

The wheel pattern, entered from a loose trail formation, was used when there were no friendly troops nearby. The fighters would fly in a circle around the target and roll in from random headings. When the fighters flew a box pattern, the base and final legs were always the same. For radio silence, the flight

Australian FAC
Anthony Ford with
an O-1 Bird Dog at
Camp Bearcat,
1967.
Anthony Ford
Collection

leader could signal by fishtailing to spread out, or nose bobbing to fly in loose trail, or wing rocking to close up the formation. A sharp dip of the wing signaled the pilots to form an echelon on either side.

After marking the target, the FAC took up a position where he could see both the fighters and the target area, adjusting his position according to the type of attack (high or low), terrain, and friendly/enemy troop dispositions. If the fighters dropped slicks (low-drag or free-fall ordnance), the FAC held high. If the ordnance was drags (drogue-retarded or parachute-dropped ordnance), napalm, or BLUs (Bomb, Live Unit of special purpose bombs), the FAC held at a lower altitude. An outside, or overhead, pattern was used with variations.

The type of ordnance dictated the order of the strike aircraft's run-in. General purpose bombs were usually followed by CBUs (Cluster Bomb Units) and napalm. CBUs were tubes that contained hundreds of softball-sized bomblets that dribbled out of the tubes with little wing-like vanes causing them to float downwards. They contained either high explosives or white phosphorus. The bomblets would explode into hundreds of pellets on contact with the ground. One pod could cover an area the size of a football field. Pilots put them on target from straight-and-level

flight at 450 knots at 300 feet AGL. If the release altitude was too high, the bombs would drift away from the target. If it was too low, the bombs would not arm. Whenever tactical conditions permitted, the fighters made a "dry" pass — an orientation pass with no ordnance dropped — to pinpoint the target for the "hot" pass — a run-in pass with ordnance armed — that followed. The FAC had the authority to omit the dry pass and send the fighter in "hot." If the FAC thought the fighter would imperil the troops or hit the wrong target, he could send the fighter in "dry" or pull him off the target. The fighter pilot also could call off his drop if he saw a problem. During the rest of the strike, the FAC adjusted each pass so that it would be more effective. In high threat areas, the FACs would have the fighters use random pass headings.

If flareships joined the FAC and strike aircraft, spacing took on special importance. The FAC stacked and offset the aircraft at separate altitudes. The flareship usually flew a tight pattern on the side of the target opposite the FAC and 1,000 feet above. It dispensed flares every two and one-half to three minutes on a heading reciprocal to the strike aircraft's. For a continuous view of the fighters, the flareship set its heading 90° to the fighters' course. From a perch above and outside the FAC and flareship, the strike aircraft dove between their orbits during run-ins on the target.

When a gunship linked up with the FAC and fighters, it usually flew a circular pattern, firing at enemy guns while dispensing flares, ceasing activity during airstrikes, because on roll-in the fighters passed 500 to 1,000 feet below. After pull-off, the fighter pilot had to stay clear of the bigger, slower gunship as he climbed through its altitude. Danger of collision decreased in an offset pattern that put the gunship on the opposite side of the target from the controller to enhance the FAC's view of the entire operation.

Australian FAC Flight Lieutenant Anthony Ford commended the O-1:

IT WAS A DAMNED good aircraft. You could do practically anything with it. Apart from running rough, the engine never failed me. I was hit many, many times. Our tactics were sound, especially the 1,500-foot limit. The time I was hit so many times, I was forced to fly low, and was very lucky to come out of that operation.

⁂

Flight Lieutenant Ford's citations for medals all note his professional skill and airmanship. The citation for action near Bear Cat, on 12 January 1968, supporting troops in heavy contact reads:

Throughout this time he was receiving light to moderate ground fire which greatly added to a difficult situation. Disregarding his own safety,

he directed two airstrikes causing the enemy to break contact and silencing several automatic weapon positions. After daylight, the ground troops credited the airstrikes with saving a lot of American lives and destroying many enemy positions.

Australian Flight Lieutenant Garry G. Cooper (*Tamale* 35, supporting the 3rd Brigade, 9th Infantry Division) also distinguished himself on many occasions, both in the air and on the ground. Cooper, who was working extremely low, decided to lessen his chances of being hit by ground fire. Cooper's action report for 4 October 1968 described his procedure and made evident his skills:

He would put in his smoke markers using a shallow approach so that the trees would block the enemy gunners' vision, leaving himself exposed to gunfire a minimum amount of time. This proved most effective as the ground fire, although just as intense, was not very accurate until the aircraft was directly over the target. The only reason Flight Lieutenant Cooper did not receive hits must be attributed to his skillful rocket delivery techniques, changing attack direction on each pass as much as possible. . . . So close did he monitor the target that one fighter pilot reported hearing gun fire over the radios.

Cooper's dossier is full of descriptions of flights during which he saved hundreds of lives, disregarding his own personal safety. He often flew low to draw enemy fire away from the friendlies, using his O-1 as bait. On many occasions he made repeated low passes over enemy gun emplacements to draw fire, forcing them to reveal their positions to the attacking fighter aircraft. Many of the reports state it was miraculous that he was not hit. He was "daring and skillful" as he performed day after day in extremely hazardous and adverse conditions. Many fighter pilots that he worked with, and ground commanders, wrote letters of commendation regarding his "professional ability, valorous

The flight line at Tan An Air Base, 1968.   Anthony Ford Collection

performance, gallantry and devotion to duty."

Flight Lieutenant Cooper was recommended for the Medal of Honor for his actions on 18 August 1968, even though the medal cannot be given to a foreigner. From the USAF commendation:

On that date two of my F-4 pilots were working with Tamale 35 on a heavily defended target at Gai Be, near Rach Kein, when Captain Cooper's helicopter crashed very close to the hostile position. Without FAC direction, the F-4 pilots could not provide the close air support and circled helplessly. When last seen, Tamale 35, distinctive by his Australian flight-suit, was half-carrying an Infantryman toward an embankment under what must have been highly hazardous conditions. The situation as viewed did not seem survivable. We of the 12th TFW [*Tactical Fighter Wing*] sincerely hope that Tamale 35 will soon return to provide us with his exceptional Forward Air Controlling.

Cooper also spent long hours in the Tactical Operations Center (TOC) planning and coordinating air power. Throughout the offensive in the spring of 1968, his

aggressiveness and initiative, under conditions of continuing stress, were instrumental in obtaining clearances and fighter allocations to support 3rd Brigade ground units. In addition, he spent many nights traversing an insecure road, to the airstrip, in order to ensure that the ground forces would have the support required regardless of the time of day.

Flight Lieutenant Cooper developed a valuable FAC navigation aid, a convenient map directory that enabled pilots to fly to any target in III or IV Corps areas of operation with a minimum of notice. This system did away with the ungainly method of refolding maps in flight and enhanced high navigation

Robert Monroe, ready to launch a FAC mission in July 1969.   Robert Monroe Collection

efficiency under all conditions, as reported in the Aircrew Record of Operational Tour, signed by Lieutenant Colonel James T. Patrick.

Then Major Robert Monroe (*Jake* 74), flying O-2s, related his own FAC experiences:

GENERALLY I FLEW once or twice a day, each flight two to four hours depending on the mission. We always had one or two FACs over Quang Tien Province during daylight hours. I was checked out combat-ready in five days. I flew alone and usually solo. Primarily I did visual reconnaissance, airstrikes, put in RANCH HAND [*defoliation and herbicide*] spray missions, convoy patrol, artillery adjusting, and I even shot the guns off a carrier sitting off the coast. One of the roads of the Trail in Laos came through the mountains in Quang Ngai Province. We got involved in interdiction along that road. We usually had a lot of preplanned strike areas for the F-100s coming back off the Trail.

Whenever we were airborne, we had another FAC on the ground at the command post talking to us on the radio. The pilot was working three radios at once, talking to the fighters and the ground commander. With one toggle switch, you were really busy. There was a lot of trim-and-rudder flying of the airplane.

I liked to start an airstrike at 2,000 feet because I didn't want to go below 1,500; you would lose about 500 feet of altitude setting up a strike. If I got below

San Sok flies as the backseater in an OV-10 Bronco with FAC Doug Aitken.

doing his run-in before you can clear him hot to the target. It's a VFR operation. I have run it below ceilings of 2,000 feet, and it gets to be a little easier because fighters are not as maneuverable down that low. There are fighters I loved to work with and some I hated. I liked the F-100 [*Super Sabre*] the best. The guys generally put their bombs or strafed where you told them to. The worst planes to work with were the F-4s [*Phantom II*]. They were very maneuverable. A pair of them would just about run you ragged trying to keep up with them. They would turn such a tight pattern that before I could get one around and check his bomb to see where it hit, and make adjustments off that bomb for the next guy, and check to see if the run-in line is clear, the second guy would be looking for the cleared-in hot clearance. Sometimes the guys would shift the run-in line, so you couldn't clear them hot until you visually checked to see where he was running across the ground. If anything went wrong, the FAC was responsible. The FAC was the ultimate guy.

1,000 feet I was easy prey for small arms fire. They told us in-country that any time Charlie could read the numbers on the airplane, you were within range of his weapon. So, if you got down that low you could expect to come home with some bullet holes in the airplane.

The technique for shooting a rocket pass was, more or less, to get on crosswind or base leg to your run-in line and then just pull up the nose, wing-over, and dive and roll out real quick and line it up. We had a sight, kind of like a gun sight, that sat up on the windscreen. It was a series of cross-hairs on glass. You had to neutralize your rudder pedals. If you had any one-sided rudder pressure, you would throw your rocket off, even though your gun sight was straight, because the plane would be cocked. So it was quickly get the thing off, arm the rocket, shoot, pull-off. Generally you did a 180 to fly downwind of your run-in line because now you have to talk to the fighter, tell him where your smoke is, and do your adjustments off the smoke. He saw you make your run-in, and you wanted him to use the same run-in line. You are responsible for his ground track, and just in case he gets an early release, you don't want him to run over friendlies. You brief him. It has to be quick because usually the fighters are tight on fuel.

The fighters sit at an orbit of 10,000 feet or higher, holding high and dry, anxious to get to work. You have to have a visual sighting of the fighter as he's

---

French-speaking Doug Aitken (*Rustic* 16), who flew an OV-10, explained how a FAC would adjust his attack strategy according to the type of fighters he was working:

I ALWAYS TRIED to give the fighters random direction attacks unless friendly positions dictated otherwise. The A-37s [*Dragonflys*] loved this, and expected it. When we did start working with the F-4s, they were used to north/south, east/west type run-ins, and though we would clear them for random attacks, they would still use only one direction. With the F-4s, you could hold in a looser pattern than for the A-37s. You did not hold over the target with the F-4s unless they were releasing stuff like finned nape [*napalm*], high drags, etc. If they were dropping

Mishyou, the *Rustic* Mascot, walked down to Ops every morning prior to the first launch and didn't leave until the last recovery. She slept in the squadron hooch and would drink Miller beer, but no other brand.   Doug Aitken Collection

that which made it a much more rewarding job. It helped living next to the A-37s at Bien Hoa and rehashing the day's strikes over a beer. When the *Rustic* FACs moved to Ubon, there was a general change in effectiveness.

Generally I worked from 1,500 feet AGL as a bottom altitude. We might work from 3,000 feet, roll-in to mark, and bottom out no lower than 1,500 feet. In areas where Intel [*Intelligence*] had the .50 cals [*caliber guns*] located, we worked from 4,500 feet or higher. We got very good at FACing and marking from there. The OV-10s always lost a lot of altitude at every pass, so the best technique was to start high and let the fighters pass underneath. Most of the A-37s broke left because they flew from the left seat. They didn't want to worry about the FAC being in the windscreen when they pulled up.

There were times when the FAC would not allow a fighter pilot to drop his bombs, because he was afraid that the fighter would be inaccurate, causing friendlies to be injured. Joe Madden (*Cider* 10) recalled a time when he was working fighters in support of a U.S. Army Battalion on 8 November 1967:

slicks [*low-drag, straight-flying weapons*], I held them off to one side and would set up to come "down the chute" with them to keep them in sight and watch results. With gunships, since they would orbit over the target, we would mark and then hold off to one side. With the A-37s, we had mutual respect.

We were not as close with the F-4 drivers. I felt they were the ones losing out: buzz in, drop your bombs, and buzz home. They did not see the situation develop, know its background, what was at stake, or the folks on the ground. We got into all of

THEY WERE ALL there at once, a flight of A-1s, a flight of F-4s, and three flights of F-100s. I briefed them all at one time on the target. I sent the A-1s down to the south to hold at 6,000 feet. I had a flight of F-100s ready to go to work. Their base altitude is 9,000 feet, their base leg altitude, so I stacked the other flights of fighters at 1,000-foot separation at 15, 16, and 17,000 feet. It happened that the F-4 flight was at 16,000 feet. So I put the first flight of F-100s in and then the A-1s had nothing but napalm. I was going to put them in, but then the next flight of F-100s was hurting for fuel, so I said,

Captain Doug Aitken (*Rustic* 16) May 1971-May 1972, patches and plaque.   Doug Aitken Collection

"OK *Hobos*, hold it off." The second flight of F-100s had 500 pound bombs. I put them in on some mortar and 12.7 [*antiaircraft*] sites. Then I brought the *Hobos* (A-1s) up and they napalmed around both sides of the perimeter.

Meanwhile the other fighter pilots were sitting up in orbit, listening to my instructions to all the other flights. Then it was time for the F-4s to go to work. I said, "Okay, you see the western fire where the napalm is?" And one of the pilots said, "I don't know, I want a briefing." I said, "What don't you

The Douglas AC-47, *Puff the Magic Dragon,* gunship at Cam Ranh Bay, 1966.   John Taylor Collection

know?" He said, "Well, I don't know where the target is." So I said, "Get your ass out of here. Clear the area." He said, "I think I know where it is." I said, "Think is not good enough. Get the hell out of the way and get off the frequency."

I started talking to the next flight of F-100s. "Miss that flight of F-4s and come on down." The guy in the F-4 piped again, "Well, I think I know where you want the bombs, I'm ready to go to war." I said, "Get your ass out of here. You're not dropping your damn bombs anywhere in Southeast Asia as far as I am concerned." And, I sent him home. I wouldn't let him drop. Here's a guy sitting up there half an hour, flying around with nothing to do but fly in circles and look at the ground, listening to all that damn war going on, and he doesn't know where the hell the war was. I don't know what he was thinking, but his thoughts certainly weren't on the job.

Bomb Damage Assessments (BDA)

The FACs were called on to fly down after an attack and do a bomb damage assessment — a damage tally by all the types of ordnance — which would be reported to headquarters. When a FAC flew low, the only way he could survive the ground fire was to never fly straight and level for one second. He kept his aircraft jinking all the time and pulling Gs. Fred

McNeil (*Covey* 502) described how he sent fighters up on the perch to wait for their turn at assessment:

ONE TIME I WENT down to do BDA, and it scared the hell out of me. I had two Navy [*Vought Corsair II*] A-7s come up behind me to strafe. They told me I was taking ground fire and I didn't know it. They came down right behind me without being asked. Maybe they just wanted to strafe. Anyhow that's how they did it when we were taking fire.

ARC LIGHT Missions

The Boeing B-52 Stratofortresses conducted their bombing missions from extremely high altitudes — so high that the enemy couldn't see or hear them. Robert Monroe (*Jake* 74) described these missions, called ARC LIGHT:

THESE FLIGHTS WERE kind of hairy. We had to fly over an area and do visual recon before an ARC LIGHT mission, without giving away what was going to take place. The guys on the ground were used to hearing FAC planes all day, so we kept all our passes the same to look normal. We were checking for anything unusual and to be sure no friendlies had strayed into the area to be bombed. Ten minutes before the ARC LIGHT took place we had to be in

LT-6G Texans (49-3557 and 49-3579) of the 6147th TACCON at Chun Chun.    Dick Phillips Collection

that area, announcing the coordinates on guard. We also watched for stray aircraft so they wouldn't fly into the drop zone.

Sid Johnson, who was a *Mosquito* FAC in Korea before going to Vietnam, flew in a C-47 that was equipped with special electronics (installed by Sanders Corporation):

WE FAC'd B-52s from C-47s. We were the primary source for locating targets for heavy bombers. These B-52s were standby over a position in the South China Sea waiting for somebody to have a target of opportunity. Our RC-47-P carried a lot of classified audio and visual equipment. We carried different services in the back. We could locate targets within a few feet. We flew in the DMZ, North Vietnam, Laos, and Cambodia.

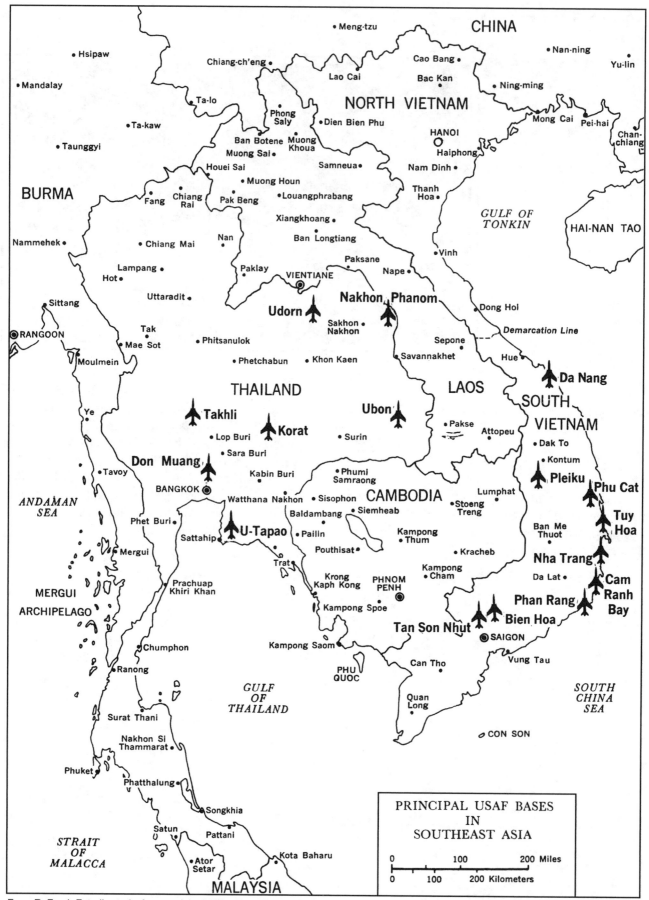

PRINCIPAL USAF BASES
IN
SOUTHEAST ASIA

0   100   200 Miles

0   100   200 Kilometers

From R. Frank Futrell, *et al., Aces and Aerial Victories: The United States Air Force in Southeast Asia 1965-1973* (Washington, D.C.: GPO, for The Albert F. Simpson Historical Research Center, and Office of Air Force History, Headquarters USAF, 1976), p. 23.

Chapter 3

U.S. Involvement Stepped Up

$\mathcal{T}$HERE WAS ONLY LOW-KEY USAF involvement until the August 1964 Gulf of Tonkin incident. The North Vietnamese attack on U.S. destroyers resulted in reprisal attacks that were formalized in the "Tonkin Gulf Resolution" passed by both houses of the U.S. Congress on 7 August. Contingency plans for airstrikes already had been drawn up. Isolated reprisal attacks were made until February 1965, when President Lyndon B. Johnson decided to inaugurate a sustained, limited air attack against North Vietnam, an operation called ROLLING THUNDER.

In May 1964, the USAF had begun flying reconnaissance missions over the Laotian panhandle to obtain information about the supplies and troops traversing the Ho Chi Minh Trail. Many footpaths had been enlarged to become main arteries for North Vietnamese trucks and heavy equipment in order to bypass the DMZ on the way to South Vietnam.

By the end of 1964, OPERATION BARREL ROLL was involved in interdiction operations in Laos. The U.S. Ambassador to Laos approved all targets before they were attacked. BARREL ROLL provided strikes in northern and southern Laos to support the RLAF and Hmong forces. The bulk of the airstrikes took place out-country, but some hammered enemy supply routes in central South Vietnam.

The USAF again needed the FACs in their low-flying, slow-moving aircraft, to serve as a liaison with the ground troops and the fighters. This was especially critical with Troops In Contact (TIC) with the enemy or near friendly villages.

In early 1965, the enemy carried the initiative in Vietnam as the Viet Cong increased its attacks throughout the countryside. The 7 February 1965 attack on the U.S. air base at Pleiku caused President Johnson to order new air attacks on North Vietnam. Large contingents of U.S. Army and Marine troops were ordered to Vietnam. On 2 March 1965, the USAF instituted OPERATION ROLLING THUN-DER, the systematic bombing of North Vietnam starting at the DMZ.

General William C. Westmoreland had decided to change the nature of the U.S. involvement in February 1965. U.S. markings were restored to the A-1Es, and the requirement for Vietnamese observers in American planes was abolished by General Tran Van Minh. On 9 March 1965, the Joint Chiefs of Staff decided that U.S. aircraft could be used for combat operations in South Vietnam, but with no strikes originating from Thailand. The USAF now had a new system for improved air-to-ground communication. Ground or airborne FACs could send a ground commander's request for immediate air support directly to the Direct Air Support Center (DASC), and DASC would send appropriate air to the waiting FAC for a rapid response.

On 3 April 1965, the U.S. began STEEL TIGER, an operation over the panhandle of Laos and the DMZ, to locate and destroy enemy forces and troops that were being moved southward at night. Laos was still neutral, thus target approval had to come from Washington. The U.S. Ambassadors in Laos, Vietnam, and Thailand were also involved in these U.S. air operations

12th Air Force Tactical Air Control Party (TACP) Deployed to Southeast Asia, August-September 1965

This subordinate operational component of the Tactical Air Control System (TACS) provided air liaison functions and coordination for the control of strike aircraft. Consisting of Air Liaison Officers, Forward Air Controllers, radio operators, and other personnel as required, Tactical Air Control Parties operated at the corps, field force, division, brigade, or cavalry squadron and battalion levels, as well as province and regimental levels of the ARVN forces. In the fall 1965, one TACP was assigned to each maneuver battalion, two to each brigade, and four to division headquarters. Eleven of these people were F-100 Super Sabre pilots from Cannon Air Force Base. Others were F-4 Phantom II and F-105 Thud pilots from stateside McDill Air Force Base, Tampa, Florida, Seymour Johnson Air Force Base, Goldsboro, North Carolina, and McConnell Air Force Base, Wichita, Kansas, thus providing a wide range of experience and talent. Each TACP was assigned an MRC-108 radio jeep complete with a MD-28 generator and a full range of portable gear.

The first O-1 Bird Dog arrived 11 November 1965, and by 28 February, the full strength of Bird Dogs had arrived, 22 in all. Using the call sign *Sidewinder*, two were assigned to each of the five brigades, one to the cavalry squadron, and two to the division.

The O-1 had three radios, FM, VHF, and UHF, allowing the controller to call the DASC for his area to get approval for an airstrike. These requests could be relayed to Tan Son Nhut where the TACS could dispatch fighters. In an emergency situation, the FAC could call any fighter that was nearby. When the fighters arrived, he orchestrated the attack, swooping in low to mark the enemy position with his smoke rockets. In some instances, a fire support coordinator on the ground would provide target location information.

More than 7,000 combat tours were flown without incident or accident, although three pilots were wounded while airborne, and there were five dead-stick landings. One controller received a .30-caliber round through the floor and seat of his O-1, which lodged in his rear end. After that, many FACs started sitting on their flak vests instead of wearing them. Another *Sidewinder* received a .50-caliber round, but did not fare as well. The armament went through the floor and seat of his O-1 and continued up through his body, destroying bone, tissue, and organs, but stopping just short of his heart. Luckily, he was able to land at a nearby Army field hospital where there just happened to be a surgeon who specialized in such wounds. After a few anxious weeks, he was relocated to a hospital in the rear. Another FAC had a fuel line in his O-1 cockpit shot out, which began dumping raw fuel down his back — definitely a hazardous situation. He was able to get it plugged and land safely.

The *Sidewinder* FACs had support from McDonnell RF-4C Phantoms and RF-101 Voodoos, Martin RB-57 Canberras, and Douglas RB-66 Destroyers, and had Army Grumman OV-1 Mohawk aircraft to support recce requests. To fulfill airlift requirements they called on 30 C-130 Hercules and 43 C-123 Providers.

During ground alert, the FAC's response time matched the needs of the Army commander in that it took about 20 to 25 minutes from initial call to bombs on target. In an emergency, it took the commander from 20 to 25 minutes to establish the position of his troop, identify the threat, and have his troops dig in and mark their position. Response time with aircap (aircover rescue) over the requesting brigade was about four minutes.

On one occasion there was a target just off the south end of Bien Hoa. The fighters were rolling when the call was received, the FAC made contact as they retracted their gear and marked the target as they were inbound, allowing an immediate strike.

In 1965, two-man teams had been sent on temporary duty (TDY) to Udorn for operations in northern Laos. These teams, under the call sign *Butterfly*, consisting of an Air Liaison Officer and a FAC, worked from forward operating locations. *Butterfly* FACs, who were Air Commando Combat Controllers, flew as unrated FACs in Air America (CIA contract) aircraft to direct strikes in Laos. The ALO stayed on the ground to handle communications with the Laotian troop commander. When the FAC borrowed an aircraft, a Laotian crew member went along to interpret conversations between ground commanders and RLAF strike pilots. Later, the *Butterfly* FACs were replaced by the *Ravens,* the young USAF volunteer pilots who flew in civilian clothing from bases in Laos.

Technical Sergeant James J. Stanford (*Butterfly* 22 and *Butterfly* 44) flew as a backseater in an O-1E Bird Dog and in Air America aircraft:

IN APRIL 1966, I was sent to Nakhon Phanom (NKP), Thailand on project LUCKY TIGER. I flew in the back seat of O-1Es whose job was to look for targets on the trails coming from North Vietnam

through Laos into South Vietnam, then request fighter support and direct these fighter aircraft to the discovered targets. After a month of flying these missions I was taken, in civilian clothing, to Vientiane, Laos. From there Charlie Jones and I went to Long Tieng, also known as 20 Alternate, or simply Alternate.

Charlie had been working missions using the Pilatus Porter [*STOL aircraft*]. Earlier, because of the lack of UHF radio equipment in the aircraft, Charlie had obtained some antennas from Udorn and installed them on the Continental Air Service [*privately owned and under contract to CIA and other U.S. agencies*] and some Air America aircraft so we could get better reception from our portable equipment. We also installed a portable HF radio each day in the aircraft that we used with a long wire antenna strung to the wing strut.

Our call sign was *Butterfly*. The number designation depended on which zone we were flying in: *Butterfly* 22 in northwest Laos; *Butterfly* 44 in MR [*Military Region*] II, Sam Neuva Province; *Butterfly* 33 in MR III, Xieng Khouang Province; and the U.S. Army advisor attached to the Thai artillery battalion at Moung Soui used *Butterfly* 99. Our call sign could be said to have originated in the bars, as the girls used a phrase with the GIs when they would move around to different bars [*like*] butterflies, always moving, never staying in one place .

We were non-rated enlisted so we weren't flying the airplane, even though we were working on civilian licenses (I like to think that's why we were picked to do this mission, but in reality it was performance on other missions). We would fly in the right seat with either Continental Air Service or Air America pilots on the strike missions. The missions started the night before at General Vang Pao's house for debrief and the usual White Horse Scotch. We would debrief him on the day's operations, and with his messages from the field he would tell us what his plans were for the following day and in which areas his operations were being conducted.

Back in our operations hut we would encode our request for air support and include any new information obtained about bomb damage or kills from previous operations. During this period our support came from two flights of F-105s [*Republic Thunderchiefs, nicknamed the Thud*], one flight in the morning, another in the afternoon. The same would be true for the Thai T-28s [*North American Trojan*] that would cross over the border each day and unload at

The entrance to Ubon, Royal Thai Air Force Base.

Doug Aitken Collection

Discussion would get around to the next day's operational areas for the aircraft and determine who would fly with us on the strike missions. Our preferred aircraft was the Pilatus Porter. The pilots would be paid more for these missions, so the pilots would mostly rotate this mission among themselves. It was more challenging working with the fighters and provided a break from their routine.

We would take off at daybreak, proceed to the operations area, and land at the site to talk with the site commander. We would have a Thai interpreter with us who spoke Lao and would work as the FAC for the Thai T-28s. The site commander would have agents who had returned from the field with an eyeball account of targets, truck parks, bridges, troop locations, and gas barrels. We would then take off either with the agent or the information and do some target reconnaissance. The aircraft had a big side window on which we would draw an outline of the target site with a grease pencil. The agent would use the grease pencil to place the information on what he had seen and where. Next, we would go

Vientiane. Other aircraft could be obtained from the ABCCC [*Airborne Command and Control Center*] aircraft, which at this time was a RC-47, call sign *Dogpatch*.

We would get something to eat, then go up to the Air America porch, sit around and talk, have a few drinks, and play with the dogs or the caged bears.

Flying over a Viet Cong-infested area along the Republic of Vietnam coast, an Air Force C-47 crew fills the air with psychological warfare leaflets designed to persuade insurgents to turn themselves in, 10 March 1966. During and after the New Year holiday season in January, more than 1,600 Viet Cong defected, using "psy war" leaflets as safe-conduct passes.

USAF

F-105 Thunderchiefs, nicknamed the Thud.

back to the site, drop the agent off, then proceed to an area near the target, establish communication with *Dogpatch*, and await the arrival of the fighters.

As the fighters proceeded inbound to the target they would tell us what ordnance they had on board. We would describe the target area and the location of friendly troops. We couldn't mark the targets because Air America and Continental Air Service used the same aircraft to drop rice and other civil aid functions. We didn't want to make them targets for these missions. Later, because of fuel constraints for the fighters, we would occasionally drop smoke grenades but this was rare.

At one location, site 59, we had heavy troop concentrations trying to overrun it. We called ABCCC for support. It worked out because of weather problems in North Vietnam. Aircraft were airborne with ordnance and nowhere to dump, so they were diverted to us. Within 30 minutes we had flights all day. We ran out of fuel three different times and had to dead stick back to the landing site. Fuel was in 55-gallon drums, which we hand pumped into the wings. At times we would only get enough fuel in the aircraft to take off, direct the fighters, and head straight back to start the hand pump all over again.

At other locations there were lots of caves where the bad guys stored ammo, food, guns, and medical supplies. We preferred using the A-1s that flew the roadwatch missions, call sign *Firefly*, for cave strikes because of the amount of ordnance they carried and the longer time on target. These aircraft were very accurate and could put rockets right into the cave entrance. The fast movers were not as accurate and would only have time to make a marking pass, drop the load, then proceed directly to a tanker. We rendezvoused with these fighters using the TACAN [*Tactical Air Navigation*] near 20A on Skyline Ridge to give them a radial and a distance.

There were limited navigational aids in the Porter. Most of the time you would have to use plain old dead reckoning. The Air America pilots were very good at knowing where they were. Weather was a constant problem along with the terrain. It wasn't uncommon to break out of the clouds, beneath a 100-foot ceiling, in narrow valleys, and still be able to find your way back to the airstrip.

20A became one of the busiest airports in the world. The runway ran east to west in a valley, with a tall karst at the west end of the runway necessitating short field approaches. There were no roads into the base, only small trails. The landing strip was dirt, until early 1968 when it was paved. The maintenance area was PSP [*pierced, interlocking steel planking*].

In late June 1966 I was sent to work for Tony Poe in western Laos because he needed air support. He was based at LS118A, Nam Lieu, which had a clay

USAF B-57 Canberra tactical jet bombers over Vietnam.

runway 2350 feet by 60 feet at an elevation of 1,900 feet. It was a little harder to obtain air support because of the location. You couldn't get the fast movers because it was too far from their fuel supply. Some of my FAC missions were from H-34 [*Sikorsky Choctaw*] helicopters because they had UHF radios, which were an advantage.

Tony Poe was not one to sit idle if there was no fighters available. We would load rocks over the drop door of the Pilatus Porter and drop them on trucks. We also had these tubes that were about three inches in diameter. We would take about a hundred and lash them together and fill them with hand grenades with pins pulled with a little tape on the spoon so they would pop when falling or hitting the trees. Our biggest was lashing 100-pound high-explosive bombs with 100-pound white phosphorus bombs with time fuzes.

In August 1966 I returned to 20A to help Charlie Jones, as the operation was getting bigger. We were able to get more fighters including F-4s, A-4s, and, F-105s with different kinds of ordnance. We didn't

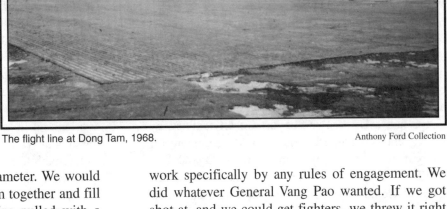

The flight line at Dong Tam, 1968.

Anthony Ford Collection

work specifically by any rules of engagement. We did whatever General Vang Pao wanted. If we got shot at, and we could get fighters, we threw it right back at them. It was a lot better fighting this way. The Laotians were different people, and it was totally different than Vietnam. The country was beautiful, as many who would come after us would say it is Shangri-La. While Vietnam was a political war run from Washington, Laos was the real thing. Nobody from outside the field was influencing the minute decisions that had to made in the field.

Jim Stanford with a FAC-equipped radio jeep, Laos 1967.

The adventure was there. Sure you were being shot at, but the excitement was tremendous. Here I was just a sergeant in the U.S. Air Force and had the power of a general. You were getting to do everything that you were trained to do. You had people down south that had the confidence in you to make the right decisions while operating at times alone. It was one of the my best fulfilling times in the service.

———— ✇ ————

The military divided South Vietnam into four corps tactical zones: I Corps, II Corps, III Corps, and IV Corps, and 214 Areas of Operation. Each Corps had a Direct Air Support Center manned by USAF and Vietnamese personnel to coordinate air support for the ground forces. Each DASC forwarded requests for airstrikes to the Tactical Air Control Center (TACC) in Saigon where air assets were (theoretically) assigned to each corps. The U.S. Marines controlled their own assets in I Corps. Even though there were conflicting command arrangements at the top, it was actually the local FACs who controlled the air war. Many times they made the difference between life and death for the embattled ground troops.

The enemy was reluctant to fire on the Forward Air Controllers, knowing that it would bring instant retaliation. However, once the enemy knew they had been spotted, they didn't withhold their fire, and many times the controllers swooped down through a hail of bullets while marking their targets.

USAF ground FACs, who used a specially equipped radio jeep, were assigned to Army units, who began using the air mobility concept in Vietnam. The FAC was assigned to the Army commander to advise him on the use of air attacks and how to request them. The Army used aircraft, primarily helicopters, instead of ground-based vehicles, to move troops from one place to another.

At first, the Army didn't comprehend that the FAC could have airstrikes almost immediately, but when they learned how the system worked, they appreciated it, especially the small gray O-1s flying overhead, keeping the enemy off their back. At night, these airplanes operated under the flares of the gunships. Joseph V. Potter had to call for a flareship while flying in the battle of Tong Le Chon Special Forces camp. He received the Silver Star and Vietnamese Cross of Gallantry for his actions that night.

On 11 August 1967, Potter had flown 250 combat missions:

I CONSIDERED MYSELF bullet-proof. Tong Le Chon Special Forces camp was specifically built to provide a blocking obstacle to protect An Loc. Manned by 300 Cambodian mercenaries and led by a Special Forces "A" team, it was cut out of triple canopy jungle just south of the "Fish Hook" jutting out from Cambodia (a prominent North Vietnamese staging area) and situated in the middle of the "Iron Triangle" [*south of Ben Cat, near Lai Khe, and Ben Suc, about 21 miles northwest of Saigon*]. A model Special Forces camp, it contained two reinforced perimeters ringed by mine fields, barbed wire, and overlapping fields of fire. If it fell, it would provide the enemy with a clear psychological advantage and a clear path to roll over a key provincial capital.

It was pitch dark as I flew toward the camp, but the sky was lit with the red glow of numerous explosions. There was no moon and no horizon. My O-1 was not equipped for instrument flight, but I kept flying in and out of low-lying clouds. I was sitting on my flak vest with no parachute — because flying between 100 and 500 feet, a parachute would have no time to deploy. I flew on, a rock-hard FAC, "armed" to the teeth with awesome destructive power, including a ten-inch Marine Corps combat knife, complete with "blood grooves."

As I approached the battle site, the continuous white fire of the explosions on the ground were almost blinding. I began to attract intense ground fire. The dull, low thuds were delayed by several seconds. Tracers from numerous .50-caliber machine-gun emplacements pierced the sky. I turned off my running lights and began jinking erratically with great flying skill and involuntary hyper-apprehension.

I contacted the ground commander. He said they were being attacked by two crack North Vietnamese regiments (about 3,000 troops), that their outside perimeter had fallen, most of his command was decimated, and that the survivors were trying to hold the inside perimeter against human wave assaults. The commander was badly wounded, almost hysterical and half-crying with panic. There was desperation in his voice as he told me the Army did not intend to reinforce the camp as this would amount to more American casualties.

Flying a semicircular horseshoe pattern, I began adjusting a 155mm long-range artillery battery located ten miles to the east. I gave the command "fire

An F-4C airstrike, less than five miles from Tam Ky. The tremendous amount of smoke made target marking by the FACs very difficult.
Robert Monroe Collection

on for three hours. I whirled the O-1 around, dodged ground fire repeatedly, while briefing the fighters and helicopter gunships and reassuring the ground commander. The tide of battle seemed to be turning. I had expended all my rockets and my fuel level was extremely low.

The first rays of dawn cut through low clouds and steam rose from the green jungle on my flight back to Phouc Vinh. My voice was hoarse, eyes burned, and hands were still shaking. Visions of the battle flashed in my thoughts as I planned my return to Tong Le Chon

for effect" and one side of the enemy camp received a continual pounding with devastating accuracy as I bracketed the target.

I called for a flareship for USAF tactical bombers, and while waiting, briefed the flight leaders of several Army helicopter gunships. They darted in and out at low level, stinging the enemy with rockets, grenades, and machine-gun fire. Probably the most unsung group of heroes, the Army's helicopter crews displayed raw courage, operational responsiveness, and disciplined airmanship. In this battle, they were particularly effective as they dodged low clouds and constantly shifted flight patterns to confuse enemy gunners.

With several flights of F-100s and F-4s at high altitude overhead, I instructed the C-47 *Spooky* flareship to orbit the battle area upwind and to keep two flares burning at all times. The fighters were briefed on the ground situation, fire-control lines to avoid incoming artillery, and helicopter patterns, as well as attack headings and pulloffs. The ground commander continued to scream, asking for bombs to be placed as close as possible to their position.

I rolled in and fired marking rockets and began directing flight after flight of tactical fighters, expending their ordnance as quickly as possible. We had 500-pound bombs, napalm, and 20mm from sets of fighters on all sides. This intensive fighting went

after refueling to mop up retreating enemy units. I knew they would be making their way north to the "Fish Hook" sanctuary in Cambodia. I would have to catch them before they could get to the border.

I did a quick turnaround and launched with full fuel and rockets. Arriving over the battle site, I saw a smoking camp in rubble. Bodies were scattered everywhere, both enemy and friendly. The ground commander, with a weak voice on a crackled radio frequency, still tried to maintain contact. Other than a red and gold South Vietnamese flag hanging limp at the flagpole and black smoke rising from several fires, there was no movement or sign of life. The few remaining friendlies were wounded or completely exhausted, hiding in underground bunkers waiting for medical aid. The Army choppers began bringing in help and supplies, kicking up dust as they landed in the camp.

I received sporadic fire, but after directing several more airstrikes into the jungle surrounding the camp, it stopped. I adjusted long-range artillery fire into likely assembly locations and directed helicopter light fire teams along possible escape routes into Cambodia. The battle had ended.

The airborne FAC took on additional importance

as the Army moved into mountainous territory or thick jungles, where the ground FAC couldn't see very far. The role of the ground FAC became that of an Air Liaison Officer, counseling ground commanders on air support. The North Vietnamese waged a very different form of war than what our air forces had encountered in previous conflicts. The enemy attempted to make itself immune to airstrikes by moving its troops at night and using varied techniques for camouflage. They also used numerous underground tunnels to keep out of sight during daylight hours.

In April 1965, there were four O-1 Bird Dog Squadrons in Vietnam. One year later, there were 250 FACs in South Vietnam. These numbers increased substantially as the war continued. In addition to the 19th TASS at Bien Hoa, the 20th TASS was at Da Nang AFB, the 21st TASS at Pleiku, the 22nd TASS at Binh Thuy, and the 23rd TASS at Nakhon Phanom. All were grouped under the 504th Tactical Air Support Group (TASG) at Bien Hoa Air Base for administrative, maintenance, and supply support. The 504th reported to Seventh Air Force headquarters at Saigon. The Seventh Air Force was under MACV (Military Assistance Command Vietnam), which reported to CINCPAC, who answered directly to the Secretary of Defense Robert McNamara. The main operating bases for maintenance were Nha Trang, supported by the 20th and 21st TASS, and Binh Thuy, supported by the 19th and 22nd. However, limited maintenance was performed

The 20th Tactical Air Support Squadron maintenance crew kept their aircraft flying for 250,000 hours.

at the various forward operating locations. The 19th, 21st, and 22nd Squadrons operated almost entirely in-country, while the 20th flew both in South Vietnam and out-country.

Keo Neva Pass, Laos 1966.
Jim Stanford Collection

A massive enemy attack, 19 October 1965, on the Plei Me Special Forces camp in the Central Highlands of South Vietnam had required Tactical Air Command air for the survival of friendly troops that were caught off guard by the enemy's sophisticated weapons and large ammunition supplies. The troops and their weapons had come from a sanctuary in Laos where the North Vietnamese had started the Ho Chi Minh Trail in 1959 as an infiltration route to South Vietnam. The main passes were at Mu Gia and Ban Karai, as well as at Deo Keo Nua (Nape Pass) and Ban Raving Pass. From the passes, the Trail fanned out in three directions through the Laotian panhandle into Cambodia, and had choke points that could not be bypassed. The Ho Chi Minh Trail skirted the DMZ, which cut Vietnam in half, and was North Vietnam's main supply route to its military offensive in South Vietnam.

A-1E and A-1H Skyraiders at Ubon, Thailand, with an F8F Bearcat in the background, September 1966.
Frank Kricker Collection

Enemy supplies were delivered by ship to Hanoi and then moved south by road or rail to Route 12 to the west into the Annamite Mountains and down the Trail.

The bloody battle of the Ia Drang Valley, in November 1965, had sent the enemy back to Cambodia, and as the year progressed, the North Vietnamese increased their use of the Ho Chi Minh Trail. Thus, the U.S. decided to concentrate operations on the part of the Trail closest to South Vietnam. This venture, named OPERATION TIGER HOUND, utilized USAF, Navy, Marine, VNAF, and RLAF aircraft. TIGER HOUND began operations 6 December 1965 to conduct an interdiction campaign in Laos to impede night operations on the Trail and river complex nearest to South Vietnam, with FAC O-1s controlling the strike aircraft. The operation brought together Air Force FACs, Airborne Battlefield and Command and Control Center aircraft, Army OV-1 Mohawks, flareships, and C-123 defoliation aircraft. U.S. B-52s were called in on 11 December 1965, the first time they were used in tactical operations over Laos.

By early 1966, the TIGER HOUND O-1 FACs had been augmented by A-1E Skyraiders, from the 1st Air Commando Squadron. They were to be used for a short time, until the planes were needed more as strike aircraft. The Skyraider could carry a tremendous ordnance load — more than a B-17 Flying Fortress in World War II. The A-1 could deliver accurately and loiter in the target area, and had the capacity to sustain battle damage. The aircraft was also used for search and rescue under the call sign *Sandy*. In the FAC role, the A-1Es carried 14 marking rockets in addition to other munitions.

The Army OV-1 Mohawks used side-looking airborne infrared radar (SLAR) to detect the enemy along the roads and trails. An Army unit based at Phu Bai in 1968, with the call sign *Spud*, flew almost exclusively the OV-1. The pilots all wore black flight suits. Their primary mission was locating movers — trucks or tanks — in the RP-I/DMZ (Route Package One/Demilitarized Zone) area using side-looking radar.

The FACs were usually part of the search and rescue task force, especially in the early stages of a recovery mission. The FAC was often the first aircraft in the area, and thus he assumed the job of on-scene commander until the Douglas A-1, call sign *Sandy*, arrived. Often it was the FAC who first spotted the survivor. After the *Sandy* reached the Initial Point (IP), the controller assisted by directing jet fighter-bombers if they were needed.

The FAC aircraft staged from Special Forces airstrips near the Laotian border, including Dong Ha, Khe Sanh, Kham Duc, and Kontum. At first, the O-1 TIGER HOUND controllers worked by day patrolling from dawn to dusk. The enemy holed up during the day in camouflaged truck parks until dark. By

January 1966, the night interdiction operation commenced. C-130s lumbered alongside the OV-1s dropping flares when told of potential targets. Next, the O-1 FACs moved in to mark the target and request strike aircraft. When bad weather grounded the O-1, AC-47 *Spooky* aircraft with a controller aboard took over. The *Spooky* marked targets with minigun tracer fire. The controllers on the AC-47s could get fighters from the ABCCC and direct them in the target area. The AC-47 pilots were also checked out as "target identifiers."

Out-country tactical air couldn't be controlled by the Direct Air Support Centers, so an ABCCC flew as a relay aircraft. The first was *Dogpatch,* an RC-47 that had worked the BARREL ROLL area in northern Laos, pending the arrival of a big ABCCC. By the fall of 1965, *Hillsboro,* a EC-130, was on-station carrying a Lao officer for swift approval of strike requests. This coordination was so successful that a second EC-130 ABCCC, *Cricket,* came on line in 1966. By late 1966, the RC-47 was operating opposite the DMZ, where it was called *Alleycat.* It was replaced in June 1967 by an EC-130, which worked strikes in North Vietnam and Laos. In February 1968, the Seventh Air Force divided *Alleycat's* operating area, with the EC-130 *Moonbeam* taking over the STEEL TIGER area in Southern Laos. Day and night coverage by ABCCC was a backbone of the war.

TIGER HOUND night FAC operations were coordinated with the EC-130 ABCCC *Moonbeam,* which could throw out flares, each shining with two-million candle power to illuminate the target. The FACs flew at night over the Ho Chi Minh Trail and rivers looking for trucks and sampans. At that time, each *Moonbeam* sortie carried two Royal Laotian officers, who had to get approval for each target from the Laotian government by communicating with centers at Vientiane or Savannakhet. In emergencies they could evaluate targets on the spot.

Living Arrangements

Some of the FACs lived in tents with the Army while others enjoyed more luxurious accommodations, depending on where they were based. Richard Clements (*Covey* 243, with the 20th TASS, 1967-1968) commented on the daily routine:

AT HUE PHU BAI I was living in a compound where I had a refrigerator and a stereo set. Boredom was a problem. We had lots of books. We would fly one mission a day and then wait. We drank and played basketball and handball. During the siege of Khe Sanh I flew 68 days straight. The most exciting time for the FACs was the Tet Offensive. That's when most of us worked our butts off.

Paul Burrows, during 1968-1969, started out with the 1st Air Cavalry at Division Camp Evans near the village of Phong Dien, and moved with them to Bien Hoa and Quen Loi (call sign *Rash*). Later, he was assigned to the 1st Australian Task Force out of Nui Dat (call sign *Jade*), and he finished up with the 82nd Airborne out of Phu Loi (call sign *Gimpy*):

WE ENVIED THE FIGHTER types with their air-conditioned quarters, but our situation wasn't always bad, depending on how permanent the base camp was and how long the FACs had been there. Showers ranged, for instance, from a five-gallon jerry can with holes punched in the bottom and tied to a tree, to a drop tank with an immersion heater and nozzle, to a real French or U.S. made shower. Some of the chow provided by Army cooks at a base camp, consisting of doctored up C rations, was surprisingly good. FACs, given the time, usually scrounged stuff to improve their living conditions because in the Air Force, we like to be comfortable. Some Army units liked to use the term "hard core" and seemed to try to live in misery if they could. Aussies differed in this regard and tried to make their surroundings liveable.

Duane Aasted (*Cider* 11), who worked for the 1st Brigade, 4th Infantry, at Dak To in 1968, described living arrangements:

OUR LIVING QUARTERS were excellent. Our men in Dak To put up a building to live in. They obtained (swiped) everything they needed throughout the country. The Army commander made a special trip to view the standard porcelain urinals with deodorant cakes. The hooch [*living quarters*] also had a nylon parachute ceiling. It was first-class. No one worried about having "USAF DAK TO" on the roof, because the enemy's aim was poor. Our bar was the "Dak Tiki." The Montagnards made lampshades for us from bamboo. We had a GE pink refrigerator. The bar had a tile top (a chapel being constructed in Phan Rang came up short for that one). We had lots of new furniture that was officially listed as destroyed in a rocket attack on Pleiku. Wayne Abbey painted a nude mural, that must have been eight feet long, over the bar. It was a very nice bar.

John Rogers (*Nail* 68) was at Nakhon Phanom, Thailand, from 1968 to 1969:

ALSO KNOWN as NKP, it was out in the country. The red clay roads were paved by 1969. The hooches had two men to a room that had a refrigerator and air-conditioner. It was much better than Vietnam, because there were no mortar attacks. You could take a bus or taxi to Mekong. The food was good and the ladies were friendly. Some of our guys lived in town with local Thai girls.

Richard Gary Mucho, a *Toy* FAC at Di An 1969 to 1970, recalled his primitive living conditions:

WE DIDN'T live in Bien Hoa, Cam Ran Bay, or Da Nang in nice huge air-conditioned units in rooms with clean sheets. We lived on a primitive basis. It was hot and muggy. Our uniforms would last a couple of months before they were in shreds. We used two holers and four holers. We had to beg to get a fan for a commode.

David L. "Dutch" Helms, *Bilk* 37, assigned to the 20th TASS in 1969, was based at Camp Evans working with the 3rd Brigade of the 101st Airborne Division. Camp Evans was a forward operating location right outside the village of Phong Dien, midway between Hue and Quang Tri. Helms flew O-2s from a 2,200-foot PSP runway that had mine fields for over-

Duane Aasted, call sign *Cider* 11, flying over Dak Seang Special Forces Camp just after wiping out a mortar west of the camp that had been bothering them for several days. Upon seeing a large secondary explosion, the Special Forces radio operator said, "*Cider*, that was better than peanut butter."

Duane Aasted Collection

Duane Aasted at Dak To, 1968, ready for a mission in his O-2.

The 4th of July party, 1968, at Dak To. All outfits had a dog. This one was named Waldo, and Waldo later had puppies. Duane Aastad says, "The name was probably due to poor Intelligence."
Duane Aasted
Collection

FIVE FAC OFFICERS lived in our sandbagged hooch, and obviously it was not first-class living, but that was how the Army liked to live, so that's how we lived. We stored water in a big gray tower. We had 55-gallon drums with gasoline-fueled water heaters. We would light that thing up in the winter to heat the water to 45- to 50-degree temperatures in order to take showers. We had two Army generators. We ran each one 12 hours a day to provide minimal power inside the hooch. There was a central bar area with refrigerator and sink. There were six bedrooms, and off the bar a small room for another guy. The whole building had slits in it through which you could point M-16s or CAR-15s if you were so inclined. A couple of times we did just that when Camp Evans was hit by "sappers" — sneak attacks — but no one was killed around the hooch. Inside each little room was an old desk, chair, and bed, and a place to put a trunk. It was constantly damp in that place.

Living quarters for five FACs at Camp Evans was a sandbagged hooch.   Dutch Helms Collection

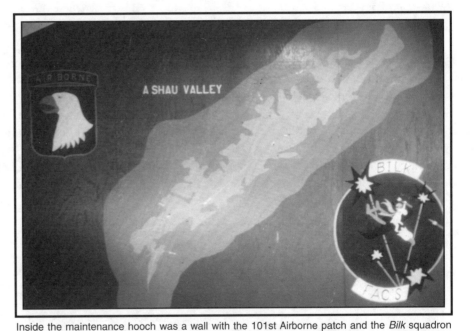

Inside the maintenance hooch was a wall with the 101st Airborne patch and the *Bilk* squadron patch designed for their "party suits." The A Shau Valley was *Bilk*'s favorite hunting area to look for "bad guys."

Dutch Helms Collection

The toilet facility was basically a one-holer outdoor john, a little shed built around a sawed-off half of a 55-gallon drum. Every week or so one of us had to go outside, pour diesel fuel in it, stir, and burn. That was standard plumbing at Camp Evans.

We constructed the TACP building ourselves (our five officers and six enlisted guys) next to our revetment area. Before that our enlisted guys lived in a tent. Other than flying, there wasn't much to do. We would go back to the hooch, crack a beer, grab something to eat — C rations or alert meal which is basically all we had — and sit around and play cards, shoot the bull, or write letters. At dinner time we'd go to the officers' kitchen/bar and then come back and play bridge until we got tired and went to bed. Occasionally we got X-rated movies when some-

body came back from R & R in Hong Kong. In the year I was at Camp Evans, two or maybe three shows made it up from Da Nang. Bob Hope never came to Camp Evans. In fact, no one came to Camp Evans unless you had to.

CW2 Jim McDevitt, U.S. Army FAC (*Headhunter* 35), went to Vietnam in 1970 and was based at Pleiku:

THE COMPANY BUILT its barracks out of rocket boxes. We had hooches with wooden floors, and generators for electricity. We flew for the 173rd Airborne. The [*DeHavilland C-7*] Caribous dropped supplies every week. We got some of the best steaks in-country and fresh beer.

⚒

Doug Aitken (*Rustic* 16) was impressed with his living conditions at Ubon RTAFB when compared to the grunts in the field:

IT WAS TOUGH to get serious about anything but staying alive when you knew you were there for one year, with air-conditioners, freezers, maids, bars, steaks, and lobsters. No wonder our logistical tail was so long. I never expected to go to war in such splendor with an air-conditioned room to myself, with a bed and chest of drawers, and a maid for $10 a month to do the laundry.

⚒

A FAC hooch at Dong Tam, 1968.

Anthony Ford Collection

Michael E. "Scoop" Jackson lived at the other end of the scale. Assigned to the 20th TASS from June 1971 to June 1972, he lived with the 101st Airborne Division at Camp Eagle:

LIVING AT CAMP EAGLE was like returning to the Stone Age. They definitely did not believe in overdoing creature comforts. Even taking a shower and washing flight suits were not to be taken for granted. Our hooch, which was handmade, had a 75-gallon water tank on top of it that was filled once a week, no more, no less. We soon discovered that four or five FACs couldn't shower and wash clothes without running out of our water allowance before the week was over. Solution: we would put all our clothes into a wash tub and walk around in the tub while we took our showers.

⚒

Grove C. Norwood, *Walt* 75, lived at Ban Me Thout in the Grand Bungalow, a long "A" frame teak or mahogany structure that some king had built:

YOU WOULD GO up the stairs and it had a porch the entire length of it, across the front, maybe a hundred yards down the back and along the sides. The

The pilot team at the "Nuoc Mam Bowl," Christmas Day, 1972. The building in the background was the only club at Phu Cat. Bottom row (l to r): Hank Nietergeisis, Ralph Kunce, Joe Arbuckle (token Army "wienie"). Standing (l to r): Craig Dunn, Bill Leatheredge, "Flash" Gordon, Ray Hain, Larry Clements, Dick Chapin, and Finn Gutaas.

Ralph Kunce Collection

Bilk FACs at Camp Evans. Dutch Helms calls them "The Fearsome Five": l to r, Captain Mike Berguson (Mormon chap from Salt Lake City, a super guy, one of the best FACs we had with us); Captain Jim Evitt (became a SAC Wing Commander), was the Brigade ALO at Camp Evans, our boss; Lieutenant Art Gaspart (ex-B-52 pilot); Lieutenant Charlie Artardo, excellent FAC; and Lieutenant "Dutch" Helms.

Dutch Helms Collection

Below: Four O-2s taxi out for the "air show" at Camp Evans.   Dutch Helms Collection

hallways were actually outside (we're in the tropics). We would sleep on the floor in our rooms.

⌇⌇⌇

Camp Evans Air Show

Dutch Helms did something about the lack of entertainment at his camp:

A HIGHLY UNUSUAL event was staged at Camp Evans in the spring of 1970. We had four 0-2s assigned to us. Most of the time two were operational and two were broken. On this day, and it was something we had looked forward to for some time, all four aircraft were operational. We decided to put on an air show for the Army at Camp Evans. We taxied all four O-2s out to the 2,200-feet long and 65-feet wide runway, lined up on the PSP as a "four-ship," and made a formation take-off, two by two. We rejoined turning out of traffic and formed up and put on the O-2 version of the USAF Thunderbirds. For about an hour and a half we did as much aerobatics as you can in an O-2, including flying the diamond formation and low passes across the runway. The Army went absolutely nuts. They just couldn't believe it, and we had an absolute ball. Fortunately, nobody got killed and no one let Da Nang know that we did it.

We landed. One of the guys refueled for his regular missions and the rest of us went back to the hooch and celebrated, got shit-faced, and were worthless

for the rest of the day, because we thought we had put on such a great job flying as Thunderbirds. For this mission, instead of our normal flight suit, we all dressed up in our yellow party suits, and if something had happened, the Air Force would have had a cow when they found out about it.

Busting my ass flying the old Oscar Deuce [*O-2A*], I had two things happen that might be of interest. One day I was flying around Khe Sanh putting in air. I didn't think there was any appreciable AAA in the area so I was down around the trees doing my normal thing. All of a sudden I saw some red smoke and thought it had to be friendlies, so I went down to take a peek. When I got down there I flew right into a trap. The North Vietnamese or VC had set up three .51-caliber pits so when I went down to look at the red smoke they just hosed the hell out of my airplane. The result was the front engine totally knocked out. I lost the prop off the front. It was an unbelievable experience, needless to say. It was a hot, humid, summerish day and here I was on the back side of the mountains, around Khe Sanh, knowing full well that I didn't have the power to climb on just the rear engine up over the mountains, so I ended up flying up north of Khe Sanh and down the valley until I found the Song Thach Han Lo River. Following the river, I flew along it 20 to 25 feet above the water to the coast. I never thought of landing the O-2 at Quang Tri for some stupid reason. I figured I had made it that far so I could make it all the way back to Camp Evans. Reaching the coast, I turned right and headed down the beach towards Camp Evans. I had plenty of gas, so just zipped in and landed without a front prop. Why I never landed at all the other fields that were available is just beyond me, but I felt embarrassed and just wanted to get it home and hide it in a revetment before somebody saw it.

The other classic was an administrative run up to Quang Tri to deliver parts just as a courtesy to the OV-10 guys up there. I volunteered to do it just to get some flying time. It was a very windy day, gusty winds, but Quang Tri was only 30 minutes north and I figured it couldn't be much worse up there, so I took off and about ten minutes out of Quang Tri called the Army tower there, told them where I was, and requested landing instructions. The tower guy told me where to land, and I said, "It's kind of windy, what kind of winds do you have out there?" He said, "About 30 knots down the runway." So I said, "That's great," came down to initial, to do a normal approach with a pitch out and turn to land. When I came down initial, I noticed that to stay lined up with the runway I was carrying about a 20-degree crab into the wind. I said, "This doesn't seem right." So just before I pitched, I called the tower again and said, "Say again the winds?" The tower operator said, "Down the runway at 30 knots." So I said, "OK," and pitched up, did the 180-degree turn, rolled out, and dropped gear and looked at the runway.

Things are looking good. I dropped flaps and

started my final turn. It was taking me forever to get around that turn. It was like flying into a 50-knot headwind. I called tower again and said, "Say the winds," and again he said, "Rog, down the runway at 30 knots." I said, "OK," and rolled out on final. In order to stay lined up with the runway, I had one wing low, all the crab in the world to stay lined up, and I'm still drifting off runway center line. So I said it must be a wind shear, and once I get below 100 feet the winds will be down the runway. I asked for another wind check and tower said the same thing, "Rog, 30 knots down the runway."

So I said, "OK," and I'm coming in wing low, full rudder trying to hold that O-2 steady, pulled the power off, crashed onto the runway, bounced a few times, and then just lost control. The wind started dragging my airplane to the right across the runway and the runway lights and I'm headed right towards their GCA (radar) tower, so I said, "Oh shit," added power, saw that wouldn't do any good, so pulled power, added brakes, and finally the airplane did two 360-degree turns in the combination cinder-dirt junk. I finally got back on the runway and taxied in. I about wet my pants doing this thing.

Tower and ground control were on the same frequency. I said, "Damn, the wind can't be 30 knots down the runway, I almost killed myself with this landing." Then another voice came up saying, "Say Bilk, I'm sorry about this, the winds really aren't 30 knots down the runway. I had to go and take a piss so I gave it to this new guy and he asked me, seriously, 'What shall I do if someone shows up?' I said, 'Just tell him the winds are 30 knots down the runway.' I knew no one would show up. Well, just as I went to piss, you came, and I'm sorry."

So I said, "What are the winds?" He said, "It's 90 degrees across the runway at about 45 knots steady state." I said, "Holy smokes! That's totally out of limits and I almost busted my ass doing it." But Murphy's law strikes again.

Chapter 4

The Forward Air Control Aircraft

The O-1

Engine: One 213 hp Continental 0-470-11, 6-cylinder, air cooled; **Wing span**, 36 ft; **Length**, 25 ft, 10 in; **Height**, 7 ft, 4 in; **Weight,** Empty, 1,614 lb; loaded, 2,400-2,430 lb; the F model, 2,800 lb; **Maximum speed**, 115 mph; **Cruising speed**, 85 mph low level, 104 mph at 5,000 ft; **Diving speed**, 130 mph; **Cruising range**, 530 miles; **Service ceiling**, 10,000 ft.*

*Weight and density altitude cause variations in service ceilings.

*T*HE O-1/L-19 all-metal monoplane was manufactured by Cessna Aircraft Company, originally as the civilian Model 305. In June 1950, a U.S. Army contract called for the modification of the two-place tandem tailwheel aircraft to serve as an observation platform for artillery spotting and adjustment. By October 1954, Cessna had delivered 2,426 L-19As to the Army and 16 O-1Es to the USMC. By the time production ended in 1961, a total of 3,431 had been built. O1-As through O-1Gs served throughout the Vietnam War.

A Cessna O-1E Bird Dog from the Marine Corps Aviation Museum, Quantico, Virginia, maintained in operational condition.

An O-1F Bird Dog at Phu Cat Air Base, 11 October 1970.

David Menard Collection

The L-19 designation was changed to O-1 when the U.S. Air Force acquired the Bird Dog. It was a rugged, single-engine, high-wing aircraft for slow speed visual reconnaissance (VR) in a benign combat environment. Using the control stick, the pilot could turn the aircraft on a dime. However, it had several shortcomings. Its slow cruise speed hindered response time.

Because of this, the O-1 was based at many of the 53 Forward Operation Locations (FOLs). There weren't enough aircraft for each FOL, so the Army 2nd Air Division authorized the use of Army Huey UH-1B Iroquois helicopters for carrying the FAC and the Province Chief, who approved requests for immediate airstrikes. Army units utilized their own L-19s, painted olive drab, for artillery spot-

Over the jungle somewhere in South Vietnam, an O-1E rolls into position to fire a smoke rocket to mark the target for an air strike.   USAF

ting, but they could not put in airstrikes. Sometimes the Air Force and Army pilots traded airplanes to confuse the enemy. The enemy thought the olive drab airplanes couldn't put in airstrikes, so they would shoot at them. This resulted in immediate strikes.

Climb performance at sea level was 500- to 700-feet per minute (fpm), which was hardly adequate, and it was less than that at higher altitudes. Because of its slow speed, making it vulnerable to AAA, the O-1 pilots developed a weaving flight path where neither heading, altitude, nor aircraft attitude remained stable enough for an enemy gunner to draw an accurate lead on the aircraft. The most vulnerable interval was during the marking pass to deliver the 2.75-inch Willie Pete rockets. The FAC would roll his aircraft and dive toward the target, after having aligned the aircraft to the target using a grease pencil mark on the windshield. The alignment required a rather stable diving attitude in relation to the target, which gave the enemy gunner an advantage in computing the lead necessary to have his rounds impact on the aircraft. After firing the rocket, the FAC would begin a rapid climb to reach a relatively safe altitude away from the defending weapons. This "pull-off" climb left the aircraft in an extremely vulnerable position because the FAC was trading airspeed (of which he had little) for altitude. He thus remained within the effective range of any AAA for long periods of time. Furthermore, airspeed and rate of climb decayed rapidly when G forces were imposed on the aircraft. Wind shears in the mountainous areas added to the hazards.

The O-1 grossed out at 2,600 to 2,800 pounds when combat equipped, including four shackles for rockets and flares, as well as ordnance and survival equipment. Each of the four ordnance stations was rated at 200 pounds and could carry four 2.75-inch white phosphorous marking rockets and two Mk-24 flares, or eight rockets or four flares. Smoke grenades were carried in the cockpit, along with pistols and rifles. On many missions the smoke rockets were used up early, but after finding more targets, the FAC could open the side window and pull the arming pin on the smoke grenade. He would then make a low pass over the target, which required an excellent sense of timing, not to mention intestinal fortitude in the face of automatic weapons fire. (Some pilots carried hand grenades in peanut butter jars to drop out the window.)

Colonel Franklin Fisher designed *Little Puff*, an O-1 with a machine-gun installed in the rear seat and fired sideways like the miniguns on the big *Puff, the Magic Dragon*, the AC-47. It was an interesting innovation, but was not widely used.

The O-1 had no armor to protect the pilot, the engine, or the fuel tanks. More than one FAC was killed or seriously wounded when the belly of his aircraft was raked by automatic weapons fire. To provide protection, some controllers would wear one flak vest and put another on the seat. Others had a piece of armor plate welded to the seat. In 1967, the ballistic helmet was provided for more protection.

On 1 January 1965, the Air Force owned just 22 O-1s in Southeast Asia. This indicated quite a shortage since each TASS was authorized 30 aircraft. By July, the Army had transferred 49 O-1s to the USAF and by November, the quota was filled.

The USAF O-1s were painted gray with Air Force markings for most of their work. Some had artwork such as a tiger's mouth with teeth, or a Snoopy character, and some were painted black, with no markings, for clandestine missions into Cambodia under the *Tum* call sign.

The communications package in the O-1 was also somewhat of a shortcoming. It was basically a frequency modulation (FM) liaison set (AN/ARC-44): VHF (AN/ARC-73), UHF (AN/ARC-45), and, for navigation low-frequency, ADF (Automatic Direction Finder) (AN/ARN-59) — the O-1's only navigation tools besides a compass and a marker beacon (AN/ARN-12).

The O-1 had a difficult switching system between its ancient radios. The switching panel was overhead to the side, with the volume control elsewhere. The ARC-44 and ARC-45 radios had limited preset frequencies so that several operations could be going on at once over the same frequencies.

The Seventh Air Force requested the ARC-54 radio, and on 22 May 1968, Warner Robbins Air Matériel Area, Robbins AFB, Georgia, informed the Seventh that it could furnish 25 tunable AN/ARC-51BX radios a month to replace the ARC-45s. The ARC-51BX was chosen because it also had guard (emergency) monitoring capability. Installation of these radios began in January 1969, and by 1970, all the O-1s were equipped.

The ground visibility looking straight down in the O-1 was excellent, but there was limited visibility above the wings, which created a safety hazard. The O-1 had clear plastic panels overhead for upward visibility from the cockpit, but the FAC had to continuously have the target and strike aircraft in sight. During steep turns, the pilot could lose as much as 70 percent visibility, which contributed to a substantial number of in-flight collisions with fighters and other aircraft.

In spite of its deficiencies, the O-1 was considered by many as the best FAC aircraft, because it was relatively easy to fly and had sufficient endurance for four hours. It could take off and land using short, rugged, unimproved strips. Maintenance was simple. It could take innumerable hits as long as the rounds didn't strike the few vital areas. One O-1 returned to base with a five-foot section of wing shot away by a 57mm shell.

An eight-mile glide with no engine power and a perfect dead stick landing culminated a flight by Captain James L. Champlin, a 21st TASS FAC, assigned to the 1st Air Cavalry Division in support of OPERATION CRAZY HORSE in 1966. He was conducting an airstrike in support of the Republic of Korea's Capital Division. His quick analysis of his aircraft's mechanical problems and his subsequent fast actions saved himself and the airplane.

Champlin had taken off from An Khe in his O-1 Bird Dog. While climbing en route to the target area, he reached 1,500 feet and noticed his generator was malfunctioning as well as a slight engine vibration. Champlin

An O-1 departing Nakhon Phanom, Royal Thai Air Force Base, in northeastern Thailand, 1966.   Jim Stanford Collection

An O-1E Bird Dog with the pilot's personalized markings.   David Menard Collection

Captain James L. Champlin, a FAC serving with the 1st Air Cavalry Division, flying the O-1.

James L. Champlin Collection

correctly assumed that more trouble would follow. At the time, he was flying over a friendly convoy of motor vehicles. Champlin recalled, "I knew it would be difficult to land on the highway in the midst of the convoy, so I took her up to 3,500 feet and headed over a ridge that would put me in friendly territory and give me a downhill shot at An Khe."

About eight miles from An Khe the engine stopped. Champlin immediately salvoed his rockets and set up a glide. "After I cleared the ridge, I thought I could make it. The landing turned out to be easy enough, and in fact, I had to use my flaps to slip in." Post-flight investigation revealed that the engine had broken completely in two and that the propeller hub was resting on the cowling.

Captain Champlin took the incident in stride and continued to fly from either An Khe or Pleiku AB every day for the remainder of his tour.

Weather was always a factor for the little O-1 in combination with distance limitations. When the 20th TASS had out-country missions from Da Nang through the A Shau Valley to Laos and back, the O-1 could only be on-station from 45 minutes to an hour during its four-hour flight. It was a VFR aircraft, but the weather was not always the same in Laos and at Da Nang, as the O-1 had to cross a chain of mountains.

The O-2A

> **Engines:** Two 210 hp Continental IO-360-C/D air-cooled engines in tractor-pusher arrangement; **Wing Span**, 38 ft, 2 in; **Length**, 29 ft, 9 in; **Height,** 9ft, 2in; **Weight,**: empty, 2,848 lb; loaded, 4,850 lb; **Maximum dive speed**, 199 mph; **Cruise speed,** 144 mph at 1,000 ft; **Range,** 1,120 miles; **Service ceiling**, 14,200 ft (front engine only, 5,100 ft; rear engine only, 7,100 ft).

The Air Force needed an interim aircraft while the OV-10 was being developed. Cessna submitted an unsolicited proposal of its 337A twin-engine Skymaster to be evaluated as a replacement for the O-1. The aircraft, to be known as the O-2A, was an off-the-shelf configuration of the civilian Model 337. Changes for the military included windows in an area at the top and right side of the cockpit for better visibility of other aircraft and the targets, ordnance stations on the wings, and military instruments and avionics. The O-2A's maximum loiter time was just under seven hours, with fuel tanks that held 122 gallons. Each wing had a main tank holding 44 gallons and an auxiliary tank holding 17 gallons. The O-2A is a twin-boom aircraft, with two rudders, and has push-pull engines placed one in front and the other at the rear of the fuselage.

The push-pull twin engine and twin boom design

An O-2A escorting plane flown by Lieutenants Rich Silver and Ross Leanard to Da Nang. They lost their right window while making a rocket pass, which tore off and damaged the leading edge of the wing.

Dale Kingsbury Collection

provides such advantages as drag reduction and the ability of the aircraft to cruise on one engine, without adverse yaw effects, if the other has stopped running. And the tandem engine design made it possible to mount hard points on the wings for rockets and flares.

The O-2 has two propellers, one for each engine. When they are turning at the same rpm they are said to be "in sync" and the engine sound is very smooth. When they each turn at a different rpm they are "out of sync" and make such a noise that it is difficult to tell which direction the aircraft is coming from.

The Sikorsky S-64 Skycrane, designed for heavy military transport duties, became a workhorse for the U.S. Army.

Richard Clements, *Covey* 243, compared the O-1 and the O-2:

THERE WAS NO QUESTION that the O-1 was better for the job, but the O-2 had more capability overall. The O-2 had more power, climb, and endurance as well as Instrument Flight Rules capability. I flew IFR a lot, especially at night climbing out of Da Nang during the monsoon season to get up on top in the clear. The O-2 was a beautiful flying airplane. We would take off, set the throttles for cruise, and use sync during the day. We just flew the devil out of it, . . . mostly at 1,500 feet AGL. Our contention was they know we are up here, and we know they are down there. They seldom shot at a FAC. Our job was to find them, not shoot at them, but we had guys who would shoot their rifles out the window.

At night we flew with Starlight Scopes [*the vision enhancers, developed in the U.S. Army, that allowed the operator to see movement on the ground at night*] hanging heads out the windows and steering with our knees. Night missions were flown out of sync; the noise harassed the North Vietnamese Army. It was psychological. We would drop flares occasionally or fire a rocket. It was reassuring to the Marines to know a FAC was up there. At places like Tam Ky, with no runway lights, we used jeep lights at night when coming in for a landing.

I knew one guy who had a problem with the O-2. The airplane quit on him coming back from Khe Sanh, so he landed on Highway 1 in the daytime, and had just enough rolling speed to taxi into the entrance of a Special Forces camp. He blocked the whole entrance. The Special Forces were furious at him. The next day an Army [*Sikorsky S-64*] Skycrane came in and picked up the O-2 to haul it to Da Nang. The Skycrane got out over the bay at Da Nang and something went wrong; it started vibrating and dropped the O-2.

Another guy had the rear engine and most of the stabilizer blown off, but not the elevator. He managed to bring the O-2 back. I had occasion to fly the O-1 into Special Forces camps. There was a camp east of Tam Ky that previously was a hunting lodge for tigers. We would go up there and land. I had to scrape the mud off the wings so I could take off. The mud was really thick so it would disrupt both the weight and distribution of the airfoil.

The O-1 was an aircraft you could horse around all over the sky. You could see out of both sides,

whereas in the O-2 you were in a left turn most of the time.

The FACs had a tremendous effect on the Army. We pulled them out of conditions they never should have been in, and we helped Long-Range Reconnaissance Patrol (LRRP) teams to navigate.

The initial Cessna contract, dated 29 December 1996, was for 145 O-2As. Another contract awarded in June 1967 brought the total on order to 192, all of which were delivered by early 1968. An additional 154 aircraft were ordered later in 1968.

A contract placed 31 December 1968 ordered O-2Bs, which were used for psychological warfare missions. These were equipped with advanced communications systems and a high-power broadcast system utilizing three 600W amplifiers with high-directional speakers. There was also a fitting for leaflet dispensing. A combined total of 510 O-2As and O-2Bs were delivered to the Air Force by December 1970.

The communications package on the O-2A included two UHF/AM command radios (Wilcox 807 and an AN/ARC-51BX); two VHF/FM sets (Magnavox FM-622); one LF/ADF navigation system (AN/ARC-83); one tactical air navigation system (AN/ARN-52); an IFF/SIF system (AN/APX-64); and a crash and/or ID beacon (Motorola SST-181). The TACAN-DME (Distance Measuring Equipment) teamed with the VOR (VHF omni-directional range) to tell the pilot distance and direction from the VOR. Pulses from the Identification, Friend or Foe (IFF) helped ground control radars to identify and plot the plane's position.

The O-2A has four underwing armament pylons capable of carrying 350 pounds each and two minigun stations capable of handling two guns (7.62mm SUU-11) each. It used the LAU-59/A rocket launcher (seven 2.75-inch rockets, single-fire or ripple), an MA-2A launcher (two rockets), and an SUU-14A bomblet dispenser. It had a noncomputing gunsight for ordnance delivery. (The O-1 sight was actually a grease pencil mark on the window!) To facilitate rendezvous with other FACs, a one-gallon fluid reservoir and a pump on the firewall of the rear engine injected oil into the hot exhaust manifold, providing continuous smoke for approximately two minutes.

A remotely controlled strike camera (KB-18), holding 250 feet of 70mm film, was located immediately aft and slightly to the right of the pilot. It provided fore and aft 180-degree photographic coverage along the line of flight and 40 degrees laterally.

The O-2A had enough navigation and communications equipment to allow it to operate in almost any area of conflict. However, the avionics equipment weighed over 300 pounds which put a limit on the amount of fuel carried (avgas weighs 6 pounds per gallon).

The initial rate of climb was double that of the O-1 (1220 fpm *vs.* 650 fpm). But in extreme heat, and when heavily loaded, neither aircraft had that rate of climb. The O-2A's initial higher maximum speed provided fairly decent zoom capability during the pull-up from an ordnance pass. After a steep dive, the initial pull-up rate was 2,500 fpm. As in any underpowered aircraft, airspeed and rate of climb decay when G forces are applied. Gross weight was sometimes restricted to 3,500 pounds due to the heavy avionics and poor single-engine performance.

Visibility problems were also a disadvantage in the O-2A. With two side-by-side front seats, even though the pilot sat ahead of the wing, it was difficult to see the action to the right, and there was no visibility to the rear. Windows were placed on top of the cockpit and in the right door to alleviate this problem.

Fully loaded, the takeoff runs rarely exceeded 1,800 feet. The extended landing gear only slowed the aircraft about five knots, but considerable drag (240 fpm) was created by opening the gear doors to retract the landing gear after takeoff. Added to the drag of the rocket pods, this was a critical factor. The doors are large and act like speed brakes, so the pilot must wait until a proper rate of climb has been established, and both engines running normally, before putting the landing gear switch in the up position. Although both engines have the same horsepower, the rear one is the critical engine.

Jim Oliver was the manager of the Cessna Delivery Program, which started in 1967, with civilian pilots under contract to World Aviation Services:

THERE WERE 264 O-2s at Aircraft Facilities International, Newton, Kansas. We test-flew the aircraft and then sent them out to fly to Vietnam in flights of six. They carried a total of 465 gallons with extra fuel tanks in the cabin. They also carried 5-gallon jerry cans of oil to pump to the engines en route. The pilot had to crawl up and over a tank to get in. With the extra fuel weight, the O-2 needed an 11,000

foot runway to take off. It was a long, slow climb out. And almost two hours would pass before the aircraft reached 8,000 feet. A pilot would be lucky to complete the trip in a week.

The phase-in of the O-2A commenced on 1 July 1967 with the 20th TASS at Da Nang and its forward operating bases at Khe Sanh and Dong Ha. By the end of the year, the 23rd TASS at Nakhon Phanom, Thailand, was fully augmented with the O-2As, using them mainly in the out-country war. Some of the O-2s at Nakhon Phanom and Ubon were painted glossy black with red markings for night FAC duty over the Ho Chi Minh Trail, but the majority were gray with solid white, or a wide white stripe on top of the wings for easy recognition by the fighters flying above them.

The advantages of the O-2A when compared to the O-1 were two engines, improved zoom and climb rates, greater speed (up to 150 knots), an aiming device for target marking, four ordnance stations, night operation capability, smoke-generating capability, strike camera, and better radios. Disadvantages included poor visibility with the side-by-side seating (the pilot had to make right turns to see in that direction — the enemy learned to predict this), marginal operation on the front engine alone, insufficient armor plating, landing gear not stout enough for rugged FOLs, high gross weight that limited FOL operation (as the O-2A needed a minimum 2,000-foot runway), too little electrical power to run all the electrical equipment simultaneously, and TACAN reception weak below 1,500 feet.

Tom Milligan, *Sun Dog* 29, commented on the O-2:

WE COULD loop the O-2 in a tactical situation although the O-2 was not placarded for aerobatics. It was just as easy to go up over the top as to let it fall off. You could almost do anything with the airplane if you were careful.

David L. "Dutch" Helms, *Bilk* 37, also liked the aircraft:

THE O-2A WAS FUN to fly; you could loiter forever and missions of four to five hours were common. Thanks to the windows cut in the door and top, we had relatively good vision, although the high wing did sometimes present a problem putting in fighters onto a target. [*The pilot's seat in the O-2 is out ahead of the wing, not under it like the smaller, single-engine O-1.*] The engines were reliable, and, in general, the radios were reliable. The biggest problem was that the "Duck" [*nickname for the O-2*] was really underpowered for the hot, humid, short runway mission that we had in Vietnam. I can remember really getting excited on takeoff. If we could get gear and flaps up and have a 200- to 300-fpm rate of climb, that was really terrific. We were very heavy when fully fueled with rockets, radios, parachutes, and all the gear we were supposed to take with us. On hot summer days we were 200 to 300 pounds over max gross weight. It was really tough in the summers because Camp Evans only had 2,200 feet of PSP. On some of those hot humid days we needed it all just to take off with the stall warning horn beeping. You would taxi to the end of the runway, as close as you could get to the edge (there was no overrun), hold the brakes, run it up, lean the engine out so you got full power, release brakes, and roll it to the end. When you got to the end you just took off, regardless of what the airspeed indicator said. Normally in the summer you'd be taking off right on the stall warning horn.

The navigation aids were great in good weather, but in bad weather, especially rain, they didn't really work very well. During rainstorms the circuit breakers tended to pop out constantly and you would have to hold them in with your fingers while you were flying — very cute! Due to the weight and lack of power, rocket-marking passes in the O-2 were always altitude-losing maneuvers. You could never get a net gain on a rocket pass. You were always losing altitude. In general, after six or seven consecutive passes, you were always down in the treetops, always in range of not only small arms fire, but also Montagnard bows and arrows. A couple of guys in our outfit did have arrows sticking in the bottom of the aircraft when they came back from a mission.

The hydraulic power pack for the landing gear was always breaking. I don't know if they solved that on the later 337s or not, but a typical situation that occurred during my tour, at least a dozen times to me, was taking off, raising the gear handle, the gear doors would open, the gear would come up, the doors would close, there would be a slight pause, the doors would then reopen, the gear would come down, and then the doors would close. All this time the handle was in the up position. This was especially testy during hot weather max gross takeoffs. No one that I know of during my tour bought the farm taking off that way, but it certainly got your attention. This really worried us at Camp Evans since at both ends of the runway there was no overrun, and off each end there were mine fields and barbed wire concertina and everything. If you came clunking down after takeoff, you were probably done for, but luckily it never happened.

On maintenance, any aircraft we had that really broke was flown back to Da Nang for repair. Stationed with us at Camp Evans were six Air Force enlisted troops who were basically mechanics. We normally cannibalized on a daily basis and jury-rigged various fixes just to have two aircraft out of the four assigned to us flying. I remember flying several missions, as did some of the other FACs at our base, putting in strikes with the landing gear down. Probably the hydraulic power pack was broken, and all the other aircraft we had were fully red-X'd at Evans or down at Da Nang. We just flew with the pins in. Da Nang maintenance was great if they had the parts, but a lot of times they had to wait for parts at Da Nang for two to three weeks.

<hr />

Even though the O-2 was designed for civilian use, it turned out to be rugged when coping with battle damage. Many planes managed to return to base with severe damage, sometimes requiring the replacement of major sections. Staff Sergeant James W. Swanson, with the 20th TASS in charge of site maintenance, remembered the first field-level wing change in an O-2:

LIEUTENANT COLONEL QUANDT was getting his second TIGER HOUND orientation area ride from Captain Sansanowich, when they took a round that split the leading edge seam on the right wing, leaving a large section of sheet metal peeled back on the upper and lower surfaces of the wing. Somehow they managed to bring the O-2 back home.

John Heimburger in typical FAC garb at Khe Sanh in the fall of 1967.
John Heimburger Collection

There was a time when we ran out of daytime aircraft, so we took a black bird and painted it gray for a daytime mission. As soon as it landed, we painted it black again. I also remember instances when the pilots leaned the engines out for maximum en-

Pete Conforti in an O-2A, ready to fly over the Ho Chi Minh Trail in 1969. The enemy had 23mm and 37mm guns, which explains the Army ballistic helmet. Conforti notes, "We carried at least two survival radios on our vests."
Pete Conforti Collection

durance and then flew so long that they landed and ran out of gas on the runway or while taxiing in. Another time Captain Sam Deichelman, previously a C-130 *Blindbat* pilot, bellied in an O-2 gear up. The hydraulic pack that operates the gear had taken a round. A friend from the 8th TFW instrument shop helped us bend wrenches (we had no proper tools for this job nor had anyone changed a hydraulic power pack) and spent many off-duty hours changing the pack to get this aircraft back flying again after Da Nang had written it off for battle damage. And, it was returned to action.

⎯⎯⎯⎯ ⎯⎯⎯⎯

John Heimburger, *Covey* 77, was putting in strikes from F-4Cs on 16 December 1967 up around the DMZ. When he rolled in on his third marking run, a fan of .50-caliber tracers zapped past the front prop and both engines missed and surged:

I CALLED OUT a quick "I think I'm hit!" and I think I also got out a Mayday. No maneuvering of the prop levers or throttles or mixture levers could restore normal power. We began a descent for a forced landing in a clear area atop a high plateau. A thousand thoughts raced through my mind . . . the beeper on, alert *Jolly Greens*, get Special Forces passengers to fasten their seat belts. Select landing spot, full flaps, jettison ordnance, but most of all, I thought how inadequate I felt, that I was experiencing war and the sudden awareness of helplessness and fright in its most potent form.

I remember *Covey* 234 saying, "I'm over him, scramble the *Jolly Greens*." Everyone was calling me for my position and status. *Covey* 251 was already hustling up some fighters for an armed retaliation of the tracer source. The F-4Cs were circling overhead. Finally after about three minutes, I realized that my aux tanks had run dry in the rocket dive — a very poor time and unusual happening for both to run dry at the same instant. Switching to main and hi-boost on a downwind for the forced landing had no effect for better than two minutes. The Special Forces passengers had their weapons ready and it was all up to me. Suddenly the fuel pumps caught and the engine cleared and the beautiful whine filled the air once again. With much relief, I called off the helicopters.

⎯⎯⎯⎯ ⎯⎯⎯⎯

Some pilots weren't that lucky. John Rogers, *Nail 68*, described an unfortunate ending for an O-2A:

A MARINE LIEUTENANT was flying for the Air Force in an O-2, putting in his first airstrike. He had a major in the right seat. He was flying straight and level, writing down his BDA, when suddenly an enemy gun blew the tail off the O-2. There wasn't any doubt in his mind about bailing out because the yoke came right back into his lap. They were at 5,000 MSL [*Mean Sea Level*] and about 1,200 feet AGL in a flat spin, with effectively no forward velocity. The major kicked the door off and went out. The lieutenant, wearing a parachute, survival vest, and gun belt, had to move across the seats, out the door, and get enough downward velocity to get his chute open. (The O-2 had only one door, on the right side.) The lieutenant got one swing and hit the ground running, and went about 100 yards. His big concern was ditching his chute. He came to a road and crossed it. He said this was a dumb thing to do as he left one footprint. Anyhow, it got to be night. There are no rescue crews late afternoon or at night, so he got into the bushes. He could hear mechanical stuff going on. It turned out there was a weapons machine shop less than a quarter-mile away. When the rescue guys came the next morning, the lieutenant FAC put in an airstrike, blew the place up, and then the helicopters took him away.

In another instance, a tail boom was severed, except for the structural longeron, and both elevator cables were cut. There were also hits in the wing and vertical stabilizer. The pilot was able to control the O-2 by using the elevator trim tab for pitch control.

Will an O-2 fly on one engine? That depends on a number of factors, especially altitude, temperature, and weight. On 8 June 1970, First Lieutenant Gary J. Pavlu, *Covey* 259, was flying a FAC mission in an O-2A with an Army observer in the right seat. As Lieutenant Pavlu was preparing to put in an airstrike with A-1 fighters holding overhead, a sudden loss of power was noticed. The rear-engine instruments indicated zero rpm, rising manifold pressure, and zero fuel flow. Lieutenant Pavlu immediately attempted restart, using the fuel boost pump and starter. No sign of ignition was observed and rotation of the engine stopped as soon as the starter button was released.

The external stores were jettisoned, the fighters circling overhead notified, and the engine failure in-flight checklist complied with. Maintaining altitude was a problem, as the engine failure occurred at 4,600 feet MSL over a terrain elevation of 1,950 feet. Level flight could not be maintained so Lieutenant Pavlu headed for the lower ground around Khe Sanh. At the lower altitude, his O-2A could maintain level flight at an airspeed of 65 to 75 knots, just a little above stall speed, 2,400 feet MSL over 1,600-foot terrain. Because the weather was getting worse, with rain to the east, and there was rising terrain to the south and north, Lieutenant Pavlu decided to hold over Khe Sanh.

With one A-1 holding overhead, another A-1 flew on to look for a clear route to the east. By this time, an Army helicopter had been notified and was also holding in the local area in the event the O-2 crew would have to bail out. After 20 minutes of holding, the weather lifted slightly at the destination airfield. The A-1 was back, having found a clear route for the O-2 to fly. Lieutenant Pavlu went on to land without further difficulty.

After only 15 minutes on the ground, Lieutenant Pavlu took another aircraft and completed his mission. The 20th TASS Flying Safety Office reported on June 1970:

Lt. Pavlu's professional handling of this emergency through knowledge of procedures and close coordination with other aircraft allowed him to return safely and saved a valuable aircraft.

The same report described a landing gear malfunction. On 23 June 1970, First Lieutenants Donald Voyles (pilot) and Jerold Benson (copilot) took off from their FOL on a scheduled FAC mission in an O-2A. During the landing-gear retraction cycle, a loud snap was heard from the rear bottom of the aircraft, and no-gear-up-and-locked indication could be obtained. Lieutenant Voyles repositioned the landing gear handle to the down position and found that the left main landing gear would not extend to the down-locked position. The left main gear was observed to be in the trail position with the nose gear and right main in the down-and-locked position. All gear doors were open after attempting several cycles and pumping the gear down. The crew, in coordination with their Tactical Air Control Party, determined that the best course of action would be to divert to Da Nang for better airfield facilities. En route, the crew again tried recycling the gear in addition to using the hand pump with negative results. G maneuvers and yawing of the aircraft were also tried.

At Da Nang, the runway was foamed in preparation for a gear-up landing. While the foaming was in process, the external stores were jettisoned in the designated area. As a last attempt, Lieutenant Benson left his seat and removed a portion of the floorboard above the universal joint. The pins in this universal joint shaft were found to be sheared, and an in-flight fix was impossible due to the small access area allowing insufficient leverage to move the gear.

After Lieutenant Benson assumed his seat, several rapid negative acceleration maneuvers were tried again with negative results. Lieutenant Voyles landed in a smooth, flat attitude on 2,300 feet of foam with both engines shut down in accordance with the manual — DASH-1 operating procedures. The pilot kept the aircraft straight and in the center of the foam, sliding the entire available distance of 1,500 feet. Both pilots egressed without difficulty or injuries. The aircraft damage was minimal, requiring only 15 man-hours for repair.

Through their professional handling of this emergency by exhausting all possible methods of lowering the gear and by flying a perfect approach and gear-up landing, the crew kept aircraft damage to a minimum and avoided injury to themselves. WELL DONE!

Mid-airs were always hazardous, especially at night. Richard Clements, *Covey* 243, remembers the time when a 1st Air Cav Huey and an O-2 had a mid-air:

IT WAS ONE of the few mid-airs when everyone was killed. I was sent to investigate. The O-2 was hit and landed in a canal. The twin-booms and rear engine were sticking out of the water. The Army came in a Skycrane and tried to pull it out. It peeled the top off the fuselage. The pilot was in there — dead. He was jammed in the cockpit. We came under fire about that time. We had an Army platoon surrounding our investigating team to protect us while we tried to get the pilot out. We tried . . . and couldn't. We came under attack again. This time I said we might as well get out of here. The Army said, "No way, we never leave a man behind." They had to cut

the pilot in half to get him out, and left half of him there; the Army did.

The OV-10 Bronco

Engines: two 715 hp T-76-G-410/411 turbo-prop AiResearch engines with Hamilton-Standard three-blade propellers; **Wing span,** 40 ft; **Length,** 41 ft, 7 in; **Height**, 15 ft, 2 in; **Weight,** 6,969 empty, normal takeoff 9,908 lb, overload takeoff weight 14,466 lb; **Speed,** maximum at sea level without weapons, 244 knots, cruise speed 177 knots; **Range,** 1,200 nm; **Fuel capacity,** 402 gallons; **Service ceiling,** 19,200 ft; **Initial rate of climb**, 2,300 fpm.

In July 1968, the North American Rockwell OV-10 Bronco was introduced into the war. The OV-10A had been designed from the start as a Forward Air Control/counterinsurgency and conventional limited-warfare airplane. It had all the desired characteristics of a FAC aircraft: short takeoff and landing (STOL) capability, outstanding visibility, simplified maintenance, and the ability to operate from rough strips. The Bronco had armor protection for both crew ejection seats, twin-engine reliability, and better ordnance. The OV-10 is a twin-boom, two-seat tandem aircraft with high vertical stabilizers and a top-mounted horizontal stabilizer. The wings are shoulder-mounted, with the cockpit protruding well in front of the engine mounts to provide good visibility.

North American's entry in the Navy design competition for a light, armed reconnaissance plane was the STOL aircraft, with the ability to carry heavy armament and to evacuate casualties. Marine Colonels Rice and Beckett had the idea for a light reconnaissance plane known as LARA. The OV-10 developed from the LARA concept — the Light Armed Reconnaisance Airplane — only it was bigger and more complex than the original idea.

The first prototype, the YOV-10A, flew on 16 July 1965, followed by the second in December 1965. After some modifications, production started after the first OV-10A had been flown on 6 August 1967. The first OV-10 Broncos arrived in Da Nang on 6 July 1968 and began operations with Marine VMO-2 Squadron at Marble Mountain. A second Marine unit was equipped by October 1968. The

North American Rockwell OV-10 Bronco.

Marine Corps had 114 in service by September 1969, of which 18 were on loan to the Navy.

In 1971, the Navy acquired OV-10As for a special light-attack squadron, VAL-4, called the "Black Ponies." Operating from 28 February to April 1971, the Black Pony OV-10s were configured with rocket pods and a 20mm gun pod mounted on the fuselage centerline station. As a STOL aircraft, the OV-10 could operate from helicopter carriers without the use of catapults or arresting gear. VAL-4 provided protection for river convoys along the Mekong River in South Vietnam, as well as support for ground operations. The USAF had 157 OV-10As for its FACs.

The OV-10 communications package included one UHF/AM radio (AN/ARC-51BX); one VHF/AM (Wilcox 807A) and one VHF/FM (FM-622A[2]) radio; one HF/SSB (HF-103) radio; TACAN (AN/ARN-52 [V]); one UHF/ADF (Automatic Direction Finder; AN/ARA-50); one LF/ADF (AN/ARN-83); one VOR (51R-6); an ILS Glide Scope (51V-4A); and IFF/SIF (AN/APX-64[V]).

The OV-10 Bronco could carry up to 3,600 pounds of ordnance, including four forward-firing

M-60, 7.62mm miniguns, bombs, rockets, gun pods, and flares. It has five armament stations; the four outboard stations are capable of handling 600 pounds each, while the centerline station permits it to carry an additional 1,200 pounds of munitions or an external fuel tank. The Bronco used four LAU-59, LAU-68, LAU-32B/A, and LAU-56A rocket launchers (seven rockets each), or four B-37K flare dispensers (eight Mk-24 flares each), or a combination of both. The back of the aircraft has a rear bay which opens up to allow the loading of two stretchers or six paratroopers.

Doug Aitken, *Rustic* 16, explained the effect of ordnance upon the OV-10's performance:

THE OV-10 WAS UNDERPOWERED before any ordnance was hung on it. It only had 715 horsepower engines when it needed 1,000. *[The Marine version had 1,000 hp, more armament and additional systems.]* We carried two LAU-57s (seven rockets each) and two LAU-3s. We used about half the available 24 tubes per mission. At Ubon we had longer takeoff rolls than fully loaded F-4s. We were off the drag charts with much longer takeoffs than we were

The left-front view of an OV-10A, 1967. U.S. Marine Corps

supposed to have. This was due to our desire to get to 110 knots before liftoff so that we were above our single-engine failure speed. This was in the 110- to 115-knot range while the computed lift-off speed was more in the 92- to 97-knot range. With the counter-rotating props, the OV-10 only had 40 percent lift across the wing, so if you had an engine failure you had big torque problems, especially at low speeds. We held the aircraft on the ground until we had well over 105 knots, and then it would leap off the ground.

There was an RSU (Runway Supervising Unit), a little mini-tower, at each end of the runway. They would check for hung ordnance or gear down. They had a guy out there looking with binoculars. The town of Ubon was right off the end of the runway, so the OV-10s and F-4s took off one way and landed the other way. The RSU was 1,500 to 2,000 feet from the end of the runway and we'd still be on the ground going past it.

The front cockpit of the OV-10. Doug Aitken Collection

Roll-in altitudes were 2,500 to 3,500 feet using a 130 to 150 KIAS (Knots Indicated Airspeed) entry airspeed. Power settings were 95 percent and 1,100 ft/lb. torque. Firings were at approximately 1,500 feet AGL using dive angles between 30 and 45 degrees, at release airspeeds of 250 to 280 KIAS. Pullouts were made at four Gs, and the initial rate of climb was well in excess of 6,000 fpm.

An OV-10 Bronco piloted
by Major Everett Vaughn.
Dale Kingsbury Collection

Other features were 328 pounds of armor plating, adequate single-engine capability, multi-target marking ability carrying more rockets and flares than any other FAC aircraft, high-altitude (10,000 feet) rendezvous capability, and a choice of a 150- or 230-gallon centerline fuel tank.

Flight characteristics were excellent. The OV-10 had better maneuverability and evasion action than the O-1 and O-2. The aircraft could jink while gaining altitude, although it could not turn as sharply as the smaller, slower O-1. It made less engine noise than the O-2, making it harder to detect. Even though the OV-10 was vulnerable in a high-threat environment (AAA of 12.7mm and up), the aircraft could take its share of punishment. The FACs found that when the OV-10s were jumped by Russian MiG jets in Laos, they could easily out-turn them. (It could actually turn sharply within the mil rings of the gunsight, going right back into the track of the enemy fighter.)

The OV-10 could land in and fly out of a 2,000-foot strip. It has trailing absorption gear, which can really take punishment during a hard landing on any surface.

Using its FM homing, the OV-10 could follow a radial right to the transmitter, which was a help in identifying ground troops. The Bronco also had a smoke-generating capability, which made it easy to spot by the strike aircraft during rendezvous. A 3.2-gallon oil tank with the necessary switches and plumbing provided two to three minutes of continuous smoke. Chemicals were used to change the smoke color to red, green, orange, or yellow, which was extremely effective in aiding the strike aircraft to locate the FAC. However, the smoke was more effective when the strike aircraft was at high altitude (15,000 to 20,000 feet) and the controller was low.

The OV-10 did have disadvantages. The large canopy let the sun shine in mercilessly, creating a greenhouse effect, and poor ventilation heightened the crews' discomfort on hot days. In addition, the front-seat communications were located on the right panel, which required the pilot to either release the flight controls or switch hands to make radio adjustments. The cockpit was noisy, and with the canopy closed during flight, it was hard to hear the ground fire. And though it was an advantage in certain situations, the Bronco had trouble getting in and out of FOLs safely because it needed a 2,000-foot runway.

Robert C. Miller, Jr., *Issue* 24 and *Rash* 03, commented on the Bronco's visibility:

IN THE OV-10, vision in the cockpit at night was somewhat distracting. We were flying in support of the Army and for all practical purposes their missions ended at night. They camped out and waited for day. A couple of missions scared the daylights out of me. I was an IP [*Instructor Pilot*] checking out a guy at night, going up for a little no brainer, when all of a sudden a TIC [*troops in contact with the enemy*] broke out and we had to scramble over to this other area and put in fighters. Trying to find the friendlies on the ground was very difficult. They only had a little blue strobe light. I finally had to call this strike off. We just couldn't identify the friendlies. (There were battles when the friendlies said put down your ordnance, no matter what, because if you don't, we're gone anyway.)

It was so hazy I couldn't see the fighters either. They would roar above my wing. It was kind of scary that night, but more than that, it was really frustrating for me because I was sitting in the backseat of the OV-10. A new guy was in the front and he had control of all the ordnance.

The Starlight Scope — a smaller version of the Eyeglass Scope — operation was marginal due in part to the glare from the front cockpit panel lights. Although the scope picked up lights and streams when aimed at a 45-degree angle, when rotated up toward 90 degrees, its picture dimmed. To deal with the problem, the OV-10 was flown at a 20-degree bank with curtains hung between the two cockpits. OV-10s equipped with the Pave Nail night observation system enabled the crews to locate targets.

The OV-10 FAC (and the O-1 and O-2s in high-threat situations) rolled in at 5,000 to 6,000 feet to mark targets which kept them from deadly AAA fire in Laos and North Vietnam. In these instances, the controller favored stand-off marking, lobbing the marker rocket from several miles out. This method's shaky accuracy led to rocket impacts being used chiefly as reference points. The FACs also relied on prominent landmarks to locate targets for strike pilots.

The Bronco was the only FAC aircraft (not including the Fast FACs — in jet aircraft) that could perform the daylight Strike Control and Reconnaissance (SCAR) mission over the heavily defended Ho Chi Minh Trail in the early 1970s. The OV-10s also worked with the search and rescue HH-53 aircraft. The "Jolly Green Giant" pilots preferred the OV-10 over the slower O-1s and O-2s because they were armed with 7.62 machine-guns.

Combat Cover

During the Vietnam War, the effectiveness of an armed Forward Air Controller was tested under the code name "Combat Cover" in May 1968. The test combined the armed FAC aircraft and fixed-wing gunship to supply limited firepower for hard-pressed ground troops until strike aircraft arrived. The O-1 clearly couldn't measure up to the Combat Cover test. The aircraft's role and the weight of the extra armament overtaxed the O-2A. The OV-10 best filled the bill, having been designed for the armed concept. Despite these assets, TAC did not want to use the Bronco as a fighter or attack aircraft.

The OV-10 and the AC-119G Flying Boxcar were tested during 40 missions at Eglin AFB, Florida, in August and September 1968. Their response time was excellent. The tests proved that the OV-10's high-noise level compromised the element of surprise, making it easier for the enemy to locate and fire on it. They also found that the AC-119 was vulnerable to enemy ground fire larger than .30 caliber. Its rather slow turn rate to the left of 140 knots also made it susceptible to enemy fire.

The USAF also scheduled the OV-10 for combat test and evaluation, code name "Misty Bronco," from 4 April to 13 June 1969. Six OV-10s and nine FACs were assigned to the 25th Infantry Division's 2nd Brigade at Cu Chi. Averaging seven missions a day, these FACs flew 508 sorties, carrying out visual reconnaissance, strike control, and emergency support of ground troops. Only a small number of missions were flown at night. It was found that the OV-10's firepower could usually destroy or neutralize troops in the open, but could only harass troops that were dug in.

The best feature of the Bronco was the Low-Level-Light Television (LLLTV) equipment and laser-guided bombs. Late in the war, the invaluable Pave Nail system was introduced, which would be used in future conflicts. When it was first initiated, an OV-10 FAC would search out and pinpoint a target with a laser range indicator. This controller then directed another FAC flying an OV-10 into the radio cone that stretched from the designator to the target. The pilot then dropped his bomb, which rode the conical beam all the way to impact. The system was also used in search and rescue operations. By July 1972, the OV-10 FACs handled about 60 percent of the laser-guided bomb drops in Southeast Asia. Subsequent laser systems did not need help from a target designator in a separate aircraft.

Byron R. Tetrick, a *Nail* FAC flying out of Nakhon Phanom from April 1972 to January 1973 commended the performance of Pave Nail OV-10:

THE OV-10 WAS excellent for the job with good visibility and was fully aerobatic. You could Split-S if necessary in a rocket pass. It had a zero-zero ejection seat and good loiter time. The accuracy of the

A Douglas A-1 Skyraider with pilot Dick Walter.

Author's Collection

Laser OV-10 allowed it to drop one 2,000-pound smart bomb, which would destroy a hard target, whereas several F-4s dropping many Mk-82 500-pound bombs had low probability of destroying the same target. The LORAN computer tie-in helped in search and rescue efforts.

But there were weaknesses. The navigator had to have pinpoint knowledge of the target location since he illuminated it with the Laser. The fighters also had to be talked in very close and needed good parameters or the bomb would miss. While the Laser system was reliable, the LORAN navigation computer tie-in was not as good. Night drops were very difficult because of coordination. Only the backseater of the OV-10 had night-scope visibility; the OV-10 pilot,

the front seater, who directed the aerial airstrike, couldn't see the target, and neither could see the fighter.

Another weakness was the OV-10's turboprop putting out a strong heat source for the SA-7 heat-seeking missiles. We lost about ten OV-10s while I was there due to that very missile. The slow cruise speed was also a weakness. It also was difficult to determine if targets were already destroyed or damaged by using binoculars. In many cases, airstrikes were put in on already dead targets.

Other FAC Aircraft

During 1965 to 1970, the O-1 Bird Dog, O-2 Skymaster, and OV-10 Bronco formed the backbone of the slow FAC operations in Southeast Asia. When the need arose, however, other aircraft performed FAC duty in addition to their primary role: the T-28 Trojan, A-1E Skyraider, U-17 Skywagon, OV-1 Mohawk, A-26A Invader, C-119 Flying Boxcar, C-123

Opposite: New Zealand FAC Darryl J. McEvedy signing off an OV-10 at Bien Hoa, March 1970. Note the empty left pod and one rocket fired from the right pod ("Willie Petes"). Both center pods are still carrying high-explosives intact, which would indicate that the mission had ended with a Troops in Contact (TIC) airstrike. Normally they never returned with any ordnance.

Darryl J. McEvedy Collection

The memorial made for an OV-10 pilot shot down by Communist Khmer Rouge soldiers: *"In Memory of Joe Gambino Who Lost His Life Honorably in Combat 7 April 1972."* Gambino, who was shot down on his 24th birthday, was a close friend of Tom Yarborough, FAC and author of *Da Nang Diary*.

Mark Berent Collection

FAC role, the A-1E was armed with 14 marking rockets, in addition to other munitions. The T-28 was also used in FAC and strike roles in Laos.

The A-1Es and T-28s ventured into areas too dangerous for O-1s and O-2s. The A1-E FACs used stand-off marking in hot areas. The nose of the aircraft was pointed at the target at 60 to 70 feet, raised 20 degrees above the horizon, and then three or four rockets were ripple-fired. Another technique was to dive in low, pop up, and lob rockets into the target area. In less hostile areas, the A1-E FACs rolled from a left turn into a 30- to 40-degree dive toward the target. Rockets were released from 4,500 feet, just prior to pull-up, and then the controller swung into a racetrack pattern to the side of, and parallel to, the strike aircraft's approach.

Provider, C-130 Hercules, and HUP-1 Piasecki helicopter. Navy helicopters were also used on occasion, but controllers had trouble marking targets from helicopters, and their slow speed and hovering operation made them fair game for enemy gunners.

The Grumman-designed OV-1 Mohawk was a battlefield reconnaissance aircraft. Redesignated in 1962 as the OV-1A, the aircraft was equipped for night, radar, and photo reconnaissance missions. The OV-1B carried SLAR in an under-fuselage mounted pod that could scan on both sides of the aircraft, producing a radar map that could be reproduced photographically while the Mohawk was in flight. The OV-1C carried infrared sensors with a forward-aimed camera for night surveillance. The OV-1D carried all three kinds of sensors: cameras, SLAR, and infrared sensors.

Specific guidelines were issued for these substitute FAC aircraft by the Seventh Air Force. T-28 and A-1E, for example, flew in pairs and acted as controllers for one another. If they flew singly, both crewmen needed to be FAC-qualified before directing their own strikes. The A-26 was allowed to furnish its own controller support if a navigator was in the crew. The C-type (C-119, C-123, C-130) aircraft carried a Forward Air Controller with them. A-1 pilots flew dual missions, especially in Laos, completed their own strikes, and then directed other strike aircraft to the target area. When used in the

The U-17, the military version of the Cessna 185 Skywagon, was used primarily in psychological warfare by the VNAF 23rd Tactical Wing, operating out of Bien Hoa Air Base, to drop leaflets and make broadcasts from special speakers.

The A-26s performed their first FAC duty in July 1966. Operating out of Nakhon Phanom, they controlled their own strikes in STEEL TIGER, supported by a C-47 flareship.

During the 1968-1969 interdiction campaign, the AC-119G *Shadow* gunship rendered FAC service when it performed reconnaissance, dropped flares, marked targets, and directed airstrikes. The *Shadow*'s performance was marginal and dangerous, because the gunship had to fly a continuous orbit to keep strike aircraft and the target in view. Its size and slow speed invited enemy ground fire. In March 1969, Colonel Conrad S. Allman, 14th Special Operations Wing (SOW) Commander, recommended that the *Shadow* no longer do Forward Air Control duty.

In 1967, jet Fast FACs operated in the high-threat and heavily-defended areas of North Vietnam and Laos. The F-100s of the 37th TFW (*Misty* FACs) began operations in June. By 1968, the 366th TFW and the 8th TFW had Fast FACs, with the 388th TFW and the 432nd TRW being supplied with jets in 1969. Airstrikes in North Vietnam were considered twice as effective when conducted by a jet FAC. The F-4D *Stormy* FACs flew night-fighter operations in Laos with support from the C-123 *Candlesticks* and the C-130 *Blindbats*. The *Night Owls* were F-4Ds flying the area near the Mu Gia Pass, the Ban Karai Pass, and the Ban Raving Pass. The *Falcon/Laredo* FACs flew out of Udorn. The *Misty* FACs extended their operations into the Echo area of STEEL TIGER to hit choke points such as Mu Gia Pass and Ban Karai Pass. By 1969, the *Mistys* were flying in the Golf Sector of STEEL TIGER. *Wolf* was the call sign of the 8th TFW flying F-4D/Es out of Ubon RTAFB.

"Took a round in the wing," Dong Ha Air Base, Republic of Vietnam, 1966.   James F. McMurray Collection

Chapter 5

The War Expands

$\mathcal{B}$Y 1966, the Southeast Asia ground operations had accelerated. U.S. strength had grown to 385,000 personnel, augmented by additional forces from Australia, New Zealand, and South Korea. There was a massive air build-up. Air power, directed by the USAF Forward Air Controllers, was vital to the success of Allied operations which had regained control of the countryside. The Viet Cong's only significant victory that year was in March when their forces overran a Special Forces camp in the A Shau Valley. North Vietnam had to commit more than 58,000 of its regular troops because of heavy Viet Cong losses.

The FACs developed an effective system of visual reconnaissance. Assigned to fly over specific areas, they were able to identify changes in the landscape caused by surreptitious enemy movement. The North Vietnamese waged a very different kind of war, unlike anything the USAF had encountered in previous conflicts.

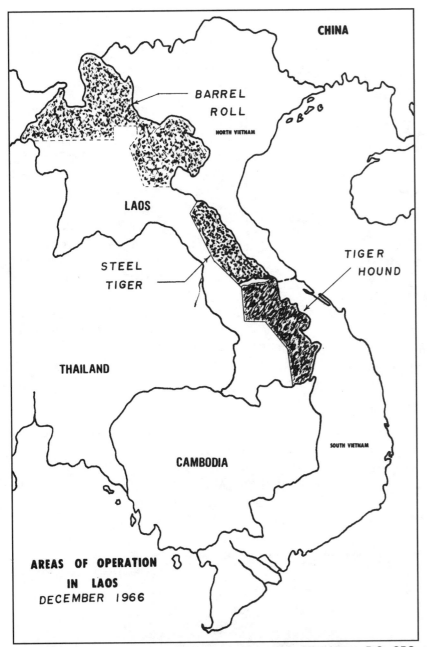

CHINA

BARREL
ROLL

NORTH VIETNAM

LAOS

STEEL
TIGER

TIGER
HOUND

THAILAND

CAMBODIA

SOUTH VIETNAM

AREAS OF OPERATION
IN LAOS
DECEMBER 1966

From General William W. Momyer, *Airpower in Three Wars* (Washington, D.C.: GPO, 1978), p. 198.

TIGER HOUND flying O-1 Bird Dogs over the Ho Chi Minh Trail in Laos from Da Nang, Dong Ha, Kham Duc, Khe Sanh, and Kontum."

On 20 July, following the North Vietnamese invasion of Quang Tri Province, the USAF and the Marines launched a new campaign, TALLY HO, against infiltration routes and targets between the DMZ and the area 30 miles northward in Route Package One (RP-1). O-1s were flown out of TIGER HOUND forward air strips, but not with the same success as the CRICKET operation due to the strong enemy defenses in the coastal area which forced the controller to fly too high for optimum visual reconnaissance. The minimum operating altitude for the TALLY HO FACs was raised to 2,500 feet AGL with a resulting drop in accuracy. By the end of the year, the O-1 aircraft had to be replaced with A-1s which in turn gave way to the jet Fast FACs.

Stuart E. Kane, formerly an F-105 pilot, flew O-1s in support of the 1st Air Cavalry Division:

WE USED THE TEAM concept for FACing in the early stages of the war with the O-1. We always kept two FACs in the O-1 because of the kind of communication you needed between air and ground to get effective coordination. In the early stages of the war, we had an additional FAC on the ground with the battalion as part of our team. There were four-way conversations including the battalion commander. We got into the team concept exploring night capability. Our night missions in TALLY HO in 1966 used the Starlight Scope in the back seat of the O-1. We could find targets but didn't have the ability with TAC air to strike them effectively. Bad weather at night was a problem. The high-speed aircraft had difficulty with the winding roads in mountainous terrain.

Frequently, we would rendezvous with the fighters out of our area so the guy on the ground didn't know explicitly that he was going to be attacked. The

Night reconnaissance operations were enhanced by several research and development programs and by refinement of existing instrumentation. The Starlight Scope was especially useful. Infrared viewers also assisted night aerial reconnaissance detection. STEEL TIGER operations continued in the Laotian panhandle with special emphasis on the TIGER HOUND area where the NVA were moving most of their truck traffic at night. James F. McMurray, an Intelligence officer with the 20th TASS out of Da Nang, stated: "One of the projects I worked was

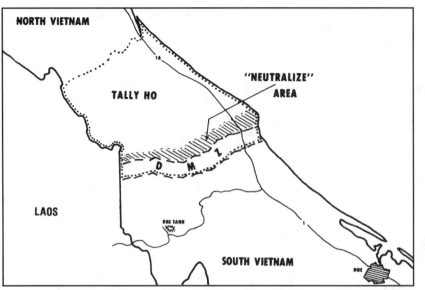

From General William W. Momyer, *Airpower in Three Wars* (Washington, D.C.: GPO, 1978), p. 304.

ample, 285, so the fighters let down right over the lake which was secure, and took up the assigned heading as they got under the clouds. They were a bit off, so the FAC said go back to the lake. From there he gave them the correct heading to fly. They had CBU. The FAC said, "On my command, I want you to pickle [*drop the bomb*]." The fighters turned and came in straight and level. The FAC said, "OK, pickle now." The fighters laid the CBU right across the path of the on-coming NVA. In this case the fighters never saw the target at all. They were just responding to the FAC. They really broke up the attack as they put the ordnance right down across the line of attack. The FAC was intimately familiar with fighters' capability and ordnance.

ideal situation was getting the fighters in without any mark at all. Other times we would have targets off-set from the mark. Sometimes we used our O-1s as bait. . . .

There was a FAC in III Corps working F-100s for a company that was severely under attack near the Cambodian border. The weather was extremely bad, with ceilings below what the fighters were supposed to go in on. The troops were about to be overrun. Through a few breaks in the clouds the fighters could see a lake. The FAC said take a heading of, for ex-

A TALLY HO FAC, James F. McMurray, described a TALLY HO mission:

PROJECT TALLY HO was flown out of Dong Ha into and above the DMZ. Our missions were intelligence and controlling strikes against targets of

TALLY HO FAC living area, Dong Ha Air Base, Republic of Vietnam, 1966.
James F. McMurray Collection

TALLY HO FACs, Dong Ha Air Base, Republic of Vietnam, 1966.   James F. McMurray Collection

opportunity, supply caches, and rolling stock. In addition, TALLY HO directed naval gunfire against land targets in North Vietnam with a Marine artillery spotter in the back seat.

OPERATION CRICKET

In January 1966, OPERATION CRICKET, using the 23rd Tactical Air Support Squadron, began to provide strike control and visual reconnaissance against the North Vietnamese Army and Pathet Lao insurgent forces in Central Laos. O-1s and A-1Es based at Nakhon Phanom RTAFB near the Laotian border began flying visual reconnaissance and serving as FACs in the northern STEEL TIGER area to Nape Pass and the southern BARREL ROLL sectors. In the BARREL ROLL area, the mission was primarily support of friendly ground troops while in STEEL TIGER, it was primarily armed reconnaissance. The aircraft covered an area about 300 miles from Nakhon Phanom, concentrating on the roads south of Mu Gia Pass — Routes 12, 23, and 911. The FACs flew in pairs, one high and one low. The high FAC would accomplish strike control while the low FAC spotted AAA fire and marked the gun's position.

Royal Laotion Air Force observers flew with some of the USAF FACs to authenticate targets before the F-100s, F-105s, and AC-47s were allowed to strike. The Forward Air Control pilot worked with both the ground Air Liaison Officers and the road reconnaissance teams inside Laos who helped pinpoint enemy targets. The FAC teamwork with the ground observers exceeded all expectations. Enemy daytime traffic virtually ceased.

U.S. Ambassador to Laos William H. Sullivan requested gunships for CRICKET. To support his request, aircraft based at Nakhon Phanom and Udorn flew continuous coverage, day and night. In addition, they shared Airborne Battlefield Command and Control Center functions with the C-130s. Later that year, when enemy defenses improved, they were withdrawn from Thailand because their slow speed made them vulnerable to enemy firepower.

The CRICKET FACs found significant infiltration routes by using visual mapping techniques from Nape Pass to Ban Raving Pass. It was difficult to determine exact locations because the old maps provided to the controllers lacked the accuracy needed to determine precise locations. All the new routes had to be meticulously plotted by the FACs, and in so doing, an extensively used route from North Vietnam through Ban Karai Pass to the intersection of Route 911 was found. Portions of this route had been extensively trellised — a camouflage technique where the NVA would build a wooden trellis over the road and cover it with vines or other growing vegetation. When they used cut vegetation, it was changed frequently to make sure it did not turn brown. But the top of a live leaf looked different from the bottom and gave the camouflage away. The controllers could detect changes of color in these leaves. This camouflage method was used by the NVA in Vietnam, Laos, and Cambodia. The CRICKET FACs also noted heavy activity on the major routes from the passes to Central Laos where they merged with the north-south route structure. They found the heaviest concentration of enemy infiltration through the Mu Gia Pass.

When looking at a map of Central and Southern Laos, there is a tendency to think of rural two-lane gravel roads. From the binocular-equipped FAC in his small aircraft, the view was entirely different. Several of the roads that had been constructed by the French were surfaced with hard-packed gravel, and occasionally asphalt or concrete. However, the majority of the infiltration routes were mostly single-lane dirt roads hacked out of the jungle. There were no neatly groomed shoulders along the roadside, and in many cases the trees were so thick and so tall that the pilots had to be directly over a road to see it. In several areas of Laos, the roads would disappear into the thick triple-canopy jungle. Most of the NVA-constructed roads followed the natural terrain features such as stream beds (where bridges might be constructed below the surface of the water to avoid detection), valleys, and along the sides of steep hills. The maps did not show the many hidden bypasses, turnoffs, and, later, connecting roads that appeared as the war progressed. It has been hard for many people, both military and civilian, to understand what confronted the FAC as he participated in the war over this unusual and constantly changing battlefield.

Because of the extensive number of route segments available to the enemy and the fleeting nature of the targets, a "choke point" concept of operations was recommended by the FACs in 1966 and adopted by the Seventh Air Force. The choke point theory involved controller-directed airstrikes that cratered and made impassable selected route segments. These areas were located in narrow valleys with very steep sides, along steep sides of cliffs, and at fording points through deep streams and rivers, such as the Ban Hieng and Se Pone Rivers in Central Laos. One example of the choke point was along Route 9 from Tchepone (Muang Xepon) east to the South Vietnam border. The road was cratered by bombs and seeded with mines at impassable points. As long as the choke points were under observation both day and night, the concept was effective. However, when the NVA felt the pressure of the choke point operation, they began to use countermeasures.

The NVA reaction came with the deployment of ever-increasing numbers of AAA weapons along the route structure. These weapons consisted of 12.7mm machine-guns, 14.5mm ZPU heavy machine-guns, 23mm twin-barreled rapid-fire AAA guns, and later the 57mm, 85mm, and 100mm weapons. The Soviet SA-2 surface-to-air missile and the SA-7 shoulder-fired, heat-seeking missiles were not deployed in Laos until 1971-1972. The densest concentration of antiaircraft fire affecting FAC operations was located in the vicinity of the passes, the choke points, and the sections of the route structure that were most susceptible to controller-directed airstrikes. In addition to the proliferation of antiaircraft artillery defenses, the NVA began to increase their use of camouflage to conceal caches of supplies and mask fording points from visual air observation.

In spite of the growing number of Allied aircraft, the infiltration of the North Vietnamese into South Vietnam strengthened. The enemy's most effective tactical change was moving the majority of supplies at night.

Night Work

Forward Air Control forces, early in 1966, had little or no night observation devices with which to observe the enemy's movement. Multi-engine aircraft, acting as flareships in the night, were utilized over choke points to provide night surveillance. The *Nimrods,* flying A-26s, performed their first FAC duty in July 1966. Operating out of Nakhon Phanom, they controlled their own strikes in STEEL TIGER, usually supported by a C-47 flareship.

During 1967, the C-123 *Candlestick* FACs worked with the T-28 *Zorros.* The C-123 Provider could loiter for hours, carrying many flares, while working with the *Zorros*. They did this at night, using the Starlight Scope. Later, the Air Force expanded these operations using tactical jet fighters.

In early 1967, the O-1 FACs had begun limited night operations using the Starlight Scopes borrowed from the Army. The Starlight Scope worked best in moonlight but could be used only when the line of sight to the ground was devoid of visual obstructions, such as heavy haze or cloud layers. During the rice-burning season the smoky haze was very thick.

The Starlight Scope consisted of an objective lens, a three-stage, image-intensifier assembly, and an eyepiece. Powered by a 6.5-volt battery, the scope collected available starlight and/or moonlight and amplified it up to 40,000 times by passing it through several lenses to the operator's eye. With the Starlight Scope, the operator could see people moving about, canals, tree lines, buildings, trucks, roads, and sampans moving along waterways. However, the aircraft vibration was a problem, and if the FAC was peering through an unopened window, the Plexiglas would distort the picture. Despite these shortcomings, the Starlight Scopes were very helpful in night reconnaissance.

On night missions, a two-man O-1 crew would depart at dusk for their assigned sector accompanied by T-28, A-1, or A-37 strike aircraft. This was no

small feat because the Bird Dog was not designed to be flown at night in a hostile battle environment. Its vacuum-powered flight instruments were very susceptible to failure and the effects of moisture. There was little or no instrument lighting and no navigational equipment to fix the aircraft's position. This was literally seat-of-the-pants flying by a highly dedicated group of aviators. The pilot flew the aircraft from the front seat while the observer stuck the Starlight Scope through the side window and peered down at the ground. A green-hued image of the ground would appear on the tiny cathode ray tube of the Starlight Scope. When the ambient light was sufficient, trucks moving down the road, without the use of their headlights, would show up on the scope. Infrared viewers also assisted night aerial reconnaissance detection. In Red Haze Recce Missions, the VC were tracked by infrared emissions. Large units could be pinpointed.

There were several techniques of directing airstrikes during the hours of darkness. When the target was visible to the unaided eye, the O-1 FAC would roll in and fire a marker rocket. As he passed over the target, he would release a flare during the pull-out. The strike aircraft would then attack as soon as the controller cleared them in hot. If the target was not visible to the unaided eye, a flare would be released and the target marked with a rocket. In many

Spade, a prominent landmark in the STEEL TIGER area in Laos.
Byron Tetrick Collection

A USAF KC-135 Stratotanker refuels a flight of F-105 Thunderchiefs on their way to a strike in North Vietnam, 25 November 1966.   USAF

cases, flare illumination had to be provided through-out the attack. Because the O-1 could only carry a few flares, it had to rely on the illumination provided by the flareships. Between January and March 1967, the night FACs from the 23rd TASS sighted approx-imately 500 trucks of which 70 were destroyed and 45 damaged. This may seem like meager results, but the O-1 had its limitations. Many valuable lessons were learned and applied to future night FAC opera-tions.

Jay Mengel, with the 20th TASS out of Da Nang, explained a Red Haze Mission:

AT NIGHT we used the Starlight Scope. . . . We used ground-burning flares . . . , red or green, drop-ping one or two in the target area. Parachute flares

were not used in the dry season. It was like flying in haze. If you lit a flare, you couldn't see anything. Also, the flare would highlight the aircraft at night in the haze.

Shortly after the night O-1 operations began, it was clearly apparent that the aircraft's gray paint scheme allowed it to be seen by enemy gunners dur-ing the flare illumination period. A limited number of aircraft thus were painted black, and a shielded rotating beacon was installed on top of the aircraft to facilitate a rendezvous with the fighters and to main-tain a safe separation from the strike aircraft, and to prevent the enemy gunners from using it as an aiming point. Originally this beacon had been located on the bottom of the aircraft.

The enemy took every advantage of the time lapse between the arrival of the flare and the strike aircraft. Trucks would drive under the jungle canopy, or attempt to get away down the road as fast as possible. On moonless nights, they would simply turn their lights off and drive under the trees. The O-1 night FACs began to use ground-released markers to keep an element of surprise. These markers would be released from the cockpit or from the pylon under the FAC aircraft's wing and would free fall to the ground where they would ignite and burn with a small intense light for about 45 minutes. The early ground markers were actually Navy floating distress signals in the shape of a small wooden box; they were called "logs" because of their shape and packaging. A log would be dropped in the foliage near the road and ahead of the moving trucks and served as a reference point for the strike aircraft that moved in on the attack. The logs weren't especially accurate, so the air controllers used them only as a general reference for the strike pilot.

Even though the Bird Dog couldn't carry enough target-marking and illuminating devices to conduct continuous night operations, the combined results of the O-1/T-28 hunter-killer teams were felt by the NVA, and their flak increased. Later, O-2s were used with the hunter-killer teams. While the FAC scanned for targets with the Starlight Scope, the T-28 flew at 500 to 1,000 feet above and behind, following the FAC's lights while maneuvering in slow S turns. The FAC would pick and mark the target with flares, secure strike clearance, and clear the T-28s in hot! They often surprised trucks before they could pull off the road. Eventually, the O-1/T-28 hunter-killer teams from Nakhon Phanom were forced to withdraw from operating over two of the route segments because of the increased intensity of the AAA.

The daytime O-1 FAC missions were also affected by the greater antiaircraft firepower. Because the enemy trucks were moving primarily at night, the day FACS concentrated on supply areas and choke points. The mountainous terrain in eastern Laos, coupled with the AAA fire, forced them to raise their operating altitude. In northern STEEL TIGER, the minimum operating altitude was raised to 6,000 feet, except for night operations. But the O-1 was designed to fly its maximum performance at lower altitudes, and thus the increase seriously degraded its

optimum performance. Morale suffered in northern STEEL TIGER because not one FAC who had been shot down between January 1966 and May 1967 had been recovered.

—————— ⚙ ——————

The AC-130 gunships could provide assistance for strike aircraft in Laos, because their pilots would become qualified as Forward Air Controllers after attending the FAC school at Ubon. They could drop logs to mark enemy gun emplacements and then clear fighters for the attack. USAF FACs in O-1s, A-1Es, and O-2As and Army air controllers in OV-1 Mohawks located enemy activity, contacted the orbiting ABCCC for air, and directed the fighter-bombers to the targets. C-123 and C-130 flareships mounted with Starlight Scopes flew in tandem with the FACs at night.

STEEL TIGER and TIGER HOUND areas were divided into four zones in 1966, resulting in a change in air operational rules. In Zone One, closest to South Vietnam, pilots were relatively free to strike targets of opportunity. The other three zones had more stringent rules governing strikes. In those areas, targets could not be hit unless authorized by low-flying USAF FACs, Laotian officers, or by the American Ambassador in Vientiane. In bad weather, all missions had to be under Skyspot MSQ-77 and TPQ-10 radar control. The FACs flew the same geographical area on a daily basis, which not only aided in enemy detection but also simplified command and control of strike aircraft.

The USAF MSQ-77 Combat Skyspot began operations in Southeast Asia after the Viet Cong took advantage of bad weather to overrun a Special Forces camp in the A Shau Valley. The only assistance to the men at this important patrol base was provided by FACs flying O-1s. A ceiling of 300 to 500 feet complicated the task. There was limited air space within which to guide the jets to their targets, and it also restricted the jets to shallow approaches, which hampered their accuracy. Following this inability to apply tactical air efficiently, Combat Skyspot was used to put bombs on target regardless of weather conditions. A computer accepted altitude, wind velocity and direction, aircraft speed, outside temperature, and ballistic traits of the ordnance carried, then figured the heading, altitude, and airspeed the airplane should maintain. As the aircraft approached the release point, a ground operator began a countdown

with course corrections, eventually giving the bomb-release signal.

The year 1967 found 486,000 troops in Vietnam as General William C. Westmoreland seized the offensive and stepped up pursuit of the enemy. By mid-1967, the FAC operation was in full swing as the effort quickened to choke off the flow of supplies along the Ho Chi Minh Trail. During one 49-day operation, commencing 12 September 1967, FACs played a key role, flying extremely close to enemy positions north of the DMZ. In OPERATION NEUTRALIZE, an air plan devised by General William W. Momyer, the FACs had a tremendous backup of air coming from the USAF, Navy, and Marine strike aircraft, as well as off-shore Navy guns and Marine artillery.

There were many occasions when strike fighters weren't available, and FACs took it upon themselves to create an attack in aircraft not intended for that sort of scenario. Robert C. Mikesh was tasked to perform an operational check flight in an O-2A on 13 October 1967. He took off from the gravel runway inside the walled city of Hue, at 4:30 p.m., for what should have been an uneventful 20-minute flight:

I CHECKED IN with *Big Control*, our DASC *Victor* control center for this northern sector. The tranquility of my check flight was interrupted when a desperate voice came up on the frequency using the call sign *West Gate*, a Marine reconnaissance squadron north of Hue. *West Gate* was transmitting in the blind for any *Big* aircraft, our FAC call sign, to respond. I overheard *Big* one-seven answer. The Marines needed immediate fire support to cover their position which was under intense enemy fire. *Big* one-seven was low on fuel so had to head home, but he had heard my check-in and asked if I could help. Even though I had only a partial load of fuel, and the smoke rockets (seven) left from an earlier flight, I headed for the desperate Marine's position on a high ridge asking *Big Control* for air support aircraft, hoping to have fighters on station by the time I got to the Marine's location.

Big Control gave me the call sign of the F-4s, but as soon as I made contact with the fighters I learned that they were heading north to provide cover for one of their comrades that had gone down north of the DMZ. *Big Control* said another set of fighters would be available shortly. By now I passed the top of the ridge where the Marines were in trouble. They released smoke to verify their position. The second set of fighters came up on my frequency, but just then, they too were diverted north. The only air available was now the ground-alert aircraft at Da Nang. They were to be scrambled immediately, but it might be too late by the time they arrived.

I decided to roll in and use my lightly armed FAC aircraft like a fighter. I fired off one smoke rocket and watched it hit the ground as I banked away and pulled off. The Marine radio operator reported with excitement that my hit was "right on!" Little damage can be caused by a smoke rocket, but the effect is disconcerting. I continued to make passes, alternately some hot with some dry, just to keep the enemy guessing. As the shadows deepened, I was aware for the first time that the VC were also firing at me with hand weapons each time I made a pass. I was looking right at their muzzle flashes as I bore in on them at low level with each dive. And me without my flak vest, a "must" item of personal equipment on any FAC mission.

To my surprise, a flight of Marine A-4s came on station and reported in much sooner than I expected the Air Force F-4s. I briefed them and cleared them in hot. They dropped 500-pounders right on the mark, which brought a favorable response from the Marine radioman. After the Skyhawk's second pass, a line of Hueys came into view and were snaking from the south side of the ridge to the Marine position. As the Skyhawks provided cover, a rapid extraction of the Marines took place. Quickly the Marines were on their way to Marble Mountain Marine Base, east of Da Nang, without the loss of a man.

Returning to my base with not enough fuel to go elsewhere, I made my first, and thankfully my last, night landing at Hue Citadel Airport, gliding across the protective wall that circled this ancient city, over the moat, and on to the 2,400-foot gravel runway that had no lights. With this, I had enough action for one day.

Mikesh was awarded the Distinguished Flying Cross for this air support. The citation that accompanied the medal read in part:

No air support was immediately available so Major Mikesh made repeated rocket passes at low level to impede the hostile movement to-

ward the friendly forces. He was successful in keeping the hostile forces pinned down until tactical air support arrived forty minutes later. During this entire period, he was subjected to intense hostile fire. The professional competence, aerial skill, and devotion to duty displayed by Major Mikesh reflect great credit upon himself and the United States Air Force.

In late 1967, the FACs noted a large increase in NVA activity in the area of Routes 9 and 92 just west of the DMZ. Correlated with other Intelligence information, this activity indicated that the enemy was preparing for a major attack into South Vietnam. The activity increased and culminated in the Battle for Khe Sanh, which the enemy had hoped to make into another Dien Bien Phu. Close air support, controlled by the USAF and Marine FACs, was the chief factor in beating back the attacking forces. For this battle the Marine FACs flew O-1Es that had been resurrected and certified fit after being airlifted to Vietnam. The Marines' original supply of O-1s had reached the end of their service life in September 1965.

Joe Madden, *Cider* 10, was awarded the Air Force Cross for his flying on 5-8 November 1967. Madden was assigned to II Corps field forces out of Nha Trang, the 1st Brigade, 4th Infantry Division:

I THINK WHAT got it for me were my activities at night rather than in the daytime, resupplying the perimeter. A resupply helicopter was shot down (water was always a problem for the troops). We concocted a resupply route with airstrikes on the west and artillery fire on the east. Airstrikes with napalm were very effective at night. In effect, we had a narrow alleyway on the east side of the perimeter for the helicopters. They would go in, throw off supplies, load the wounded, and bug out in a hurry, and go back the same way. The Army didn't like to send their slick helicopters in without helio-gunship support, but when you're running down an alleyway, you don't have room for six abreast. You had to do this on a one helicopter at a time basis. I ran the airstrikes to support this operation at night.

The next day the 173rd Airborne made a landing to the northwest, up near the Special Forces camp at Ben Het. They made a LZ there and got into trouble. Eighty fighters were diverted to them. We ran out of heavy close air support and could only get CBU24s. There was still a .50-caliber site up on a hill to the west, firing down on the perimeter. It just so happened that I was flying my O-1 at 1,500 feet and saw a 12.7 machine-gun being fired by three bad guys. No CAS [*Close Air Support*] was available so I whipped out my trusty AR-15 and I killed those three SOBs.

———————— ✈ ————————

During the 1968 Tet Offensive, FACs were airborne around the clock, directing airstrikes against enemy storage areas and troops as well as providing support for troops in contact (TIC) with the enemy. During the Battle of Khe Sanh, there were so many flights of fighters that they would have to wait their turn to be worked by the FACs, via ABCCC. Sometimes the holding patterns extended as high as 35,000 feet. One O-1 and three USAF O-2As, at Khe Sanh when the attack began, were flown to safety while two USAF officers, Majors Milton Hartenbower and Richard Keskinen, remained behind to serve as ALOs. Flying in the zone was difficult. Weather was always a factor. At Lang Vei, the FAC usually had to penetrate the overcast (which might be concealing a hilltop or ridge line), identify the target that might be shooting at him, climb back above the cloud cover, and lead the waiting fighters down below the murk. Once beneath the overcast, the FAC had to direct the fighters, keeping them and the target in sight at all times. In addition to bad weather and hostile fire, the FACs also had to worry about friendly artillery. During the Khe Sanh battle, friendly shells were fired from Camp Carroll, the Rockpile (a 700-foot-tall, toothpick-shaped hill with steep cliffs dominating some of the terrain south of the DMZ), or the Marine base itself.

Sometimes the FACs were able to save innocent civilians from attack. On the morning of 8 February 1968, several hundred people were spotted by a FAC moving westward along Highway 9 from the vicinity of the Marine base toward the ruins of the Special Forces camp at Lang Vei. There was talk of shelling this group that was moving in the wrong direction until the controller, USAF Captain Charles Rushforth, flew down and made a pass at tree-top level. He determined that these were really refugees as he saw only old men, women, and children. However, two days later the enemy used civilians on the same highway to move military supplies. That situation dictated an immediate attack to prevent the movement of matériel.

John Heimburger was sent to Khe Sanh on 2 November 1967. He wrote:

NEW LOCATION, Khe Sanh. Intelligence says there are four NVA Divisions in I Corps. Of course Khe Sanh has a battalion of Marines for protection. Exciting arrival in my O-1 at Khe Sanh. 1 + 40 [*1 hour 40 minutes*] en route through weather to 1,500-foot runway. Strong crosswinds 60 to 70 degrees at 15 gusting to 20 knots. Dirt constantly blowing, reminds me of Dong Ha. Typical Marine position, perimeter with claymores [*directional antipersonnel mines*]. LTC Roberts late, no landing lights here. I thought he'd not make it through the rain, but GCA [*Ground Control Approach*] talked him over the camp and a hole opened up in the clouds so he popped down for a hairy landing.

Several months later I made an interesting discovery with a civilian in the backseat. While taking an Illinois newscaster, Lavern White, for a ride in an O-1 from Nha Trang AB, near the coast of South Vietnam, he made the comment that "those Vietnamese certainly make straight rows with their crops, but must not have much success. It looks like a neat farmer planted his corn in straight rows with a rope." Looking at what he was speaking of, we descended to treetop level for a closer look at the rows.

Requesting a ground search, we learned that a huge 2½-mile rhombic antenna had been constructed on the north side of the hill. Its purpose was to receive and send messages from and to North Vietnam for the entire central region. At altitude the row guides (antennae wires) couldn't be seen or even associated with a communications network. At low altitude a single wire, or even several hundred feet of wires, did not draw interest, since they were such a small part of a huge whole.

White was a news director for radio station WLRW [*in Champaign, Illinois*]. Reporting later after his one-month tour of Vietnam installations, White said: "I'm told that the Viet Cong never shoot at the little planes. We have hovering above us at 10,000 or 12,000 feet heavy jet bombers just waiting to come down and bring wrath to the situation."

I told White I wear earplugs, so "I won't know about it. However, I must admit there have been several occasions when the ground fire was directed at my plane. A couple of times they were close enough to be a ZING instead of a POP, which is the usual indication. But I try to fly so erratically no one will be able to hit me."

White gave a ragged sigh and said, "Believe me, this has been quite a day. You can't imagine the experience of flying over enemy terrain in a single-engine airplane. At any time a rifle on the ground could take care of you without any trouble. And you're 40 or 50 miles from anybody who's friendly."

———

The Laotian portion of the battle began with the overrunning of Royal Laotian Army positions located west and adjacent to the DMZ. Known as the "elephant," this area was lightly defended by the Royal Lao BV-33 unit commanded by Lieutenant Colonel Soulang. His forces were attacked the night of 23 January 1968. The weather conditions prohibited FACs and gunships from effectively supporting the Laotians. The BV-33 unit began withdrawing toward South Vietnam.

When the weather improved, *Covey* 263 located refugees fleeing east on Route 9 toward the border with the enemy in hot pursuit, and immediately began directing airstrikes against the bridges behind the refugees, which effectively stopped the enemy. The *Covey* FACs provided continuous air cover until all the refugees had entered the Long Vei Special Forces camp.

The NVA activity kept increasing, and on 26 January 1968, the FACs began to sight truck and troop movement from Laos into South Vietnam. Their airstrikes began blowing away the jungle canopy and revealing more and more stacks of supplies and ammunition. The FACs were effective in spite of very heavy AAA fire in the Route 9 area. One night during February 1968, *Covey* 673 received accurate fire

Vietnamese Air Force A-1H Skyraiders in formation over South Vietnam, 27 September 1967.
USAF

from four positions north of Target 674. He advised that the guns were radar controlled because the fire from all positions converged in close proximity to the FAC, who was at 6,500 feet, with rounds bursting both above and below the aircraft. The line of fire from the gun positions was straight at the aircraft and came very close to hitting it. The night was dark with no moon and the aircraft did not have lights on.

During the support of Khe Sanh, the FACs flew 1,598 sorties. The enemy disengaged, but even so, the Route 9 area in Laos retained its reputation for being hostile. Major Gerald T. Dwyer, *Nail* 55, experienced this in a chilling and hostile episode while flying a combat mission in an O-2A over the extreme western end of the A Shau Valley on 21 May 1968. Suddenly there was an explosion and his aircraft became uncontrollable. A 37mm projectile had struck the aircraft and blew off one of the wings. As the O-2A began a wild tumble toward the ground, Major Dwyer released the aircraft's entry door and dove out the open hole. He pulled the ripcord on his parachute as he, too, tumbled through the sky and was rewarded by the opening shock.

Major Dwyer began to receive small arms fire from enemy troops who had observed his O-2A go down. He landed without injury, discarded his parachute, and began to evade. But within minutes, he was being pursued by five heavily armed enemy soldiers. The search and rescue forces were contacted on his survival radio, but the AAA fire was too intense for a helicopter pickup. Major Dwyer began to evade again. His attempts were successful as he wove his way through the jungle, until he was instructed to ignite a smoke flare in preparation for being picked up.

The smoke from his flare completely compromised his position and his pursuers attacked him with rifle fire, pistol fire, and hand grenades. Dwyer killed three of his attackers and forced the remaining two into an open area where they were dispatched by an airstrike. The major was rescued by helicopter without further incident.

After the siege of Khe Sanh (which began in January 1968 until it was abandoned in June 1968), the Tactical Air Commands were placed under the command of the Seventh Air Force making it essentially a single manager system for air resources. Enemy firepower was especially dangerous along the Cambodian border where the enemy used heavy, automatic machine-guns that reached above the FAC's minimum assigned altitude of 1,500 feet. To avoid being hit, the controllers kept their aircraft uncoordinated by using the rudders continuously to maintain an unpredictable flight path, thus preventing the enemy gunners from lining up on them.

The 23rd TASS aircraft loss in the vicinity of Mu Gia Pass from AAA fire placed it off limits for low-altitude operations. The operating altitude in northern STEEL TIGER had been raised to 6,000 feet, except for night operations. The O-1 was inadequate. By late December 1967, almost all the USAF FACs in STEEL TIGER had transitioned to the O-2A. The STEEL TIGER operation was now handled by the 20th TASS. The *Nails* flew in the northern sector and the *Coveys* flew in the southern sector.

Because the O-2A had side-by-side seating, the right front seat and door had to be permanently removed to move the Eyeglass (Super Starlight) Scope into the aircraft and clamp it to the seat rails. The observer squeezed around the scope to get in and out, which was a safety hazard. Sometimes rain pelted through the open doorway, splattering the Eyeglass and electronic equipment. The scope weighed 137 pounds, so together with the operator's weight, the O-2 was usually overloaded. The scope's position limited its use to the right side of the aircraft, forcing the operator to direct the pilot through most maneuvers so

Engine maintenance on an AC-47 *Spooky* used as a gunship or flareship. Armament included three side-firing 7.62mm Gatling-style miniguns and 45 flares of 200,000 candlepower.

Pleiku Airfield, South Vietnam, 1967.

that he could keep the Eyeglass fixed on the target. Eventually, the Air Force decided to use the smaller and lighter AN/AVG-3 Starlight Scope for the O-2A.

The airborne gunships were also effective. The AC-47, AC-119, and AC-130 fixed-wing transports were modified with 7.62mm, 20mm, and 40mm weapons. The guns were fixed in position to fire from specially made holes on one side of the aircraft. The guns were aimed by maneuvering the aircraft in precise left-hand turns at an altitude just above the reach of enemy ground fire. They could stay aloft for extended periods.

The USAF used AC-47 *Spooky* gunships, the military version of the Douglas DC-3, with three side-firing 7.62mm Gatling-style miniguns, each firing 6,000 rounds per minute. Each fifth round was a red-glowing tracer bullet. This stream of fire looked like a curving dragon's tongue. The Viet Cong thought it was a fire-eating dragon, and thus *Spooky* got another nickname, *Puff the Magic Dragon. Puff* carried 24,000 rounds of 7.62mm ammunition and 45 aerial flares of 200,000 candlepower that floated down in

chutes. The *Spooks* kept many Special Forces camps from being overrun at night.

In March 1968, the FACs began flying round-the-clock rocket watches of the Saigon area. Two O-1s were airborne at all times during the hours of darkness, augmented by two A-1E Skyraiders on strip alert (ready to take off at an instant's notice) and two AC-47 *Spooky* gunships on night airborne alert. After putting aside its guerrilla methods in 1965, the enemy found that mortars and rocket launchers were best for attacks because they could be assembled quickly and then moved out. Enemy planning was serious. They often used sand tables that depicted attack terrain with building mockups set in exact locations. Airbases, such as Da Nang, were particularly vulnerable because they lacked overhead revetments to protect the parked airplanes.

A Better FAC Aircraft

The requirement for a new FAC aircraft to replace the O-1 Bird Dog had been realized as far back as 1962. Numerous candidates were considered, including the T-6, T-28, A-1E, T-33, and various helicopters. All of these were rejected because of age, limited numbers, or lack of visibility from the cockpit. It was decided to develop a single all-service aircraft, the OV-10. North American Rockwell began development of the Bronco in 1964. The USAF had stated that it needed a new aircraft by 1965 to replace the O-1, and the situation that developed in eastern Laos proved them correct. But because the OV-10 would not be in the inventory until sometime in 1968, an interim FAC aircraft was needed, and thus the Cessna O-2A Skymaster was modified for FAC duty. The updated navigation and communications equipment, as well as the twin engines, provided a vast improvement over the O-1 in most respects.

At this time there was a realignment of squadrons responsible for the STEEL TIGER operation, which was now handled by the 20th TASS, using the call sign *Covey* while operating in the southern sector. The northern sectors were handled by the 23rd TASS under the new call sign, *Nail*. The Forward Operations Locations were Pleiku, South Vietnam, and Ubon RTAFB, Thailand.

The introduction of the O-2A did not significantly change the basic FAC tactics. However, it did increase the FACs' effectiveness through greater speed, the ability to carry more marking devices, and ability for night operations. The FAC was now an airstrike controller, an Intelligence officer, an ordnance expert, a radio operator, a political interpreter in applying the Rules of Engagement (ROE), and an on-scene commander during rescue operations when necessary.

When President Richard M. Nixon took office in 1969, there were 500,000 troops in Vietnam. Nixon ordered reductions in forces, and, to keep the enemy off balance, incursions into Cambodia. The Allies increased their control over the countryside despite the withdrawal of American troops. (These troop numbers do not include CIA operatives in Southeast Asia, especially the planes and men of Air America and other clandestine airlines.)

After the Easter Offensive of 1972, the FACs flew day and night. Before the spring of that year, their minimum altitude had been 1,500 feet AGL. However, after the NVA started using the SA-7 heat-seeking missile, the minimum altitude became 7,000 feet AGL. The An Loc defense in Military Region III in the spring and summer of 1972 saw the regular use of three FACs, similar to the operation at Kham Duc in 1968. One flew high and briefed the incoming

fighters, assigned holding altitudes, and managed the fighters according to their fuel states. The other two worked the strike aircraft, one on the north side of town, and one on the south side.

Sometimes pilots flying other than the usual FAC aircraft took on the Forward Air Control role. A C-7 Caribou pilot performed FAC duties for the Special Forces when a regular FAC was not present. The DeHavilland Caribou supported Special Forces operations at remote camps, as well as the roving Mike Force teams throughout the northwest Central Highlands, the mobile, elite Special Forces strike teams. Ground fire was a continuous concern. To protect themselves the C-7 crews flew, inches above the trees, where no aircraft had ever been hit before. However, hits were frequent elsewhere, due to an enemy gun emplacement high up on hillsides, for example, when the Caribous went up to 2,500 feet.

If a FAC was not available, the Caribou crews gave Intelligence to the Special Forces, as well as performed artillery spotting. The Caribous worked in areas where it was impossible to support the ground people with helicopters.

Candlesticks and *Blindbats*

The *Candlestick* FACs operated over northern STEEL TIGER, and the *Blindbats* over southern STEEL TIGER. For four years, the C-123 *Candlestick* FACs did yeoman work holding the line against enemy night infiltration in northern STEEL TIGER. Night work was extremely hazardous because of the threat of AAA and the possibility of a midair collision with so many aircraft working in close proximity to each other. Along with the O-2A *Nails*, the C-123s were the first reliable night hunters employed along the Ho Chi Minh Trail. The *Candlesticks* on station time averaged over six hours per mission, allowing better traffic-following and target development than other FAC aircraft. The whole operation was improvised when they started using the Starlight Scope in the old Fairchild C-123 Provider. The C-123 was equipped with marking munitions consisting of 50 flares and 26 ground markers that were launched manually off the cargo ramp. The aircraft lacked the sophistication of the C-130 in that it had no auto-pilot, radar, cabin pressurization, or power-boosted flight controls.

The C-123 did not have a side-mounted Starlight Scope. The navigator operating the primary Starlight Scope had to lie prone on a mattress placed over a piece of armor plate. He viewed the route structure

The newly modified C-123K Provider, with the addition of jet engines, in flight over South Vietnam, June 1967. USAF

through an open forward bailout hatch in the floor of the aircraft. From this uncomfortable position, the scope operator would call out heading changes to keep the C-123 over the route under observation. A second scope operator scanned from a door on the left side of the aircraft. Both jobs were very fatiguing and had to be rotated among the three navigators. Just in time for the 1967-1968 dry season, the Air Force was able to substitute the lighter, six-pound AN/AVG-3 Starlight Scope. Solidly mounted, it was more stable, easier to handle, and better for picking out ground targets.

The C-123 would be blacked out upon entering the Area of Operation. The scope operators would go to their positions and the loadmaster to the rear ramp, which opened in flight. The two loadmasters were responsible for launching marking munitions and calling out enemy AAA as it fired at the aircraft. The

scope operators would give aiming-point corrections after each attack by the fighters. Information would be relayed to the pilots who controlled the strike. The *Candlestick* crews preferred working with the aircraft that had the endurance to loiter with the FAC aircraft. They formed hunter-killer teams with the T-28, A-26, and A-1 sister squadrons from Nakhon Phanom. This combination allowed the *Candlesticks* to find a target, mark it, and make an immediate strike.

The *Candlesticks* worked as teams with the O-2As that used their marking rockets at night to pinpoint targets, while the C-123s and C-130s provided flare illumination and ground markers. Among their team efforts were the battles at Khe Sanh, Ban Bak, and Lam Son 719. By the end of 1969, the C-123 Providers couldn't survive the increased antiaircraft fire along the Trail in Laos, so the Seventh Air Force

shifted them to less hostile areas, which curbed their usefulness. On 30 June 1971, the 606th Special Operations Squadron was deactivated, and modified AC-130 gunships, equipped with Forward-Looking Infrared Radar (FLIR), LLLTV, SLAR, and advanced Starlight Scopes, replaced the *Candlesticks*.

Blindbat missions were flown by the C-130 *Spectre* gunships of the 374th Tactical Airlift Wing, based at Da Nang, on TDY from Naha AB, Okinawa. This temporary duty was eventually switched to Permanent Change of Station (PCS). In March 1966, the detachment moved to Ubon AB, Thailand. The transition in late 1966 and early 1967 to Forward Air Control duty went smoothly. After completing a brief FAC course at Ubon AB, C-130 pilots and navigators were cleared to direct interdiction airstrikes. The C-130s working in southern Laos were named *Blindbat*, while those that flew in northern Laos were called *Lamplighter*. Later, all C-130 flare and FAC operations became known as *Blindbat*.

The *Blindbat* C-130 aircraft carried a crew of eight, which included a pilot, copilot, two navigators — one to navigate and the other to operate the Night Observation Device (NOD) — a flight engineer, and two or three loadmasters to drop flares and ground markers. The aircraft was painted black and used a shielded rotating beacon. A typical load of marking munitions included 250 flares, 30 colored ground markers, and 36 white burning ground markers. The flares and ground markers were dispensed manually through a launcher on the cargo ramp door which opened in flight at the rear of the aircraft.

The mission of the *Blindbats* was to provide flareship support at night and strike control as well as armed reconnaissance. The *Blindbat* crews patrolled the route structures and waterways looking for vehicular and boat traffic. In the early days, this was done without the advantage of the Starlight Scope. When suspicious lights were sighted, or the crew could see a target under bright moonlight, a flare was dropped from the rear of the aircraft, and strike aircraft would be called in.

Later when the Starlight Scope became available, they found that the C-130 was not really an ideal platform for it due to the paralax from the aircraft's curved windows. However, the long station time, wide range of airspeeds, and the ability to carry large numbers of flares and ground markers, made the C-130 an ideal aircraft for *Blindbat* night operations in low-threat environments. And the Starlight Scopes were useful in target detection, in spite of the curved windows. Crews used significant offset distances from the route structure by installing a seat and Starlight Scope near the right rear troop door. When the aircraft arrived in the area of operation, it was depressurized and the right rear troop door was removed. The Starlight Scope was rotated into position and the seat locked into place for the operator, who could then sit and swivel as needed to keep the route structure under observation.

But this arrangement could be hazardous. Captain Johnson was flying as NOD operator on *Blindbat* 13 on 12 June 1970. The aircraft began experiencing mechanical difficulties, so the aircraft commander decided to return to Ubon. Captain Johnson began to reposition the NOD so that he could close the troop door in preparation for pressurizing the aircraft. As he bent over the mount, his chest-pack parachute inadvertently opened and he was sucked from the aircraft. In an instant he was swinging from the parachute's risers. He landed in the jungle with only minor injuries and was rescued without difficulty the next morning.

For precision marking, the *Blindbat* dropped a series of flares and called in an O-2A FAC to pinpoint a target with a smoke rocket. This tactic worked especially well when enemy convoys pulled off the road to hide. *Blindbat* and the fighters coordinated their positions using the clock code: "The target is at ten o'clock, 30 yards from the marker." In addition, *Blindbat* gave the strike crews a base altitude and the location of the highest terrain within a five-mile radius. The base altitude was a reference altitude assigned to the mission for control and separation of aircraft in the target area. "Flareship at base minus two," for example, meant that the aircraft was 2,000 feet below the base altitude. The frag order changed the base altitude daily for security reasons.

Limited electronic countermeasure capability was installed in some C-130s in December 1968 in response to the increasing number of radar-directed

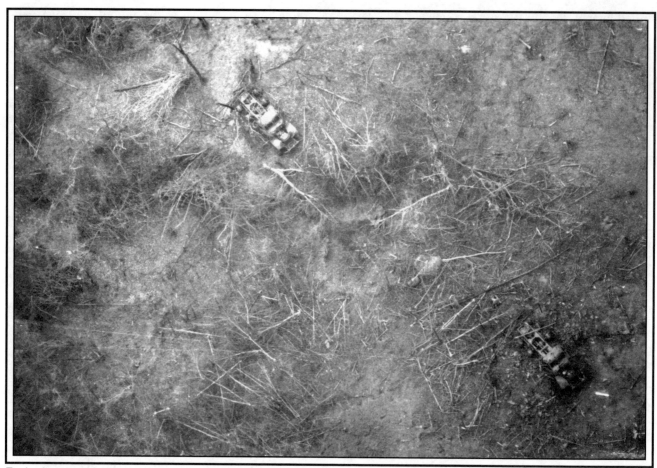

Trucks destroyed by airstrike on the Ho Chi Minh Trail.

AAA encounters. The most unique was the mounting of a laser designator to the top of the night observation device in November 1969. This successful improvement led to installing laser designators on three *Blindbat* aircraft. The operator would observe and designate the target using a right-hand orbit while the strike aircraft delivered a laser-guided bomb into the center of the orbit using a ground marker for reference. But, as the laser designators were being installed, the *Blindbat* operation was disbanded. Their role was turned over to the B-57 Canberra and the C-130E gunships, which possessed a self-strike capability.

The C-130 *Blindbats* flew their last mission on 14 June 1970 bringing the FAC/flareship era in Laos to

a close. The B-57G Canberra that replaced them were equipped with LLLTV, FLIR, and Forward-Looking Radar (FLR) with Moving Target Indicator (MTI), which had more capability to see the enemy at night and keep tabs on his maneuvers.

Shadow and *Stinger*

When the AC-119K was being developed under project COMBAT HORNET, gunship 3 eventually received the call sign *Stinger*. Previously the AC-119G was called *Shadow*. The AC-119G was in combat in 1968, followed by the AC-119K in 1969. The *Stinger* had two extra J-85 jet engines, and its gross takeoff weight was 80,400 pounds compared to *Shadow*'s 64,000 pounds.

Chapter 6

The War Winds Down

*I*N 1969, the "Vietnamization" program accelerated. Vietnamese troops were trained and
equipped so that the United States could start
withdrawing its forces. The first U.S. troops departed in
July, and by the end of the year, 69,000 had been withdrawn.

*The COMMANDO HUNT operations, begun in 1968,
continued in the Laotian panhandle to interdict troops
and supplies along the Ho Chi Minh Trail. The Communists were slowly advancing across the northern part of
Laos, defeating the Laotian forces. The North Vietnamese
even built an oil pipeline inside the panhandle to bring oil
south from Hanoi. U.S. military advice and assistance
was rendered, but U.S. ground forces could not participate in the defensive operations without violating Laotian
neutrality.*

*The enemy had been using Cambodia as a sanctuary,
crossing the border to make attacks on South Vietnam,*

and then fleeing back across the border for protection and safety. For years the U.S. military and South Vietnamese military experts, as well as ex-President Eisenhower, had urged President Johnson to allow attacks on the enemy in these sanctuaries. However, it was not until the enemy launched a nationwide offensive, 23 February 1969, that President Nixon ordered a secret two-month bombing campaign by B-52s.

In April 1970, the USAF and VNAF flew into Cambodia to strike North Vietnamese positions. USAF controllers had been monitoring the DANIEL BOONE recce teams' incursions into Cambodia, but they seldom crossed the border themselves. On 28 April, the Seventh Air Force Tactical Air Control Center alerted the Direct Air Support Centers and fighter wings. The FACs, adhering to normal Rules of Engagement, were assigned specific ground units. They operated in radio jeeps as well as aircraft and controlled all airstrikes. The 19th Tactical Air Support Squadron backed up operations in southern Cambodia, the 20th TASS in the northeastern part of Cambodia, the 22nd TASS in the eastern portion, and the 23rd TASS in the northwest.

A special task force, with an Air Liaison Officer and Tactical Air Control Party, coordinated air support. An O-2A FAC, call sign *Head Beagle*, flew out of Di An, climbed to 8,000 feet, and circled south of the Fish Hook area, just inside the South Vietnam border (the protrusion of Cambodia into Military Region III). The *Head Beagle* took fighter handoffs from the DASC and passed them on to the FACs. There was so much air support that even the *Head Beagle* couldn't handle it, so by December 1970, EC-121 Super Constellations were flown in to function as ABCCCs. French-speaking FACs were a plus to this operation, as the incursion forces often did not speak English.

By 1970, enemy activity was at a low in South Vietnam. Supplies continued to move down the Ho Chi Minh Trail. On 17 February 1970, B-52s were used for the first time to drop bombs on targets in northern Laos. Trouble erupted in Cambodia as the North Vietnamese and Viet Cong troops seized territory. On 20 April 1970, the Cambodian government called for assistance. USAF and VNAF aircraft responded by bombing targets in Cambodia on 24 April. On 29 April, U.S. and South Vietnamese troops crossed the border and hit the enemy sanctuaries. By the end of June, they withdrew to South Vietnam. At that time, the enemy, having continued offensive operations, occupied about half of Cambodia.

Richard Gary Mucho, a *Toy* FAC from 1969 to 1970 at Di An in III Corps, remembered the mission in Cambodia:

THE COORDINATION between the FACs, Army ground units, and TAC air was a masterpiece. We had less than a week to prepare for this mission in Cambodia. Hardly anyone knew about the coordinated airstrikes with the FACs in Cambodia, and the Army ground units. No one got recognition for that feat. This was a big operation with Tactical Air Support and the FACs. It was a masterpiece of planning. A Top Secret message came down. How many planes can you support in a 24-hour period? How many pilots? Is anybody night qualified? Get your Cambodian maps, that kind of thing. We had plenty of aircraft. In a ten-klick square area, which is not very big, we had three holding patterns — the 25th Infantry, the 1st Air Cavalry, and the 11th Armored Cavalry Division of the Vietnamese Marines, all concentrated in one area of land going to Cambodia. We also had the logistical support of helicopters flying in with howitzers and ammunition, dustoffs, and whatever.

The FAC that worked this particular mission relieved me. I was working a hunter-killer team just west of Tay Ninh in a place called the "Dog Face" area in Cambodia. This was well into the invasion. We only had a couple of weeks left before we had to pull back. A hunter-killer team from CHARLIE HORSE was working an area just west of the Cambodian border which we called the "Picket Fence" between Cambodia and Vietnam. We heard rumors Intelligence-wise that the NVN were making an end run around the invasion force, and they were going to make a regimental-size ground assault on Tay Ninh itself. Tay Ninh was a district capital with a big Army (U.S. and SVN) installation there.

They sent in hunter-killer teams to scout the area. We had three units, an Army LOH [*Light Observation Helicopter*] with two men, Cobra [*AH-1*] gunships with two men, and one man in an O-2. The LOH flew low and slow, the Cobra flew at 800 to 1,000 feet, always in a left turn, and the FAC flew top cover at 1,500 feet AGL, or lower, right above but behind the Cobra to check six. If the Cobra took fire, the FAC said break. There were hardly any forces in the Dog Face area. The main forces were farther north. Tay Ninh was virtually undefended.

My hunter-killer team came upon a village, actually a large-size town in Cambodia with east and west streets, like Main Street and Elm Street. There was nobody around, no dogs, no children, nobody. The Cobra rolled in and made a couple of high-speed passes. Then he slowed down for a closer look and all hell broke loose. The Cobra took gunfire and was hit. The pilot had enough momentum to overfly the village and land near a tree line. The crew got out of the chopper, one with a machine-gun, and they ran to the tree line. Another Cobra rolled in and took fire from the school, the orphanage, the church, and all kinds of buildings in this supposedly deserted village. The Army's command and control helicopter landed and picked up the downed crew. The Army commander, a light [*lieutenant*] colonel, called the FAC and said, "I want air strikes and I want the town leveled, and my initials are. . . . That was the FAC's authorization to call in everything, which he did. The fighters kept hitting the town, taking fire all the time, until the afternoon sun went down. We aborted a major attack on Tay Ninh by an experienced force while everyone else in Cambodia was making headlines.

In late November and December 1969 and January 1970, before we first went into Cambodia, we would tune in certain FM frequencies and listen on VHF. We could hear certain tones coming through when flying right along the Picket Line (Cambodian border) which were radar-tracking devices. I was always changing my altitude and attitude to lose the trackers. That was the danger of the hunter-killer missions with the Cobras. There was not much chance to move, except I would try to vary the altitude. The O-2 was pretty maneuverable, like the Cobra. We used to dogfight the Cobras all the time. The Cobra could do pedal turns, but the Cobra couldn't raise its nose up as high as the O-2 and hang on the prop like an O-2, so we stayed above the Cobra. However, we couldn't dive on it because it was sitting right there, until pretty soon it would run out of airspeed, do a pedal turn, and head down to the deck. We would do a wing-over and follow it down going rat-a-tat-tat, "beware of the gun out of the sun!" We used to have a lot of fun dogfighting those guys.

There was lots of camaraderie with Army units, especially small ones. We were close knit with the true spirit of the old Cavalry days. We were a new entity, being USAF fixed-wing guys. We used to trade things — trucks, air-conditioners, beat-up

helicopters. The Army fed us pretty good and took really good care of us. When we lost somebody over there, it hit us bad. You were probably drinking with the guy the night before. And, the next day, he's dead.

Fear was always a factor. You lived with it, day to day. You didn't know if you would get shot down during the day. You were out in the middle of nowhere, not near anybody. Just kind of cruising around looking for things when the engine craps and you have to get out. The fear was there all the time. Some people couldn't live with it and you saw it all the time. They flew higher. They were sick more times. They aborted the aircraft. That's why you hear sometimes that the O-2 was a shitty airplane. Well, it depends on whom you are talking to. My airplane was good. I probably shouldn't have taken it a couple of times. We had six O-2s that we rotated because some were always down for maintenance. Basically we had three troops of cavalry to support with five or six airplanes, so the maintenance guys did great. Sometimes we only had one aircraft out of six when the rest of them crapped out because of lack of parts, or bad weather. We didn't have to talk about fear. It was there. It wasn't like we were flying a bomber at 30,000 feet.

Some FACs lived underground at Song Bei down in III Corps. Their aircraft were parked outside in revetments and they lived underground because the incoming [*enemy fire*] was a hazard all the time. You get used to it, but the fear is always there. What is going to happen, will happen, but what you try to do is minimize the chances. Some guys took chances, I know I did, looking back on it. I'd never do that again . . . I'm lucky to be here. We did party hard; it was a release of built-up tensions, and there was nothing else to do. You had to do this in order to get up the next day and go again.

Mucho recalls another FAC, Ed, a French-Canadian American, who came to Camp Evans and went through his check-out:

HE WAS REALLY quite a guy. Ed couldn't hit the country of South Vietnam, let alone a target. We couldn't believe how bad his marks were. Normally when you'd roll in to put in smoke you'd say, "OK fighters, see my smoke?" They would say "rog" and you would say the target is ten meters to the right or

The symbol of freedom, the Stars and Stripes, waves above Hill 119, six miles southwest of Da Nang, Vietnam, and frames a CH-53 Sea Stallion helicopter on an external resupply mission, May 1970.
U.S. Marine Corps

over what he thought was suspected enemy locations. He rolled his O-2 up and threw frag grenades out the little IFR clear-vision window on the pilot's side, down to the jungle, assuming they were blowing up. He was having a great old time.

Up in the hills in one of the passes, as he rolled the aircraft up and was about to throw the grenade out the window, he hit an air pocket. The plane bounced and he lost his grip on the frag rocket, and it fell out of his hand. The pin came out of the handle part of the grenade, and the grenade rolled under his seat. Ed knew he had about six or seven seconds before that thing was going to blow his ass away. As it turned out nothing happened, but he was nervous as hell. He finally recovered his composure, got the aircraft squared away and came back and landed very gingerly only to find that the Army had given him a case of frag grenades with no charge in them whatsoever. They figured one of us FACs would do something stupid like that.

⎯⎯⎯⎯⎯⎯✈⎯⎯⎯⎯⎯⎯

Chief Warrant Officer 2nd Class Jim McDevitt was one of the Army FACs in 1970 who covered gasoline convoys from Qui Nhon to Phu Cat. From the coast, Highway 1 went up through the Central Highlands and snaked up a valley toward Pleiku:

THERE ARE two passes there. An Khe is the eastern pass and the other is the Mang Yang Pass. These are very twisty, winding trails. They tried to bring fuel convoys up from the coast to Pleiku every night. Generally they would hit them when they were on the return trip because if they hit them when they were full, they wouldn't blow up. If you put a round in them when they came back empty, it would take out seven tankers. That was the extent of our night missions unless a fire base was being overrun.

Once that happened at LZ [Landing Zone] Uplift. We did work the Air Force. It was a nasty deal. Your eyes get used to flying around real low at night pick-

north. When Ed fired a rocket, it was a complete joke. Ed would say, "Smoke's out." The fighters would say "Rog, Bilk, we've got your smoke, where's the target?" Ed would say, "From my smoke I want you to go one kilometer north and two kilometers west and that's the target." He was absolutely incredible.

Another funny thing with him. We used to borrow equipment from the Army such as RPGs [Rocket-Propelled Grenades], guns to fire out the window of the O-2, frag grenades, and smoke grenades. The Army didn't want to give us frag [fragmentation] grenades, fearing that the Air Force officers would blow themselves up, being unfamiliar with these things. None of us threw these frag grenades, except for Ed. He had a case in his O-2. One day he was up

An HH-53 Jolly Green Giant on a rescue mission over Southeast Asia.

ing out targets for them. We didn't use Willie Pete rockets for obvious reasons. You would wind up going blind from the hit and wouldn't be able to see anything, so we threw hand grenades out to mark the targets. We were flying everything from 500 feet to the deck.

We put in a lot of Phu Gas strikes. These were 50-gallon drums full of napalm with no detonator. They were sling-loaded underneath a Chinook Army helicopter. This was the Army way of saturation. They would spend all day. They would fly over and pick out a hill and cover it like molasses over an ice cream cone. They would saturate it. They would call us up in the afternoon, and we would go and punch a Willie Pete in there and the whole damn mountain would blow.

By 1971, the VNAF was responsible for 70 percent of all air combat operations. Nevertheless, the FACs were still the key ingredient for close air support. The South Vietnamese launched a major thrust into the Laotian Panhandle on 8 February 1971 to destroy the huge amount of enemy supplies that were stockpiled there. On 25 February, the North Vietnamese launched a massive counterattack, resulting in a South Vietnamese withdrawal. Heavy North Vietnamese losses forced them to postpone their planned offensive against South Vietnam.

Communist activity continued in Cambodia, eventually blocking the road to the capital, Phnom Penh, from its seaport at Kompong Som. Supplies had to be flown in or carried on ships up the Mekong River from South Vietnam. Some FACs provided aerial escort to the river convoys and aerial support to the ground operations of the Cambodian Army. Doug Aitken, *Rustic* 16, flew patrols along the Mekong River to Phnom Penh:

NINETY PERCENT OF THE time it was a boring mission because you would do right-hand orbits for an hour, and then left-hand orbits for an hour. It was a good time for a backseater to learn how to fly the OV-10. The OV-10 and an AC-119 gunship called *Stinger* worked with the Army and EC-47s, electronic snoopers. The Army had a team of five helicopters, a slick (Huey), two Cobras, and two LOHs, down in the weeds along the banks of the river looking for ambushes. We were to control the air power. We didn't always have a gunship or Army team. Sometimes we were out there by ourselves, but generally we had one or the other. The Navy right inside Vietnam had OV-10s called "Black Ponies." They carried Zuni rockets. They were available to scramble for us if we needed help. I had one boat get hit on the Tonle Sap going from there to Kampong Thom on the Stung Sen River. I was escorting a convoy when they got hit big time. I used an AC-130 gunship to blow the bad guys away. It was as close as I ever came to getting shot down that I know of.

On 1 November 1971, the USAF began COMMANDO HUNT VII into southern Laos using the new laser-guided bomb technology. With infrared sensors and night-vision equipment, attacks could be made day and night, under almost all weather conditions. This operation struck entry points from the Ho Chi Minh Trail from North Vietnam into Laos, and then down the Trail.

In 1971, the OV-10s began SCAR (Strike Control and Reconnaissance) missions for four hours each on the Ho Chi Minh Trail, using a minimum altitude of 6,000 feet AGL. They would approach the Laos border and call ABCCC in a C-130 that acted, with preplanned strikes, as a limited Direct Air Support Center and Tactical Air Control Center for Laos. The FACs used binoculars for this visual reconnaissance along the Trail. The pilots kept the OV-10's nose moving constantly by alternating rudder pressure in order to confuse the enemy gunners' tracking solutions. Violent jinking was used only after the firing started.

These FACs put in immediate strikes if they found a target on the Trail. The preplanned missions were nearly always IDPs (Interdiction Points). The vast majority of these pilots were "B" FACs (Air Force Specialty Code 1444B) with no fighter experience at all. They seldom worked with ground units, flying instead in areas with few friendly troops or civilians.

Doug Jones arrived in Vietnam in November 1971. He had trained at Hurlburt Field, Florida, and then went through water survival school, and Fairchild Survival in the Philippines. His in-country check-out was at Phan Rang. From there, FACs were assigned to one of three places: OV-10s from Phan Rang to Da Nang with the 20th TASS; the 23rd TASS at Nakhon Phanom; or if you spoke French, to

Ubon to become a *Rustic* FAC and work with the Cambodians. Most FACs there flew with a Cambodian backseater.

Jones described his duty in STEEL TIGER:

MY ASSIGNMENT was in STEEL TIGER East (the Ho Chi Minh Trail) with the 20th TASS in OV-10s. We flew day missions. We covered from the Tri-border between North and South Vietnam to area Four Bravo to area Seven. Guys from 20th TASS out of Pleiku took area Eight down through the other Tri-border area, Laos, southern Vietnam, and Cambodia. The *Covey* two zeroes, from Da Nang, basically flew STEEL TIGER, and the guys down at Pleiku were the *Five* levels with call sign beginning with *Five*.

We would get 40 hours with an IP [*Instructor Pilot*] and 45 hours in the back seat with a combat-ready FAC. Before we took our ready check, we had to know and be able to draw the major route structure and the basic Delta Points. We had to learn reference points where you got fighters to rendezvous. FACs used their imaginations. A bend in the river was called "Snoopy's Nose," a long nose and head. Another, we called the "boobs" because of the particular shape. One area up north had so many bomb craters, we called it the golf course. It was lush green with a lot of bomb craters.

We had OV-10s and O-2s working in a small area. While we were working STEEL TIGER, the O-2s had many different missions. At the 20th TASS at Da Nang, we had more planes and pilots than the wing that owned us. The O-2s worked all night from Da Nang. We had insertion FACs in Laos called the *Mike* FACs. At 20th TASS alone we had *Mike* FACs, *Bilks*, and *Covey* FACs. For the 23rd TASS at Nakhon Phanom *Nail* was the call sign. They worked STEEL TIGER and BARREL ROLL at the Plain of Jars.

The accuracy of the OV-10 was very effective at 160 to 200 KIAS. It was better than jets at their faster speeds. At the altitude we dropped the munitions from, it was like shooting fish in a barrel. When the SA-7 came along, we lost a few OV-10s until they stepped us up to 10,000 feet. There you could see the SA-7 coming and evade it.

Tom Yarborough arrived in Vietnam in April 1970. In October, he was flying with the top-secret

PRAIRIE FIRE missions involved in supporting Special Forces commandos in highly sensitive cross-border operations. There was apt to be heavy fire. On 10 October, with thoughts of a missing team and dead A-1 pilot who had crashed the day before, he almost met the same fate. It was Yarborough's second flight that day. He was heading for an especially hot area along Highway 9 just east of Tchepone, flying at treetop level, looking for likely spots for future team inserts. At the junction of routes 9 and 92, Yarborough and his backseater, Sergeant First Class Marty Martin, a *Covey* rider from the Special Operations Group, spotted a road crew at work. The crew seemed unaware of the OV-10. Yarborough wrote in his *Da Nang Diary* (1990; p. 170):

MARTY AND I decided to ruin their day. From an altitude of 1,500 feet, I rolled in on the enemy troops while simultaneously arming up my two outboard pods. Recently we had started flying with fourteen high-explosive rockets in our bag of tricks, in addition to our two pods of Willie Petes and two thousand rounds of machine-gun ammo. The scene below me seemed custom made for a HE [*High Explosive*]-rocket attack.

Pressing in from the south, I was about to fire when a .51-caliber machine-gun opened up from a pit near the road crew. The stream of tracers raced up from our left as the two rockets roared out of the LAU-68 pods. As I sucked in the Gs to start a rolling pull-off to the left, all hell broke loose. With a horrendously loud bang, the left canopy disintegrated into a thousand pieces of flying glass. Something red-hot streaked in front of my face and shattered the top of the canopy. Perhaps instinctively, perhaps out of fear, I had released the control stick and moved my right hand upward to shield my face. I winced in surprise as a dagger-shaped piece of canopy imbedded itself in my palm.

In the split second that followed, I seemed to view the hectic action in slow motion. Through my peripheral vision, I watched helplessly as the left canopy frame bowed into a contorted shape, then broke loose and flew up into the wind stream. For some crazy reason, I reached out into the blast to try to catch it, only to be thrown back violently by airstream. Under the tremendous aerodynamic force, aggravated by our nose-low, ninety-degree left bank, the top hinges snapped like balsa wood. The metal frame sailed up and over my glassless canopy on a trajectory that sent it crashing into the right engine propeller. The gnarled three-blade Hamilton prop, badly bent and completely out of balance, began vibrating and shaking us to pieces. The OV-10 felt like it was about to tear itself apart.

Yarborough got the OV-10 under control just 500 feet above the trees. As he limped off to the west, the bad guys kept shooting until he was out of range. Yarborough performed emergency procedures, punching off the heavy centerline fuel tank and all four rocket pods. At the same time, he feathered the mangled engine. Then he checked to see if his backseater was hurt. Marty answered, "Nothing serious back here. How's sir? Are we gonna make it back home?"

In addition to the missing canopy and the shut-down engine, there was a large, basketball-sized hole in the leading edge of the wing just inboard of the right engine, from where the canopy frame slammed into the wing. Yarborough twisted in his seat, and by using the mirrors, saw that the top two feet of the right vertical stabilizer had been sheared off — time to find a safe landing field.

Yarborough called the tower at Quang Tri, the closest airport, for a weather update. As luck would have it, there was a stiff crosswind of 30 knots, 10 knots above the maximum allowable limit for the OV-10. As badly as they needed to get on the ground, Quang Tri's narrow 60-foot wide runway wasn't the answer.

Da Nang was southeast, with a big runway. Confronting Yarborough was a solid wall of cumulonimbus towering to the heavens. He picked his way gingerly through the maze of build-ups and squall lines, with the rain pelting on him and Marty. He was at 4,500 feet over a solid overcast as he neared Da Nang when all of a sudden he found a hole through which he could see Da Nang Bay. He spiraled down, squawked emergency, and called Da Nang Approach:

"AIRCRAFT SQUAWKING emergency on three-five-eight radial at five miles, contact Da Nang Approach on two-forty-three-zero or two-seventy-nine point five."

"Approach, *Covey* 221. How copy, over."

"*Covey* 221, read you five by. Go ahead."

"Rog, Approach. I've got battle damage and the right engine out. Two souls on board and lots of gas.

A "Pave Nail" OV-10. Note the wing fuel tanks and laser pod.
Byron Tetrick Collection

I'd like to switch over to Tower for a long straight-in with delayed gear call. I've got a tally on the field."

"Squawk standby, contact Da Nang Tower, channel Two. Good luck." (*Da Nang Diary*, pp. 171-173.)

At one mile final approach, Yarborough lowered the gear at 130 knots, exactly 30 knots faster than normal for an OV-10. He kept the airspeed high and left the flaps up. On short final, he centered the rudder trim and shoved in on the left rudder pedal to keep as close as possible to coordinated flight. The OV-10 crossed the threshold and settled down with a solid, friendly thunk.

The laser-equipped OV-10 arrived in Southeast Asia in mid-1971. The modified OV-10 was equipped with an internally mounted night-sensor, a precision navigation device, and a laser designator. The system, known as "Pave Nail," was installed in 15 OV-10 aircraft assigned to the 23rd Tactical Air Support Squadron. Pave Nail became operational in STEEL TIGER in late 1971 under the direction of Lieutenant Colonel Lachlin MacLeay. Now the FAC had the unique capability of determining the exact location of the target and relaying that information to the strike aircraft, which had the same precise navigation equipment, so that it would approach the target at an altitude well above the FAC. The attacking aircraft would then release a laser-guided bomb well short of the target. The navigator in the rear seat of the OV-10 would aim the laser at the target. The LGB (Laser-Guided Bomb) locked itself on the reflected laser energy that guided the bomb to its impact. If the sensor display was interpreted properly, this was a deadly, accurate system.

The F-4s out of Ubon worked in pairs with a LGB known as "Pave Way." The first aircraft was the illuminator, which carried the laser gun used to direct laser energy onto the target. The second carried the LGB. After the FAC put the smoke on the target, and called "Hit my smoke," the F-4s went to work.

On one occasion the enemy attacking a Special Forces camp drove a tank on top of a command bunker. A *Covey* FAC working overhead was flying an OV-10 Pave Nail. He called for F-4s, illuminated the target with laser energy, and watched the F-4 roll in with a 2,000-pound bomb. It hit the tank and blew it back to the perimeter of the camp.

On 31 August 1971, a Pave Nail crew was sent out to destroy a 10- x 28-foot bridge. When they arrived in the target area, they located the bridge, but flight conditions in the thick overcast with intermittent rain

A USAF F-4E Phantom with bombs, enroute to a target in Southeast Asia, 28 May 1970.   USAF

were horrible. The strike aircraft checked in and reported that the thick overcast extended up more than 20,000 feet. The Pave Nail crew decided to strike and passed the target information to the strike aircraft.

The strike aircraft navigated to the release point on instruments, as they were flying inside the thick clouds. As the first bomb was released, the Pave Nail crew fired the laser while in a tight turn almost directly over the target. The bomb charged through the cloud layer past the OV-10 and impacted directly on the bridge.

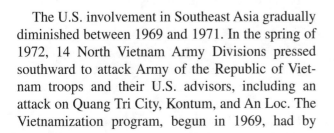

The U.S. involvement in Southeast Asia gradually diminished between 1969 and 1971. In the spring of 1972, 14 North Vietnam Army Divisions pressed southward to attack Army of the Republic of Vietnam troops and their U.S. advisors, including an attack on Quang Tri City, Kontum, and An Loc. The Vietnamization program, begun in 1969, had by March 1972 reduced U.S. manpower strength from 500,000 to 95,000, but U.S. air power was not proportionately reduced, and thus air power remained very much involved. By March 1972, there were 144 USAF FAC aircraft, including 37 OV-10 Broncos. The Vietnamese Air Force had nearly 300 liaison aircraft, mostly O-1 Bird Dogs.

Fred McNeil flew some in-country missions in the Central Highlands, especially the Tri-border area, using the call sign *Herb* 02:

WHEN I FIRST got to Pleiku, the Army still had some helicopters, the 1st Airborne Rangers at Camp Holloway. The Army would send out a LOH (pronounced Loach) — a light observation helicopter with pilot and door gunner, two Cobra attack helicopters, and a "Command and Control" bird, which was a slick or an unarmed Huey. Called the Pink Team, the LOH would go down on the deck looking for supply dumps and supply caches, bunkers, or any interesting target. The LOH was in direct contact

A FAC's-eye view of Cessna's A-37 (T-37) Dragonfly, light jet trainer and attack aircraft.

Doug Aitken Collection

with its door gunner (this was the standard way they did it) perched with one foot on the skids so he could look outside. He held a smoke grenade with the pin pulled, so if he got hit he could drop the grenade and we would know where he was.

From below the trees, this LOH said, "We've got a hooch in this grove of trees, so we'll take a look. It looks brand new, just been built, but I don't see anybody around. We're going to check it to see if food or ammunition is stored inside. I'm going to lift the roof with my skids." He took the front skids of his chopper and lifted up the roof. As he did, somebody inside opened fire with an AK [*AK-47 assault rifle*]. He yelled, and because he had a hot mike, you could hear the bullets hitting the LOH blades . . . "I'm taking fire so I'm backing out of here!" You can imagine a helicopter going down beneath the branches in a heavy grove, dragging in, and all of a sudden coming out backwards. He must have been doing 50 mph. The most amazing thing was that he didn't hit a tree. After he backed off, everybody went to work destroying that building.

with the two Cobras above him. Everyone remained silent except the LOH pilot. He kept his mike keyed all the time, so if he started taking fire, we all knew it.

A FAC always flew cover above the Pink Team. It was sort of a lazy day for us, a fun thing, because we got to watch the Army work. But, if they found a big, lucrative target, we were available to call in TAC air. Otherwise we just listened.

One day I saw an operation I couldn't believe. The Pink Team was working right along the Cambodian border. This LOH went down to a grove of trees with two attack Hueys about 100 to 300 feet above him and the C and C helicopter at about 700 feet. I was flying at 1,000 feet. The LOH went under the trees

Fred McNeil explained TAC-Es or tactical emergencies:

ONE DAY SOUTH of Fire Bases Five and Six, both on top of a mountain range on the road from Dak To to Kontum, an ARVN unit had a patrol out on a long, exposed ridge line and they got jumped by a full-size NVA battalion. The NVA were coming up all sides of the hill firing at this patrol and pouring in mortar fire. The call came and it was my mission. I knew exactly where they were.

They got me out of bed about 11 p.m. that night. They couldn't get any TAC air down to relieve these TIC. The only unit that had anything available was an A-37 outfit out of Bien Hoa. The commander was Colonel Weed. *Blue Chip* got ahold of me and I called the colonel. The target at Kontum was at the extreme limit of their range. Saigon wasn't familiar with that part of the country so I talked directly with the colonel, working out all the details. Based on the performance of his aircraft, we figured out that if I was already set up when they headed in, we could skip the normal, lengthy briefing conducted in a holding pattern above the target. Just make a straight-in pass and pull right out and fly back to Pleiku and land. The colonel decided he was willing to try it. By now these troops had taken 30 percent casualties.

The next morning I got out over the target before daylight. When you are working TIC and they are getting the hell beat out of them, one of the roles you can play is psychological, you can cheer them up. When I raised this unit when I got over the target, the radio operator I was talking to was an American, a Chicano from Tucson, Arizona. They were really scared because they were about to get overrun. I even talked Spanish to the guy and got him calmed down. The bad guys were 50 meters away, all the way around the mountain. I realized we would have to put the ordnance right on top of them, as soon as the sun came up. We were going to make two passes with two A-37s.

I got the colonel on the radio. He was inbound with his pair of A-37s. The object was to break the contact, just to get the bad guys to go away and leave the friendlies so that what was left of this patrol could pull back to Fire Bases Five and Six. So, I briefed them that help was on the way. I could hear a young American lieutenant who was with the ARVN. I made repeated passes over them at low level so I knew exactly where every American was and the location of their perimeter defense ring. I also knew where the bad guys were. This meant I could figure out exactly where I wanted to put the ordnance the A-37s were coming in with. I talked to Weed and his ordnance load was napalm, which was great, just perfect.

So I briefed Weed on what the terrain looked like. I tried to draw for him as good a verbal picture as I could. "I'll put my smoke at the low end of where I want you to put your napalm." He was using finless napalm. Finless tumble along, and you get that long, splashing fire. I said, "We're going to take the nape uphill, splash it on the guys as close as we can to the top. Not quite the top because the friendlies are there." I didn't tell the guys on the ground what the ordnance was — just told them we were going to work it as close to them as we could and they were to keep their heads down. They weren't dug in or protected.

I talked to the lieutenant on the radio, too, and made sure I had his OK to put it in. There was a limit to how close you could put ordnance to friendlies; also an emergency limit when the ground guy told you to get close as a last ditch effort. He wanted it in, "I want you to put this in, almost on top of us."

On the first pass I marked with two smokes so each airplane would have a separate target. They both came in together. It was an unusual pass, sort of a loose echelon formation. The colonel came straight in and told me he was starting down. It took some coordination because I didn't want to put my smoke in too early because it would dissipate before he got there. I held off as long as I could, working in very close to the target area, because I wanted to be absolutely accurate. They only had AK-47s to shoot at me.

I marked the two spots very quickly. The A-37s made their first pass. The nape erupted right up the hill. The A-37s pulled up and rolled right back around again and just saturated that whole peninsula with nape. Then they pulled up. I had already given them a heading to Pleiku. They left immediately. I stayed around to do a BDA and talk to the guys on the ground. .

They told me when the A-37s made their first pass. You could tell from the radio operator's voice they were scared to death because they were about to be overrun. Rightly so. When I hit my smoke on the ground, the radio operator on the ground keyed his mike and told me he saw my smoke. The moment he did the napalm hit and I could hear it on his radio! I had never had that experience before, the napalm on his mike. Instantly right after that, I heard the damnedest cheering, whistling, and clapping all over the place. The A-37s came around and did it again. Right after the napalm died down the friendlies were able to stand up. The TIC was instantly broken, completely.

We don't know how many casualties there were. I

stayed around to do the BDA. A detailed reconnaissance of the area was done later. I headed back to Pleiku. I thought that Colonel Weed had done a magnificent job. He stretched it to the limit. He got back to Pleiku on fumes. Later the maintenance people told me they dipped the A-37's fuel tanks and couldn't get any reading on the stick. Later I met Colonel Weed at the Club. I bought him lunch. He had done such an outstanding job. I reported the mission to Saigon and he got the DFC, which I thought he richly deserved. On the BDA, which they brought to us while we were having lunch, we got 335 KBA [*Killed by Air*] from that one contact. We saved probably about 75 friendlies. They had taken about 40 percent casualties by morning of which 24 percent were dead. It was an awful beating.

⬥

The 1972 Spring Invasion had many trouble spots, including the battle for Quang Tri in Military Region I and the battle of An Loc. On 30 March 1972, North Vietnam began a large three-pronged invasion into South Vietnam using tanks and mobile armored units. The biggest battle was at An Loc where, by the end of June, the enemy had lost all of its tanks and artillery.

FAC Tom Milligan, *Sun Dog* 29, described the coordinated teamwork between himself and fighter aircraft to relieve friendly troops that were being fired upon by tanks:

DURING THE BATTLE around An Loc, one day they were dropping airplanes out of the sky faster than I had seen in a long time. They were shooting down helicopters. The SA-7 Strela missile had come in. It was deadly to the O-2 because we had the rear engine. I got a call from the ground commander saying that they were under attack from two tanks. They showed me. They vectored me into where the tanks were. I saw them. I got my air overhead. At An Loc we had three FACs, a high FAC briefing the air as it came in, and then he would hand it (the fighters) off to a FAC on either side of town. We were really busy. The fighters were stacked up. We were expending air as fast as we possibly could.

I rolled in to smoke the tanks and I was shot at by guns all over the place. I rolled in from 7,000 feet. We were higher at An Loc because of the SA-7s. I pressed in quite a ways. I'm not sure of the altitude where I pulled up, but the fighters kept saying, "Pull

out, pull out, you're taking fire!" I fired my rocket and when I pulled out the fire light came on in my airplane. Of course, because things were exploding all around me. The fire light came on because I pulled out so hard, I shorted out the wire, but it took me a second to figure that out. The rocket hit fairly close to the tanks, within 20 yards, so the fighter said, "We see your smoke, actually we can see the tanks from up here."

I had the friendlies make a smoke, and it was very close to the tank position, so I told the fighters, I can't put you in here, it's too close. The fighters said, "Right, we agree." So, I called the ground commander and said, "I can't put in the air, it's too close to the friendlies." He answered, "If you don't put in the air, we will be overrun because the tanks are shooting right at us, point blank."

So I said, "All right, give me your initials." That was required if you wanted to go inside your minimum distances. That took you off the hook. And so the first airplane rolled in to drop, and his bombs were within five meters of the friendly smoke. And I thought, oh my God, we've killed some of the friendlies, so I told the fighter to hold high and dry (which means hold up in orbit until I tell you to come back).

I called the friendlies and said, "Better ring up your boys, because maybe no one is going to answer." And he said, "Yes, just a minute," and he called out there to the friendlies under fire by the tanks, and they said. "It's OK, we threw our smoke out quite a ways toward the tanks." You had to hit a tank. You couldn't just drop a bomb next to it. We continued to work and we were shot at throughout the entire engagement. When we finally finished up, we had knocked out the two tanks and saved the friendly position. The fighters went home happy. They got good BDA. We actually hit the tanks right on the turrets. It was tremendously exciting at the time.

⬥

Fred McNeil received the Distinguished Flying Cross for a flight near Kontum on 10 March 1972 aiding a long-range patrol of the ARVN 81st Airborne Division. His citation reads, in part:

Although severely hampered by smoke, haze, and ground fog, reducing visibility to under one-half mile and although constantly the object of opposing ground fire, Major McNeil directed tactical fighters onto the hostile location halting the attack and saving the patrol from certain destruction.

McNeil recounted the successful operation:

A GROUP OF TROOPS, damn near battalion size, a Long-Range Patrol (not a LRRP team) was in an open field in the Plei Trap Valley, which had steep mountains along each side. At the base of the valley is a little stream, and the whole valley is about a mile wide at its widest. The mountains start at either side and go straight up. The largest mountain, just northwest of Kontum, was called "Big Momma." It stood out above the other mountains and must have been 10,000 feet tall. There are flat lands on either side of the stream. A one-lane dirt road runs along one side of the stream with little foot paths crossing every so often. It was a major route for North Vietnamese entering South Vietnam. A big highway out of Laos terminated right near the border near Dak To. The North Vietnamese would come down and sneak into this valley and then get up in the mountains. Big Momma is where they hid all those tanks in caves.

So the ARVN sent a team down into this valley to check it out. We knew there were a lot of NVA in that valley. It was a really hot area. The extension of that valley goes up to Khe Sanh where the Marines had so much trouble.

That day, March 10, 1972, late in the day, this ARVN patrol was in an open field just below Big Momma — a big field of elephant grass, about 40 acres with not a bit of cover in it, just grass. It was surrounded by trees. The ARVN were pinned down by a battalion-sized group of NVA and maybe more. They were taking very heavy fire and heavy casualties. Most NVA were at the base of the mountain or in high ground and just knocking the hell out of them. The weather was miserable with very thick clouds, fog, rain, and smoke. It was the beginning of monsoon season with multi-layered clouds from the ground on up; generally just crummy weather. Visibility was zip, even back at Pleiku. It was IFR conditions everywhere. Nobody could get anything in there.

The FAC that day had tried but it got dark and there was no way to get in there to give them air support. *Blue Chip* called me. I talked to them on the phone and to the DASC up at Da Nang who was handling the ordnance requests and relaying radio communications from the guys in trouble down in the

Valley. We agreed to make a stab at it in the morning; try to put in some TAC air with the A-7s. The scheme was, I was going to go out there before first light to see if I could get down in the valley and then try to get the fighters in there. We wanted to do something for these guys because they were going to get wiped out that day. There was no question that the NVA battalion was going to smear them as soon as it got daylight.

Before first light I took off out of Pleiku IFR and climbed up to get on top. Big Momma stuck out above the clouds, which covered the whole valley. I figured on my chart a TACAN position for dead center of the valley at the north end. At this point I would commence my penetration of the clouds and just fly the heading down the valley to see if I could get down under the clouds and see the stream. If I could find the stream bed, then I knew I could find that field where the friendlies were pinned down. I was in contact with the guys by this time on the radio, so I refined the idea in my head as to where they were. I had a very good concept because I had worked that valley every day for several months.

Before I started my penetration into the clouds, the fighters showed up so I put them in a holding pattern up above this area and explained the situation to the four pilots. I told them I was going to go down first, because I knew the area like the back of my hand, and see if there was enough room underneath the ceiling to work. So, they stayed in holding.

I flew up to my TACAN fix. The overcast was solid as a rock. I started my descent from the point up north, and tried to time it so I would come down by the stream bed. I went IMC [*Instrument Meteorological Conditions*] and hoped to break out. I figured if I got down and didn't see anything I would just pull up straight ahead.

So down I went in IFR conditions, and sure enough I broke out under a 200- to 250-foot overcast. It was murky underneath, with about ½- to ¾-mile visibility and raining. Smoke in valley and rain (drizzle) restricted the visibility. So I climbed out. It worked like a champ! Before I began my climb, I saw the bad guys out in the open.

When I broke out on top, I told the fighters what the situation was. The fighters had mixed loads of nape and CBU. I told the fighters that under the overcast we had about 200 to 250 feet. I said, "The only way we can do it is if you guys think you can stay with me and tuck under my wings, one on each side. I'll just lead you down in formation." They said, "If

An A-7D Corsair, in the distinctive markings of the 3rd TFS at Korat RTAB, Thailand, loaded with 6 Mk-82 550-pound bombs. The 3rd TFS was re-formed and equipped with A-7s in March 1973. The squadron's main mission was the search and rescue "Sandy" operations — replacing the A-1, although it flew regular close air support bombing mission sorties as required.

USAF

you've got the guts, we'll go ahead and try it." And so, we practiced in the open to see if they could slow up. I normally went down at about 130 knots but with those guys on my wing I was 175 to 180 knots. I said, "I'll keep it as fast as I can going down; there are no obstructions at the bottom, no tall trees. It's clear at the bottom of the valley, flat as a billiard table. When we get down there, if you lose contact with me, use the valley heading, and just pull up. One pass and haul ass." The Navy pilots agreed.

I briefed them, "The mountains, at the top up here where we start down through the overcast, are about two or three miles apart. The terrain narrows to about a mile at the bottom so you have plenty of room to work, and there are no obstructions at the bottom. It is drizzly and rainy and you can't see diddley squat, but once we get under the overcast you'll see ½- to ¾-mile, so just stick with me. I will fire a marking rocket, but I'll yell on the radio at the same time so if you can't see it you can pickle your napalms and roll right over that position." They said, "Sounds good, let's try it."

So, one of the Navy A-7s got on each of my wings, tucked in really close. I got my airspeed up, all that old Oscar Duck [*nickname for O-2A*] could do, and started down like a bat out of hell right through that overcast. They tucked in right tight on me so they could see my O-2 through that thick overcast. The air was reasonably smooth. It was monsoon-like stuff, a warm front-type weather. It wasn't bouncy, fortunately, and they stayed right with me.

We went churning on down. I just got glimpses of them out of the corner of my eye. We went down and made one pass with those guys from north to south. I had put a Willie Pete on each end of the ridge line, and that's where the Navy put the napalm. I climbed back up. They did too, went by me like I was standing still. They wanted to get out of there. They met me on top.

Then I picked up the other two A-7s and came around south to north, the opposite direction. When I took the second group down, I stayed down while they pulled up, and did a BDA. I found I could orbit the valley under the overcast without too much trouble. So I stayed down there for a while. The ARVN commander told me later that there were more than 400 KBA.

The whole side of the mountain was on fire. Our attack broke the contact. Our guys were standing up in the field. Finally I got out of there when one of them got on the radio and said, "*Covey* 502, you had better get your ass out of here, everybody on that mountain is hosing you down." I didn't hear any small arms fire at all and didn't see any. So, I got up and never had a mark on the airplane. I was jinking pretty hard and had high power on the O-2. I was quite busy doing 60- to 80-degree banks all the time to stay under the overcast and keep the airspeed up. In an O-2 you work the rudders a lot. You do uncoordinated flight, which is not comfortable for a passenger at all. You cross-control a lot, trying to throw a gunner's aim off.

Armed with thousands of pounds of bombs, USAF B-52 Stratofortress bombers (called ARC LIGHTS) reached areas previously considered a sanctuary for enemy ground troops, 20 April 1967.

USAF

Chapter 7

Vietnamization and the American Withdrawal

*F*RED *McNEIL (**Covey** 502) described his FAC experiences during the build-up of North Vietnam troops and enemy camps along the South Vietnamese border:*

THERE WERE LOTS of enemy base camps along the border. At times they estimated more than 100,000 NVN in those camps, which accounted for so much activity in the Tri-border area. Just before the big offensive started in 1972, Intelligence told us that in that Tri-border area, both in-country and out-country, there were about 300,000 NVA troops (in 30 divisions).

I picked up a DFC when we found a big enemy concentration in the Plei Trap Valley near one of the biggest mountains called Big Momma, the tallest mountain in the area, a very impressive landmark. On the other side of the valley, another guy and I first spotted this big NVN buildup. When I flew that day I took some pictures of a place we called the "apartment complex." The whole top of the hill was a solid mass of bunkers. I was flying at 200 feet AGL. Until I had the pictures developed, I didn't realize I was taking fire. I was jinking very rapidly. The photos showed heavy evidence from foot marks. A very large enemy concentration settled down in this valley just north of Kontum.

We called *Blue Chip* on the phone to tell him as well as telling our local Intelligence officer. We woke up in the middle of the night with our bunks bouncing around on the floor because it was ARC LIGHT [bombs] going off. I had never heard so many airplanes, the big B-52s. ARC LIGHT is normally a long, rolling thunder that seems to go on for about one minute. The ground shakes even 20 miles away, like a giant earthquake. This went on all night. There must have been, we found out later, 20 or 30 ARC LIGHTs putting bombs in this valley. Turned out that on the basis of what I had said, they sent everything over there.

In the morning when the first FAC went out it was devastating. It was the 304th NVA Infantry that had been decimated in that valley. That was the outfit that took Dien Bien Phu. They had just moved in that day. They were the ones shooting at me when I took the pictures, but I didn't know it at that time.

That morning they found about 50 or 60 of these guys wandering around shell-shocked. The FAC put fighters on them and killed all but two of them. Then an Army helicopter went down and landed. These two came running and dove in the helicopter. They couldn't wait to surrender. They took them back to Pleiku and interrogated them. These guys said that since they had become the heroes of Dien Bien Phu, they had been kept up in Hanoi as the elite troops, and hadn't been in the war. Finally in this late stage they marched south. They had spent five months marching down. This was their first day in-country and they were detected. It was horrifying for them. They had never even heard of an ARC LIGHT. Almost every officer and NCO was killed by morning, only these few were left. They just couldn't believe it. They said it was the most devastating thing they had ever seen.

The Army left Pleiku, which made things a little spooky. The FACs at Pleiku were the last Americans left in MR [*Military Region*] II. We had no base defense at all. We were our own defense, and we knew, from having flown across the Cambodian border so many times, how many bad guys were there. We were nervous because there were enough NVA to

overrun us, and Pleiku had been overrun five times previously. Eventually they let some of us FAC in-country and that's where I picked up the call sign *Herb* 02.

Four of us were selected for that. We would go out at first light. You would see 10,000 camp fires coming up out of the jungle. The NVA weren't worried about us seeing their smoke from their little holes underground.

As we did this in the valleys between Dak To and Kontum, we spotted all sorts of activity over toward Big Momma Mountain. We saw trails on the ground in totally uninhabited areas. It looked like tens of thousands of people had been walking. I took a lot of pictures of thousands of spider holes. Then we started seeing tank tracks. We tracked tanks all over the place. Every time we reported this to Intelligence, they would reject it, and tell us there weren't any tanks. I'd say, damn it, I saw the tracks.

I had occasion one morning, because I had to coordinate a mission, to call *Blue Chip* on the telephone. I asked the colonel I was talking to, what about the tanks outside the base? I told him everybody's reporting them, but nobody believes us. He said, "Nonsense, Intelligence assures us there are no tanks in MR II, or in your region, or in the Triborder area, absolutely none." They kept that position, even though we constantly told them we saw the evidence every day, until the NVA struck in March 1972.

The next 30-day period, the 20th TASS, working with TAC air outfits, killed over 300 tanks in that area. It was incredible. Until that happened, nobody down in Saigon wanted to believe it. It didn't fit in with anything they had planned.

After the action was over, they examined the tanks, and discovered some of them had been stored for up to three years in cosmoline [*heavy grease*] in caves in the Big Momma area. They had been slowly snuck down the Trail and kept in caves. For three years, the FACs had been reporting tank tracks!

By April, the North Vietnamese Army had overrun 12 fire-support bases. Quang Tri was the next goal. Military Assistance Command, Vietnam (MACV) and the Seventh Air Force ordered continuous daylight FAC coverage for the 3rd Division's entire area of operation. Later, this requirement was extended to 24 hours-a-day coverage. U.S. Marine gunfire observers began flying with the Forward Air Controllers to direct and adjust U.S. Navy firing. The slower O-2s and OV-10s directed airstrikes near the battle, while Fast FACs went deep into enemy territory. For a while VNAF controllers, flying O-1s, provided close air support for the ARVN, but their duties had to be taken over by USAF FACs.

The enemy launched a tank and infantry attack on the north end of the bridge leading into Quang Tri City, on 29 April 1972, in the middle of the night. A FAC, using flares, put in airstrike after airstrike, destroying all five tanks and beating off the attackers. Even so, things did not go well. The ARVN commanders issued evacuation orders on 1 May. Three American FACs flew cover for the American and South Vietnamese personnel trying to escape from the walled Quang Tri Citadel. F-4s delivered many types of ordnance. The situation became desperate so the FACs called for the rescue forces to come in. Four "Jolly Greens" (HH-53 helicopters) and six "Sandys" (A-1s) arrived. The A-1s laid down smoke screens to hide the Jolly Greens who went in to pick up the trapped personnel. Minutes after they were lifted out, the Citadel was overrun by the enemy.

The North Vietnamese moved 85mm and 100mm guns and SA-2 missiles south of the DMZ to support the spring invasion. FACs, while trying to do their job, had to continuously change direction to avoid AAA and SAMs. The SAM threat was especially hazardous to the low and slow flying FACs. By April 1972, the SA-7 Strela missile was introduced to the battle. This surface-to-air missile, which could be carried by a man and fired from his shoulder, had an infrared-sensing homing system that detected engine heat for target guidance. The FACs had to raise their operating altitude and make abrupt, evasive flight maneuvers to avoid the SA-7 missile's flight path. The FACs used a steep turn, which allowed the wings and fuselage to mask the engine heat upon which the missile homed. The SA-7s shot down several FAC aircraft and an A-1 in April and May 1972. In June, an AC-130 Hercules was shot down by a Strela missile.

To help defend An Loc and Kontum, the USAF established a Forward Operating Location (FOL) at Pleiku to give the FACs more time over the target than they would have if flying from Da Nang and Tan Son Nhut. Additionally, the VNAF had 25 O-1s and U-17s at Pleiku for FAC duty. The U.S. and Vietnamese Air Forces were assigned different sectors in the battle area. Three USAF Forward Air Controllers were assigned the An Loc sector. Flying O-2s they worked with an Army advisor who was under the nominal control of the Vietnamese 5th Division commander. One FAC flew high as the *"King FAC."* He received strike allocations from Direct Air Support Center at Bien Hoa Air Base. He handed these sorties over to the other FACs as the situation required, a system which alleviated air congestion. An Loc's airfield was closed in early April due to Viet Cong daily mortar and artillery rounds, so all supplies had to be airdropped and brought in by helicopter. The FACs provided run-in headings for the C-130 air supply drop planes. When these drops became too dangerous, an alternate system was tried. Cargo was dropped from 6,000 to 9,000 feet using a Ground Radar Aerial Delivery System (GRADS) to position the aircraft.

Carl Goembel, *Raven* 40, also spent time at An Loc:

AN LOC, 70 miles northwest of Saigon, was a critical battle. It was against NVA regulars, not Viet Cong. 20,000 to 30,000 troops in that area surrounded An Loc and that was their mistake. It gave the ARVN no escape route. If they had an escape route, they probably would have run. It was a critical area at that time. It was a 24-hour operation, always a gunship or two on station. The town wasn't that large. Flying the O-2, you were constantly putting in airstrikes. There were always fighters holding, waiting to put in strikes. You were constantly talking on the Fox Mike and VHF and UHF. You did not have a break. I flew four-hour missions in the O-2, probably 95-degree heat because we were low, about 1,500 feet AGL. Very hot, very humid. In four hours, you seldom had a chance to have a drink of water, you were that busy. When you got back, you would drink gallons and gallons of ice water, iced tea or whatever. After you got in that mode, things would click and you could handle it, no problems at all.

One day we had a fighter that supposedly came in the path of the B-52s, so they had to call the ARC LIGHT off. That was three B-52s, out of Guam, flying about 30,000 feet. They had to turn around and go back to Guam without dropping a bomb. They were very upset and tried to blame some young captain. I happened to be riding with him. I was a Stan-Eval [*Standardization and Evaluation Officer*]. They called him up to the general's office. I went with him and sat in the corner. They started to hammer the guy when I said, "Wait a minute, I was with him. He did everything completely right." The general looked at me and said, "Who are you?" I said, "Captain Goembel, I'm in Stan-Eval, and here's what really happened." He said, "I'm sorry to bother you." And that was it. It was the first time the ARC LIGHT used B-52s for tactical operations. They were bombing within a mile of An Loc. Sometimes as close as a half mile. There were approximately 100 Mk-82 bombs per aircraft. That was about 300 bombs per strike.

In Laos I got a diary from a North Vietnamese soldier who had been killed in action. We had it translated. In his diary he said that these bombs coming out of the sky at night were the most fearful thing, especially with no sound. That was an ARC LIGHT. He said his buddies would die, with blood coming out of their noses and ears from the concussion. That was what they most feared.

The O-2 was an excellent aircraft to fly. I was a

First Lieutenant Ralph Kunce just prior to his last — "fini" — flight in South Vietnam.

commander for training and operations in support of Korean troops at Nha Trang, so I got to fly an awful lot of students. We had to check them out in-country in the O-2. We did a night sortie and a blackout landing. It was very simple, you set the airspeed up with about a 400- to 500-feet-a-minute descent, and they tried to hit one mile at a certain altitude, and then just

Fini — flight completion. The men didn't have a fire hose so they used buckets.
Byron Tetrick Collection

hold it until you landed on the runway. That worked out pretty well.

The only problem was flying at night, the ARVN would try to hit you with their flares, it was a game. You would be flying along and see a flare coming up at you. To them it was just a game, but we watched out very carefully. The O-2 did a super job. It was the safest aircraft we had in SEA. Very reliable, good for long missions. One time at Nha Trang, in the rear engine we had a fuel pump pumping raw fuel. We looked at that and said we had better call Tan Son Nhut. They had a lot of O-2s there while we only had five or six at Nha Trang. We did a one-time inspection of the whole fleet and found several aircraft with the same problem.

For our fini flight [*last mission*] at Nha Trang, the guy de-armed at the end of the runway, and safety up the rockets if there were any left. They would hook a drag chute onto the O-2. There was the O-2 taxiing with a drag chute . . . pretty comical. The guy would get out of the O-2 and they would throw a Nuoc Mam, a terrible smelling fermented fish sauce. What a rotten smell. The guy's flight suit would have to be burned. You couldn't get that stuff off. Then he drank a bottle of champagne. That was the fini flight.

———————⚜———————

Ralph D. Kunce was a first assignment FAC in Vietnam, going there right out of pilot training as a *Tum* FAC flying O-2s from Phu Cat, and as a *Chico* FAC flying from Saigon when An Loc got hot:

FROM FEBRUARY to April of 1972, I barely got in the five airstrikes needed to be qualified for combat-ready status. The crap hit the fan in April 1972, however, when the bad guys decided it was time to quit screwing around and win this sucker, since they knew the American populace and liberal well-doers certainly would not allow us to accomplish that end.

In May of 1972 the main squadron at Saigon needed some help because they were flying 24-hour-a-day dual FAC coverage of An Loc and Loc Ninh. I was one of three sent down from Phu Cat to help out, and things occasionally got exciting. The morning after I arrived, two O-2As and one A-37 were shot down at An Loc by SA-7s. The next three months were minimum laughs.

The area I was initially involved with was the An Khe mountain pass southwest of Phu Cat, my home-drome. This was a link between the coast and Pleiku.

Both the South Vietnamese and the Koreans were in there in a pitched battle with the NVA. Unfortunately, the ARVN and Koreans started killing each other and there was a real free-for-all, which was hard to sort out from the air. We did have several U.S. advisors to talk to, so we were pretty sure of being given a legitimate target to strike.

The fighters were now showing up with great regularity, and we were pretty sure by now that we were here for the duration. This upset a lot of guys who had dreams of an early departure for the States and tearful reunions with the Mrs. Also, another interesting thing became obvious. Not all the guys in the unit really wanted to fight what was now becoming a real war. The bad guys were really shooting at us with .50 cal., 23mm, 37mm, and SA-7s. Those are tough to duck sometimes in an O-2A mini-pig. I took one .50-cal. round in the aft part of my right rocket launcher one day. This got my attention. Some dude who must have graduated Magna Cum Laude from .30-cal. school put about six rounds through my left wing one day near Fire Base English when I was trolling around looking for non-combatants. It seems our guys were getting ready to shell a village. I wasn't sure those were bad guys there so I dropped down to take a look and got hosed. I limped my Duck home and told the Army to go ahead and level it.

One mission did some good. I was up solo early one Sunday morning in July. The ARVN and one U.S. Army advisor in a fortified outpost were taking fire from west of their location, about five miles south of An Loc. I had been working with this guy (advisor) before, and he was a pretty cool number. But this morning he was concerned because they were about to get overrun. I could tell because he was definitely more excited on the radio. I got two A-37s on station from Bien Hoa. They were carrying Mk-81s (250-pound bombs), CBU, Flechette rockets, and strafe. The advisor said the bad guys (NVA) were close to the perimeter wires, and he'd pop smoke so I could tell his location. Corrections would come from his smoke. The NVA had radio also, and they popped smoke the same time he did. This was not a new trick. It was designed to confuse us.

Unfortunately for them, their smoke was purple and the good guys' was green. I saw both and told the advisor I had two in sight and which was his? He said, "The green is us, the purple is them. Hit the purple smoke."

The A-37 drivers heard this on their FM radios. I

told them to hold for a minute, and rolled in and shot two Willie Pete rockets at the base of the purple smoke. The rockets impacted where I was shooting, and a very serious voice came up on the radio about 30 seconds later. "You'd better get those fighters in quick because your smoke just killed ten of them, and now they're charging the wire."

So we worked between my smoke and the friendlies with two very accurate A-37 pilots. The entire battle was observed by the advisor, so the results were confirmed. We killed over 100 bad guys that morning. Over ten I did myself. They pulled back and that small fortress was never overrun.

It wasn't that exciting from the air. I never saw a drop of blood. I remember thinking it was a good airstrike and buzzed on home. At the base, a lot of guys were asking me about it. Evidently the advisor had called my unit to tell the story and say thanks. The Army submitted me for a Silver Star for that mission, but the Air Force downgraded it to a DFC. I do look at that ribbon occasionally. It's probably the only one that means anything to me.

Sixty percent of Tom Milligan's (*Sun Dog* 29) flying time was in Cambodia, but a good portion of the time after the April 1972 offensive, he flew in support of friendly forces under siege at An Loc:

THIS MAJOR BATTLE was won by the skillful and abundant use of both tactical airstrikes and B-52 strikes. It was my first time to actually engage air against enemy armor.

I flew seven days a week. Up in the morning, shower, shave, and off to the flight line. Finish up administrative stuff and then go to Intel to get briefed on the day's activities. Then we got our survival equipment. I wore a chute, sat on my flak vest, carried a .38-cal. pistol or an AR-15, and carried enough maps to wallpaper the Empire State. Then we would fly the mission and debrief. Frequently during the day I stood as duty officer and monitored and controlled our FACs. At the end of the day we had dinner at the club, a drink or two at the bar, possibly a movie. Write a letter home and hit the sack. Incidentally, our unit ruled the club. There were plenty of noncombatants that would sometimes not enjoy our behavior in the club, but we ignored them. We also had "FAC Groupies," those noncombatants who liked to hang around us.

FACs knew the war better than anyone, where the enemy was moving, who the friendlies were, what happened the day before or two weeks before. If anything moved or changed, the FACs knew it. Later in the war, when the big offensive hit in '72, we sent a FAC up to *Blue Chip*, up at Tan Son Nhut, to the "cab," which is the place where the general in charge would sit. He would be running the air battle. Twice a day, once in the morning, and once in the afternoon, we would send a FAC up there to brief him on the ground war and how we were using our air assets. He loved his FACs. If the FACs were unhappy because they weren't being supported with the right air, or coordination was wrong, you were talking to the boss. Action was taken immediately. The FACs were the link between the guy on the ground and the air assets. Down south you couldn't put tactical air in without a FAC. Most FACs came back from a year's tour with 900 to 1,000 hours of flying. That's a lot of flight time in one year flying an O-1, O-2, or OV-10.

You'd fly seven days a week. When you switched from night to days, you might pick up a day off due to crew rest rules. Otherwise, you flew seven days a week. FACs came from every area of the Air Force. We had every personality and background. Most were highly dedicated and did an excellent job. I made some lasting friendships and met some people that I highly respected. On the other hand were those who had been hiding in the Air Force in an attempt to avoid combat. These folks were easy to spot. They had frequent illnesses that kept them from flying, and had frequent airborne mechanical problems, which caused them to return to base early. When they did fly, one never knew where they went or what they did. Most of these types tried to get themselves moved out of a flying job ASAP.

We were always, as a FAC, invited to go fly with other people, because we always worked with everybody — fighters and ground people. I know guys that took rides with other people and got shot. I did that a lot, but toward the end of my tour, I said this is ridiculous; I have risk enough on my missions. I got to ride in a Cobra on a mission and fire the guns and shoot the rockets. And we let them fly with us so we got to know each other's missions.

We had a mountain out in Tay Ninh Province called Nui Ba Dinh. It sticks up like a volcano. It was a cone out in the plains. We stuck a radio station up on top of Nui Ba Dinh so we could control our FACs in this area. The enlisted men assigned to our TASS were up there. Every week we would send helicopters out there to rotate them. It was a scary place because the sides of the mountain were owned by the VC all the time. We never took the sides of the mountain from them because it was volcanic and there were caves for them to hide in. But, we owned the top.

When the big offensive hit, the NVA knew what that mountain was doing. We were controlling all the FACs with it so they attacked and took the mountain. Our enlisted radio operators up there were in the middle of a fire fight. They weren't shot, but were hit by things blowing around, so they fell down and played dead. The VC went up there and kicked them, and just then we came in and retook the top of the hill. We never did get the sides. Boy, were those guys at the top of the hill happy when we came back. They got to see their own FACs put air in right on top of them.

The FAC effort at An Loc was hampered by the appearance of SA-7 missiles early in May. Two O-2s were shot down on 11 May and another on 14 May. The FACs had to raise their minimum altitude to 6,000 feet. In spite of the missile threat, Lieutenant James W. Beaubien, a controller from the 21st TASS, who was flying at 8,000 feet between cloud decks when the call for help came from the ambushed 33rd Regiment, called III DASC to launch A-37s. Beaubien, who received the Distinguished Flying Cross for this mission, dove down through the cloud deck, breaking out at 2,000 feet where he began marking enemy targets for the A-37 strikes. Lieutenant Beaubien was credited with saving the lives of most, if not all, of the 33rd Regiment's men, who were able to move to safer positions while he directed airstrikes against the enemy.

Tom Milligan (*Sun Dog* 29) also recalled a close call while breaking in a new FAC:

DURING THE BIG offensive, when the new FACs came in, we had one guy shot down on his very first mission by an SA-7. He was shot down near the Cambodian border, flying an O-2, with his instructor. They ended up lying in a rice paddy with VC all around. The instructor-FAC was directing the airstrike from the ground with his radio. He was telling

fighters when to drop right over his head. The VC were just on the other side of the rice paddy, behind the dikes, shooting at him until the helicopters flew in and got them out. The instructor wasn't shaken, but the brand new novice FAC, on his first ride, was. So, we let him take a break for about five days, and then it was back in the saddle again.

I flew with the new FAC taking him just north of An Loc which was just too busy for his second mission. I told the schedulers to try not to schedule an instructor with a new FAC in the An Loc area because you couldn't watch the new guy and monitor the battle. It was too hectic there and too dangerous. So, when we flew with a new FAC we would normally try to work around on the outskirts. We went up north a few miles and found a truck getting ready to cross a river. It was an NVN truck full of equipment. I said, "Great, you call up and launch your air."

While we were circling, waiting for the air to come in, we heard a "thunk," and I said, "What was that? Did you drop your checklist?" He said, "No I didn't," so I grabbed the yoke and pulled back hard. When you are sitting in the right seat as IP [*Instructor Pilot*], you can't see when the aircraft is circling left, although the pilot in the left seat flying the airplane can . . . I stretched to look and I couldn't see, so I grabbed the yoke and as I rolled right hard, an SA-7 went between the wingtip and fuselage. If I hadn't pulled like that, it would have gotten us. When I turned back around you could see the smoke trail right next to the truck. They snuck out from the weeds to fire at us. You could see the smoke trail just following our trail right around as the missile tracked the heat expelled from our rear engine.

I was angry. I rolled in and fired about four rockets into that area. I put them right into the place where they fired at us. When our air came in, and they were expending the air, they came out again and opened up on us. We never saw them, but some big, red fire balls were going by us. The fighters were out of ordnance, we were out of rockets, so I told this young FAC, who by then was a nervous wreck, "I think we'll leave now." We left, and that was just before I went home.

Byron R. Tetrick, a *Nail* FAC, flew OV-10 Broncos from Nakhon Phenom, Thailand:

ONE OF MY MOST rewarding missions was

working with a ground commander. I was feet wet (over the ocean) waiting for an ARC LIGHT to go up near the DMZ when I saw two triangular flashes of light. The ground commander started yelling that they were taking incoming. The spot was about ten miles away and I told the backseater to tell me when he saw the B-52 strike go in because I couldn't take my eyes off that spot. Once the B-52 went in, I turned in over the land and found the area, but all I could see were trees. But I called for air and got a couple of sets and put them in and, sure enough, there were two 130mm guns. We destroyed one and damaged the other and passed the target to my replacement who finished the job. The grunts on the ground really hated the 130mm.

We flew four to five times a week. We had different sections that we patrolled from before sunrise to sunset with occasional night missions. The first go was called the "Alpha Go." You got up about three a.m. and you were over your sector about five a.m. so that you might catch trucks, etc., out in the open when the sun came up. Usually two hours over your sector and RTB (Return to Base). Depending on your additional duties you would eat lunch, maybe take a nap and go to the party hooch about the time the last mission was coming in. We played pool, darts, gambled, and occasionally partied. There were variations from day to day depending on what time you flew your mission. Da Nang operations were similar except there was a lot less to do if you were not flying, but you usually flew every day at Da Nang.

Our Base Intel shop was outstanding. They did a very thorough pre-brief and de-brief using detailed pre-folded maps (1:50,000). The whole concept of the FAC depended on updated Intel as to what was shooting at you, and what kind of AAA or SA-7 was in the area. No FAC slighted the Intel Brief. We would rather do a fast pre-flight. I can't praise them enough.

I was proud of the job we did. There was eminent satisfaction in helping the guys on the ground and also knowing that you were the one most responsible for protecting innocents from being hurt. We had so much confidence that we knew that we were "NASH" (*Nails* are Shit Hot). I still feel that pride.

By 12 June, the last of the North Vietnamese Army were driven from An Loc. Thanks to USAF and VNAF air power, the South Vietnamese defeated

the invasion. Even so, North Vietnam occupied much of South Vietnam below the DMZ and a strip of land along the South Vietnamese border with Laos and Cambodia.

OPERATION LINEBACKER renewed bombing of North Vietnam on 8 May 1972, until a halt was ordered in October, when North Vietnam appeared ready to talk peace. By 18 December 1972, OPERATION LINEBACKER II resumed the heaviest bombing of the war against Hanoi and Haiphong after a breakdown in the peace talks. On 29 December 1972 the North Vietnamese to agree to return to the peace table.

In Laos, COMMANDO HUNT had ceased operations by the end of March 1972. Because most of the U.S. air support was involved in the North Vietnamese Spring Offensive, airstrikes in Laos dropped to their lowest level since 1965. Toward the end of 1972, the Pathet Lao agreed to meet with Laotian government representatives to discuss a cease-fire.

Byron Tetrick appreciated the trust the figher pilots had in the FACs:

THE FIGHTERS were excellent. They were almost always professional. They knew the FAC was the boss and did what they were told. In the year I was there only once did I not let a guy drop his bombs because of discipline and following instructions. The most striking incident that best highlighted the responsibility that the FAC was entrusted with took place after the cease-fire in Vietnam but bombing was still going on in Laos. I was putting in airstrikes near the five-mile buffer zone. A flight of fighters refused to drop because they were afraid that they would violate the air space. Only after repeated assurances that I knew where we were, that we had plenty of room, and I accepted full responsibility, would they drop.

During the time period that I was there, the U.S. troops had pulled out. The ARVN units had American advisors only. Usually our airstrikes were coordinated and communications were with the American advisor. I did a lot of TIC work in MR [*Military Region*] I. The advisors were topnotch and as a FAC I really tried to help them especially when they were taking incoming and needed support.

In Laos (STEEL TIGER), we usually found our own targets, and even though it was essentially a free-fire zone, we called ABCCC for approval. In northern Laos (BARREL ROLL), we got ABCCC approval but sometimes worked with Laotian ground forces and coordinated with them.

———— ⌇ ————

Fred McNeil, *Covey* 502, explained airborne control and communications:

THERE WERE FOUR ABCCCs, two C-130s in the daytime and two at night. The other orbit in the daytime was *Alleycat* in northern Laos. Up north and east Laos was all CIA country. Most operations up there were Air America and Continental Air Service. *Hillsboro* [*the EC-130 ABCCC*] selected its orbit because the majority of all TAC air strikes were coming out of Thailand from Ubon, Udorn, or Nakhon Phanom.

There were also aircraft carriers. "Yankee Station" and others launched strikes. Many times I worked as many Navy and Marine fighters as I did Air Force. All TAC air coming in (Air Force, Navy, and Marine) was allocated for out-country missions by *Hillsboro*. As they came in on the coast, *Hillsboro* knew they were coming, and what ordnance they carried. Before *Hillsboro* took off at four or five in the morning from a base in Thailand, it had a complete computer printout for every TAC airstrike in Southeast Asia for the next 12-hour orbit. Those that applied to us were torn off. That made a block from the computer printout that was called the morning "frag" (fragmentary order). *Hillsboro* would implement the Air Order of Battle (AOB) for that day that had been created by the Seventh Air Force.

Because they couldn't communicate way down in Saigon (500 miles or more away, and the war was up here) they came up with idea of an airborne battle staff that was a direct subagency of Seventh Air Force Operations. The aircraft always had either a full colonel or a one-star general on board as director of the airborne battle staff. Directly under him was the battle staff air operations officer.

Hillsboro had three or four teletype machines and wall charts illuminated from behind, giving it tremendous communications capability. There were five or six communications NCOs on board. The Ops officers sat in throne-like chairs facing all these charts of Southeast Asia. We had Intelligence officers working their own secure radios and their own teletype. We had a guy in direct communication with the

Cambodian government, another with Vientiane in Laos. *Hillsboro* was also in constant communication with Seventh Air Force in Saigon. *Hillsboro* was busy with a "frag" coming in at 15-minute intervals all day long. It was like running a control tower at a very busy airport.

In the meantime, if a FAC came up with a more lucrative target or a situation developed on the ground like a tactical emergency when some ground troops were getting beat up pretty badly, then *Hillsboro* would divert some fighters, making the decision right on the spot. *Moonbeam* and *Cricket* were the night orbits. There were very few tactical airstrikes at night when most of the gunships were working the Trail. The ABCCCs changed over at 0600 hours and 1800 hours every day.

———— ⌇ ————

Blowing off steam was important for the battle weary FACs, as remembered by Tom Milligan:

IN SAIGON WE were the only combat unit that was left over there. Before that they had F-4s and things. Most of the officers stationed there were desk drivers, pencil pushers (or pukes) we used to call them. And you could always tell the guys who came over and didn't want to be FACs. They would rush like crazy trying to get out of FACing and go up to be an administrator on the staff. They didn't like us very much because we would razz them. We would go to the Officers Club and yell and scream and drink, yell at the girls and let off steam. That was how we had to do it. Beside our barracks, we had our own little bar, the "*Sun Dog*" bar. Our call sign was *Sun Dog*. We would go in there and have barbecues and drink and have a good time. We'd shoot our pen gun flares up in the air. I think once somebody fired a round through the roof. We did carrier landings on the bar. You know, wet the bar down with your beer, and then come running at it and jump on it and slide down the bar. And then we'd say, "There's a fire on final, triple A," and we would take beans and food and throw it at the guys coming in trying to make them miss the bar, because if you missed, you fell on the floor. You fell off the bar and hit the ground.

The wing commander (base commander) there liked his FACs. When I finished my tour there was a big party for myself and several others who came in at the same time. About 20 guys were available for this going away party. We had a band that had come

"Carrier landings" outside the "Nail Hole" party hooch at Nakhon Phanom.
Byron Tetrick Collection

in from Korea. They would sing things like "Yellow River," but it sounded like "jello reever." They couldn't pronounce English very well. They would be singing and dancing while we sat there drinking wine — about three bottles for each guy. Each time we drank a bottle of wine, we lined it up on the stage. Pretty soon we had many bottles lined up all around the stage. Some of the other folks in the club were yelling for us to shut up. I guess we were getting a little boisterous.

The club manager came over and said, "If you guys don't quit this, I'm going to call the wing commander, and I'm going to have you all thrown out of here." So, we'd just say, see that mirror behind the bar. Would you like to see us hit it with this bottle of wine? That night he came over about three times, finally saying, "The next time the wing commander comes in, and he is due in about half an hour, I'm going to have you thrown out."

Just about that time the wing commander walked in through the door and said, "Hey, Terrible Tom! How are you guys doing over there?" And then he

Party inside the "Nail Hole." Front row, standing l to r: Ron Kelser, Bob Ruth, Dan Wimbelly, and Ital Michlor (KIA).
Byron Tetrick Collection

went and ordered a round of wine for all his FACs. So we knew right then, and the club manager knew, that there wasn't any way he was going to stop these FACs from having a good time.

Most of the guys handled fear differently. Anybody who said they didn't have fear over there probably was lying. Or, they had it and didn't know it. If it wasn't fear, it was anxiety. Some guys would drink it away every night. Some guys, you would never see it in them, but it probably affected them somewhere. I didn't think about it except maybe one day a month. And, then it would build up in me. And that was normally the day I was switching from days to nights or vice versa, when I knew I could go in the club and let myself go and not worry about flying the next day. That was the day I would get scared. I would get really scared, sure that on my next mission they were going to zap me. Then I would go out and fly the mission. Once you took off, you never thought about it. I was never afraid on a mission. Only before or afterwards, and then about once every month I would get scared.

Movies were my escape from the situation. No matter where they were on the base, I would try to see them, lousy or not, because it killed two hours.

The enemy was still attempting to capture the capital of Cambodia, Phnom Penh, but U.S. air power, including B-52s, continued to hammer the enemy, keeping the city out of enemy hands. In early 1973, the Khmer Rouge, Communists led by Saloth Sar, *aka* Pol Pot, kept up their attacks on Phnom Penh. The Cambodian government sent out urgent calls for help. The USAF carried out a massive bombing campaign against the insurgents on the outskirts of the capital.

On 1 July 1973, Congress passed Public Law 93-52 cutting off all funds to finance directly or indirectly combat activities by U.S. military forces in or over or from off the shores of South Vietnam, Laos, or Cambodia. Captain Lonnie O. Ratley, in an A-7 Corsair, flew the last U.S. airstrike in Cambodia on the morning of 15 August 1973. His return to home base in Thailand marked the end of the nation's longest war. However, USAF C-130s continued to deliver needed supplies to the Cambodians after that date.

A cease-fire agreement was signed in Laos on 21 February 1973, at which time the U.S. discontinued its tactical aircraft and B-52 missions over the panhandle. However, the Communists violated the cease-fire, so B-52s carried out raids on 23 February. In April, additional B-52 raids were made south of the Plain of Jars because of additional Communist cease-fire violations. Following these strikes, all USAF missions over Laos ceased after nine years of combat operations.

An agreement signed in Paris on 23 January 1973, to become effective 28 January 1973, called for the U.S. to remove all of its forces from South Vietnam and for all prisoners of war to be returned within 60 days. On 28 March 1973, the last U.S. military personnel departed from South Vietnam. Only 50 U.S. military officers and 159 Marine guards remained in the country.

Chapter 8

The *Ravens* and America's Secret War in Laos

*T*HE GENEVA ACCORDS OF 23 July 1962 had prohibited foreign military personnel from being stationed in Laos. In response to Prime Minister Souvanna Phouma's request in 1964 for help for the Royal Laotian Air Force, the USAF had deployed Detachment 6, 1st Air Commando Wing, to Udorn, Thailand. The USAF helped with RLAF T-28 checkouts and maintenance. (Detachment 6 later became part of the 606th Air Commando Squadron in 1966, and then the 56th Air Commando Wing in 1967.) As support of friendly ground operations increased, the Air Force personnel worked as ground controllers or Forward Air Guides (FAG) in Laos, because few Laotians could speak English and none were familiar with the procedures for directing airstrikes.

The **Butterflies** were Forward Air Controllers flying in the right seat of Air America or Continental Air Service, Inc. (CASI) planes, such as the Helio-Courier and the

The FAC Memorial at Hurlburt Field, Fort Walton Beach, Florida.
All *Ravens* lost in the war are listed on this Memorial.
Darrel D. Whitcomb Collection

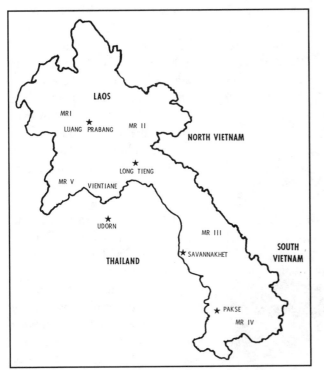

Raven FAC operating locations and military regions of Laos.

Pilatus Porter. They communicated with strike air-craft, directing them to targets. These enlisted men were "sheep-dipped," which meant surrendering all military identification and uniforms. They were issued a Laotian driver's license and wore civilian clothes, and were given papers identifying them as employees of a civilian agency in Laos. Sergeants Charlie Jones and Jim Stanford were the first *Butterfly* controllers. They were not hampered by USAF regulations as they directed airstrikes, not only for USAF and Navy jet fighters, but also for the Royal Laotian, Hmong, and Thai mercenary pilots. The *Butterfly* FAC had a pilot next to him and often a Laotian or Thai interpreter sitting in the back. The Air Commando sergeants used standard USAF procedures so well that none of the pilots realized they were being controlled by enlisted personnel. However, when General William W. Momyer, com-mander of the Seventh Air Force, found out that the FACs in Laos were enlisted men flying Air Amer-ica planes, he put a stop to the *Butterfly* program, ordering these men to be replaced by rated Air Force pilots.

On 5 May 1966, a new FAC effort was launched under the moniker "Steve Canyon," a highly classi-fied program. Pilots, as well as nonflying personnel, were attached to the "Water Pump," a part of Project 404, detachment in Udorn, Thailand. Project 404 was a covert administrative umbrella for U.S. mili-tary personnel in Laos. One hundred-twenty U.S. Air Force and Army personnel and five civilians were as-signed to Thailand, but they served in Laos.

Using the call sign *Raven*, these pilots were vol-unteers with previous experience in one of the Tacti-cal Air Control Squadrons in Vietnam. Initially as-signed to Long Tieng (and then to Luang Prabang, Vientiane, Savannakhet, and Pakse), they flew O-1s with no national markings. Experienced, elite Air Force officers, flying unmarked O-1 Bird Dogs, wore Rolex watches and gold bracelets, old jeans, T-shirts, and cowboy boots with nothing resembling a uni-form, and carried USAID (United States Agency for International Development) identification cards. Of-ficially, they weren't in Laos.

The *Ravens'* mission was unique because they operated as civilian pilots outside of normal military control. The *Ravens* were issued orders by the 56th Special Operations Wing (SOW), Detachment 1, based at Nakhon Phanom, then lent to the air attaché in Vientiane, ostensibly as members of USAID. They were given Embassy identification and a Laotian driver's license. If they were shot down, their cover story was that they were on a rescue mission out of Thailand (plausible deniability). However, cover stories ceased in October 1970 after the U.S. admitted there were military personnel at the Embassy in Laos. Permanent TDY gave the *Ravens* a two-year tour of duty under assignment for the USAF "Palace Dog" program, a subterfuge that was necessary because permanent troops were prohibited in Laos.

In the field, the *Ravens* were under the command of native generals, headed by General Vang Pao, the first Hmong to graduate from the ANL (*Armee Na-*

tionale Laotienne) or Dong Hene Academy. General Van Pao pretty much ran the ground war. All personnel, however, were under U.S. Ambassador William H. Sullivan. Some senior Air Force officers criticized the *Ravens* for lack of discipline; however, the pilots did an outstanding job under difficult and dangerous circumstances.

The senior Air Force officers in Saigon and Udorn resented the fact that Ambassador Sullivan had unique command and control authority with the U.S. Air Attaché as a key link. Sullivan received his military advice from the CIA station chief and U.S. military attachés. An Embassy-based colonel acted in place of a senior air commander. Such was the nature of the "secret" war in Laos. In order to get a handle on the situation, the Department of Defense formed a new command, eventually redesignated as the 7/13th Air Force. Even so, Ambassador Sullivan continued to make his own air power decisions. He looked to the new command only to carry out his missions. Nearly all the airstrikes required FAC control, but in areas that were designated under enemy control, approval for airstrikes was not needed.

James J. Stanford's ID card, issued 1966.   Jim Stanford Collection

There were U.S. fighters from Da Nang, in South Vietnam, Navy carrier-based fighters, and Marine F-4s at a base about 40 miles south of Udorn. (Marine F-4s were utilized later in the war.)

In support of General Vang Pao and also the CIA, however paid by the USAF, the *Ravens* were all volunteers. The *Raven* FAC had to have a minimum of four months of combat duty, at least 60 days as a Forward Air Controller in Southeast Asia, and at least 100 hours as a FAC or fighter pilot, and no fewer than 750 flying hours. He also had to have six to eight months left on his duty tour. While the *Raven* FACs were independent thinkers and somewhat irreverent, they were one of the success stories of the war in Southeast Asia. They

Lima Site (LS) 113A, Moung Chas, Laos, in 1966, elevation 3,600 feet, with a 2,700- x 85-foot clay runway with 08-26 compass headings. This runway has a medium up-slope, and was closed when wet. The Operations building is on the hill.
Jim Stanford Collection

were daring, efficient, and devoted to fighting for the Laotians.

The *Ravens* lived well most of the time. Actually, they were based at Lao Air Operations Centers in each of the five Military Regions (MR): Luang Prabang (MR I), Long Tieng (MR II), Savannakhet (MR III), Pakse (MR IV), and Wattay Airfield at Vientiane (MR V). The commander at each location reported to the Air Attaché and coordinated operations with his Air Liaison Officer and the *Head Raven* (the senior *Raven* ALO) stationed at Vientiane. At Long Tieng, better known as 20A (Alternate), the *Ravens* lived in a house on stilts with no heat (it could get very cold at night) and no bathrooms. And 20 miles northwest, over two ridge lines, was Lima Site 20, also known as Sam Thong. 20A was a secret location, not even listed in the "Airfield Site List for Laos, June-July, 1966" by the Flight Information Center in Vientiane.

Three *Raven* FACs on 90-day TDY tours borrowed aircraft and started flying cover for Lao forces in BARREL ROLL and STEEL TIGER operations. By December 1966, they had permission to install radios and marker rocket tubes in a RLAF O-1 Bird Dog based at Savannakhet to support special Lao

Army operations. A little while later, the FACs obtained two single-engine aircraft, a DeHavilland U-6 Beaver and a CAS (CIA) Helio-Courier, on loan through the Air Attaché office.

When three more TDY FACs came on board in August 1967, the Air Attaché office had no vacancies for them, and thus they were attached to Detachment 1, 606th Air Commando Squadron (later the 56th SOW), at Udorn, Thailand. From there they operated covertly in Laos, along with the three Project 404 Forward Air Controllers.

Using borrowed aircraft was unsatisfactory, so the Air Attaché asked the 7/13th Air Force to provide unmarked O-1E/Fs. He also requested that the TDY status be changed to Permanent Change of Station. The program differed from the *Butterfly* FACs in that rated officers would fly their own airplanes, which eliminated the need to use Air America or CASI aircraft. The O-1s flown by the *Ravens* did not display any national markings. They were as nonmilitary looking as their pilots. By November, there were eight TDY FACs, and the requested change to Permanent Change of Station was granted in December.

Karl Polifka, while flying as a *Walt* FAC, ran into a Holley Field, Florida, classmate around Christmas 1968. His friend, who was a *Covey* controller flying nights with the super-secret PRAIRIE FIRE teams, suggested he might want to volunteer for the Steve Canyon program. Early the following February, Polifka volunteered. Along with Dan Berry and Dan Davis, Polifka was processed through the 432nd TRW for E&E (Escape and Evasion) photos and blood chits. He soon had a ride on a clattering Air America C-123 Provider to Long Tieng.

Polifka (*Raven* 45) described Long Tieng (Long Cheng), Lima Site 20 Alternate (listed in the antiaircraft site book as LS 30):

IT IS LOCATED in a valley running NW-SE with a 4,700-foot asphalted airstrip, field elevation of 3,120 feet. The elevation and length was deliberately misstated in some Air America site books, to confuse would-be visitors. The runway length is deceptive in that the last 1,500 feet to the southeast slopes down at a steep rate. Landings are to the northwest, toward a number of karst (sheer rock formations) spires — 100 feet or more high. The "barrier" is a bunch of dirt-filled fuel drums in front of a large karst formation (C-123 wreckage at the base, a reminder that go-arounds aren't smart).

Takeoffs are to the southeast toward a close ridge about 800 feet above field elevation. An (unnecessary) attempt to land from that direction on "brick one" — the end of the runway — will require a sink rate that most airplanes can't handle. A Lao T-28 pilot tried that and drove the gear through the wings. He shot his way through his jammed canopy as the airplane burned. I landed over the burning wreckage. A takeoff using too much runway required an initial climb rate many of us can't handle.

To the north is Skyline Ridge at 5,000 feet. Site 20, Sam Thong, is on the other side. To the south is a ridge about 4,000 feet. The airfield part of the valley is perhaps two by three miles, measured from ridge tops. There is an NDB [*Nondirectional Beacon*] and a TACAN (98 or 113) on Skyline. There is no instrument approach and no runway lights, not that we didn't make night landings. The valley wanders to the northwest, a bit higher than the field, karst formations poking up here and there. Up the valley is where the bulk of the 20,000 plus Hmong (Meo) in the immediate area live.

Skyline Ridge is basically bare — scrub and grasses but not heavy jungle-type vegetation. There are heavier trees and secondary growth around the karst and the other ridges. On some days, the noise of cicadas is so loud you might think you were on the set of *Bridge Over the River Kwai*. There is real jungle out there, but it's a highland jungle.

General Vang Pao lived in a large cinderblock construction house in an unfenced compound just to the south of the central part of the runway. Almost all *Ravens* spent an hour or so of most evenings there, depending on a number of factors. Low warehouses with a variety of architectural styles surround the up-sloping ramp at the northwest end of the runway, the Air America hostel being at the highest, northern, edge of the ramp. A crushed gravel and dirt road leads uphill from the northwest end of the runway, passing more low warehouse/office buildings, mostly teak with long exterior porches outside the offices. The road leads past the *Raven* house and, next door, the large cinderblock-stucco CIA house.

The *Raven* house was, when I arrived on 1 April 1969, a weathered teak house tucked against the hillside. A crushed gravel parking area, big enough for three jeeps, was on the uphill side from which the house was normally entered. Entry was into a short screened hallway which to the left went into a large living room (about 25 x 16 feet) with a fireplace at the far end. Straight ahead, from the entry was the kitchen — fairly good-sized. To the right from the kitchen was the radio room, where the operator also slept. Straight through the kitchen led out onto another screened-in area which, on the left, was a sort of bar/lounge, and several bedrooms to the right. On the back of the house, reached through an open breezeway between the house and the shower/sinks/toilets, were three more bedrooms. Davis, Berry, and I would share a bedroom that was about 10 x 14 feet.

Later, additions were made to the house, moving the radio room to the down-slope side, closing in the bar area, and filling in the area between the new radio room and the old bedrooms with a general map, storage, what-have-you area. A second house was built behind the first, with eight bedrooms, two baths, as I recall — gave us each a bedroom and gave the three houseboys a decent place to live. All of this was destroyed/badly damaged when the NVA overran 20A in 1971.

We had an Air Force cook, Manuel Espinoza, when I arrived. He wasn't a terribly good or inventive cook (pork chops constantly) but at least we weren't cooking. He left about September and the attaché's office did nothing for us. The CIA got the *Ravens* a pair of Thai cooks in December. It was in their interest and, besides, they were tired of our bitching.

Fred Platt gave me a local area check-out on the afternoon of 3 April. After that I was on my own. The weather was off-and-on shitty during April, if my flight records are any guide. My last flight as a *Raven*, working air, was on 2 December 1969. I left Long Tieng on 17 December, the first *Raven* (I was told) to stay that long at 20A and survive. I don't know how true that is, but I was certainly a basket case. When I had arrived in Laos the MRII [*Military Region II*] *Ravens* were getting perhaps 30 sorties on a normal day, a number that grew to 100 to 120 a day after ABOUT FACE started 15 August 1969. I worked somewhere around 1,500 sorties in Laos.

A week or so as a *Raven* made you an "old head." Around the second week of April I checked out Captain John Bach. Bach was very impressed with being a captain versus us lieutenants, and was contemptuous of advice concerning defenses and mountain flying. He had spent six months in pancake-flat IV Corps. On 20 April 1969, John Bach and his backseater were blown out of the sky over Xieng Khoung.

Xieng Khoung had essentially ceased to exist the previous month. On this day, Bach had been flying along serenely in a straight line over the town remnants while General Vang Pao had helicoptered into positions some 400 meters south of the still enemy-occupied place. Bach took multiple 37mm hits and floods of 12.7 and 14.5mm before he hit the ground. Part of his spine was recovered the next day. For reasons I don't understand, he was carried as missing until 1977.

The initial call from *Cricket* was that Vang Pao was pinned down at Xieng Khoung. I was in Ban Ban, and Don Service (Dick Shubert's replacement) was in the central PDJ [*Plain of Jars*]. Don beat me there by a minute or two. I started a long full-power descent, aiming for the base of the karst on the northeast corner of the town. I reached this point at an altitude of about ten feet, coming round the karst toward the town. Of course, I was heard from the ground long before I got there.

As I rounded the karst, I looked left as a 37mm at zero elevation fired from a range of perhaps 50 meters. In my mind's eye the recoil of the gun, the rippling of the grass, and the flex of the window from the concussion remain clear. The round passed between the prop and the windshield. I instinctively turned left, dropped to perhaps a foot, and tried to be small as I flew away. They fired more rounds but missed.

On 29 April, Dan Davis became part of a tactical situation he had to hand over to me because he was out of fuel. Back to Xieng Khoung. The situation was about 300 friendlies who were advancing, steadily line abreast, from the town toward the northwest. The center of their practically Napoleonic line was aimed toward a large karst formation. Beyond that was a smaller karst formation, and beyond that the entrance to a large cave. Behind the first karst formation were two BTR-40 Soviet armored personnel carriers, each sporting twin 14.5mm heavy MG [*machine-guns*]. These were easily enough to wipe out the friendlies. Davis and his backseater couldn't raise the friendlies on the radio to give warnings and neither could I.

It was late in the afternoon, around 1700, and the descending sun was casting very sharp shadows across the valley floor. It was almost impossible to see objects in shadow unless you descended into the shadow yourself, down to about 500 feet AGL at times. At this point, I discovered that there was a 37mm with the BTR-40 hosing away at me from a slant range of less than a thousand feet. To make things more interesting, large numbers of enemy troops on the cliffs above the cave began shooting down on me. My Hmong backseater, "Scar," kept babbling about "many enemy" in a cave in the secondary karst, missing the point of the imminent disaster for the advancing friendlies. I put Scar to work trying to contact Ly Leu and his T-28 flight.

Ly Leu, thank God, showed a few minutes later and started strafing and rocketing the enemy on the cliffs. I gave general direction on VHF while coaching in a single F-4 released by a Fast FAC. I put Ly Leu and his flight of three in a clockwise pattern on the cliff tops while talking *Lincoln* down the long valley leading from the PDJ to Xieng Khoung. The 37mm kept whacking away, and we were all taking huge volumes of small arms. *Lincoln*, inexplicably, dropped 300m short from low altitude. The friendlies, inexplicably, kept advancing although I noted a wavering in their line. I was almost raving. Couldn't they understand there was something very wrong here?

"*Bobin*," two F-105s, checked in, also released from a Fast FAC, and I knew from Lead's tone of voice that this was it. *Bobin* was in at 1725 hours. I watched his progress up the valley, at some 450-500 KIAS, and rolled in to mark at minimum range when he was a few seconds out. The light-dark contrast was extremely disorienting, and must have been far worse for *Lincoln* and *Bobin*. I pulled off left, down

Looking for targets such as ammo storage in Laos, 1966.   Jim Stanford Collection

Lima Site (LS) 2 San Tiau, Laos, 1966, elevation 5,000 feet, with a 738 x 70 clay and shale runway, with 11-29 headings. This runway has a steep, rolling up-slope. LS 2 is south of Ban Ban.   Jim Stanford Collection

to about 200 feet, in time to see *Bobin* skip two Mk-84 (2,000-pound bombs) into the base of the karst I had marked. His wingman pickled off a bunch of Mk-82 short. It didn't matter.

On the ground the next day when I went in, there was the twisted wreckage of two BTR 40 and one 37mm. The personnel had disappeared in the blast. There were 27 KBA in the cave Scar had yammered about, dead from over-pressure from the Mk-84 (I would use this weapons-effect many times, becoming known among fighter pilots, without my knowledge at the time, as the cave buster). *Bobin* flight made it 25 sorties for the day. Nothing I just described could have been done in any airplane except

the O-1. It will always be, to me, one of the great planes.

Ron O. Rinehart, *aka "Papa Fox"* (*Raven* 44), served as a FAC in South Vietnam, and got into the *Raven* program because he was dissatisfied with so many rules and regulations:

EVERY TIME WE turned around we got threatened with court-martial, or got talked to about the way we were flying. Flying low was one of the things. They caught me twice and threatened to court-martial me. So I said, "How do I get out of this chicken-shit outfit?" He said, "Well, if you want to go to a different program, we got one, the Steve Canyon program." . . . That's how it all started.

I had classified orders the next day to see a Mr. Black up in Udorn, Thailand. I found him where Air America was located at that time. He said, "Do you know what you are going to be doing?" I said, "No." He said, "You're going to be doing the mission up in Laos. We are going to take your military ID card away and all your military clothes, so you need to go and get some civilian clothes."

The next day we got a briefing and went to Vientiane. They gave us an Embassy card and a Laotian driver's license. They took us to see the area. We jumped in the airplane for about two hours, and when we came back, I was checked out, combat-ready. That's the way it was.

The missions at that time were eight to ten hours a day. Basically you were on your own. We didn't have rules to go by. Always had a local in the backseat. We went and found targets and then called ABCCC, got fighters, and put them in on the targets.

My most hair-raising flight was when I got shot down. We were trying to take back Phou Pha Thi, the big mountain in the north. We had lost the radar site up there. In a matter of moments I lost two fighters and a helicopter and one of the *Sandys* crashed, all in one area within an hour. It was really devastating. That's part of war, I guess. Once during that opera-

A young guard on the trenches at Lima Site (LS) 2, Laos, in 1966. Jim Stanford Collection

was just about sunset. He came over, motioned us up the hill, where he picked us up.

So, I go back to Alternate and I'm sitting there, trying to write down what happened, when this guy comes in and says, "When's supper going to be?" He didn't even know I had been shot down. I said, "Just give me a little time. It'll be about an hour." So, I went in there and cooked supper, and the next thing, I was out flying. That's the way it was. [*Papa Fox was a gourmet cook, and no matter how long the flying day, he prepared a fine meal for the* **Ravens***, as long as the other guys washed the dishes.*]

tion I stayed on station so long that I ran out of gas on the runway as I landed.

I came out of Udorn, heading north with a new airplane. I couldn't get into our base that we normally fly out of, 20A, because of the weather. I had on this Farang Tagalog, which is an embroidered Filipino dress shirt, sharkskin pants, and alligator shoes. I went up to the forward base at LS-36 (Na Khang), picked up the backseater, and went on. I didn't have my survival gear, no radio, nothing. I ended up getting shot down and crashed in a rice paddy, way up in the mountains. Right after we landed the enemy started shooting at us. We ran for about four and a half hours through the woods.

We got about half-way up the mountain side and this guy said, "Enemy come, we wait and shoot." I said, "No," so we ran. I figured without radios, we might get picked up or we might not. So about two hours later, I said, "Somehow we have to get a signal out." We had a belt buckle and we tried shining it in the sun, but that didn't work. We were in kind of a cleared area of elephant grass, so I pulled down some bamboo about 30 feet long, tied my fancy embroidered shirt to it, let it go back up in the air, and we started waving it.

We saw two A-1 Sandys and a Jolly Green overhead, but being Air Force, they wouldn't come in without proper radio codes. About 45 minutes later we saw an Air America chopper looking up and down the mountain side, but he never saw us. He must have been about three-quarters of a mile away when he finally saw my fancy shirt up in the trees. It

Phou Pha Thi, the mountain Rinehart mentioned, was Lima Site 85, a 5,500-foot ridge about 30 miles from the border with North Vietnam, and only 150 miles west of Hanoi. The 600- x 50-foot air strip was part-way up the mountain. There was a TACAN on top. Tons of special electronic equipment was maintained there by USAF "civilians" who were supported by several hundred Hmong and Thai soldiers. From this mountain top, electronics increased the accuracy of the fighter-bomber attacks on North Vietnam. The North Vietnamese attacked and captured Lima Site 85 early in 1968.

By 1969, there were 125 USAF personnel in Laos, who assisted in establishing Air Operations Centers within the five military regions of Laos that were jointly manned by the Royal Laotian Air Force and U.S. Air Force airmen. In addition, the U.S. Air Force assigned Forward Air Controllers to Royal Laotian Army units and General Vang Pao's Hmong forces to overcome the language barrier between the FACs and the airstrike crews. The *Ravens* flew O-1s, U-17s, and T-28s on six-month TDYs. They put in plenty of flight time, averaging 183 missions per month. The CIA and Air America pilots were not on a six-month or one-year cycle, nor were they hampered by USAF Rules of Engagement.

Maintenance for the *Raven* O-1s was difficult in the field because it was performed by the pilots or untrained Lao mechanics. Phase-level maintenance

Military Regions (MR) of South Vietnam and the Ho Chi Minh Trail. From *Airpower and the 1972 Spring Invasion*, USAF Southeast Asia Monograph Series, Vol. 2, Mon. 3 (Washington, D.C.: GPO, 1976), p. 8.

was done by Air America on *Raven* O-1s and U-17s and on T-28s by Detachment 1, 56 SOW (Water Pump), on the same ramp at Udorn. After 14 engine failures between September and December 1968, the O-1s were sent back to Udorn to have their fuel tanks removed and cleaned. Mud and sludge from the unimproved dirt fields had encrusted the tanks, many of which had not been cleaned for 18 years. Also, because of the high power settings used getting out of short strips with a heavy load, engine life was shortened from the expected average of 1,800 hours to 400 hours. Air America mechanics came in to help out, and by May 1969, TDY mechanics (one for every two O-1s) were brought on board. Papa Fox Rinehart explained the difficulties he encountered:

THE FIRST MONTH I was there we had a lot of engine problems — twenty-six engine failures. The

gas wasn't strained and the tanks needed to be cleaned. They got a couple of cups of mud out of the fuel tanks. And, they had to clean out the carburetors. We got chamois fuel filters for the gas. After the carburetors were re-tuned for the altitude we were flying out of (they had previously been tuned for sea level), things were better. Our altitude was around 3,000 feet, but the temperature wasn't too hot. The density altitude was a problem. They would tune the engines down at Udorn, which was sea level, and then we'd be up in the mountains, and that made a big difference. But after we went to bat, and got more maintenance people up there, we didn't have near the problems engine wise.

⌾

Karl Polifka depended on his maintenance crew:

IT WOULD be impossible for me to overemphasize the dedication and skill of our maintenance guys. The complete standout for me was Frank Shaw, a guy in his early twenties who took his responsibilities to the max, fixed it or told you why he couldn't, and on many occasions, was found at dawn (with a couple of others), asleep on the gravel under an airplane, having worked all night to make it right.

⌾

Working with the *Ravens* was a network of native Forward Air Guides and CAS (CIA)-supported roadwatch teams. The FAGs were trained, starting in 1964, by Detachment 1, 56th SOW. They operated around the clock reporting enemy movements to ABCCCs, *Raven* FACs, or to General Vang Pao's headquarters. The FAGs were excellent Intelligence sources and had the authority to approve targets to be hit. However, the FAGs were not as far-ranging as the roadwatch teams, mainly because they stayed close to General Vang Pao's soldiers.

CAS had numerous roadwatch teams, mostly in southern Laos, working with *Cricket* and the *Ravens*. Airstrikes could be brought in within minutes as the teams followed activity along the roads and trails.

The amount of air support allotted to Laos kept the *Ravens* busy putting in strikes, and thus they relied on the Forward Air Guides and roadwatch teams for visual reconnaissance. Each new *Raven* had received some orientation training at Wattay Airfield outside Vientiane, and the rest of his training at the

Forward Operating Location, which included traffic patterns in the forward staging areas, and specifics on known enemy positions and defenses.

—⟨◈⟩—

The *Raven* drew his daily assignment the day before, or early in the morning on the day of the mission. After a preflight briefing, and study of current situation maps and the latest ABCCC log, the *Raven* was airborne at first light. He might pick up his Lao observer, who furnished him with intelligence gleaned from the roadwatch teams and FAGs, at a FOL. After takeoff, the *Raven* contacted ABCCC with his position and off time, and intended working area. From then on he checked in about every 20 minutes, or when he changed his area of operations. This would enhance rescue chances should he be downed.

In July 1969, not long before the new Communist offensive in December of that year, American Ambassador George McMurtrie Godley, III, a paramilitary man who had previous operating experience with the CIA, arrived to replace Ambassador William H. Sullivan. Godley was a real friend to combatants, especially the *Ravens*.

In November 1969, 11 of the 21 *Ravens* (there were usually no more than 21 to 27 in Laos at one time) worked in Military Region II, almost entirely in support of General Vang Pao's troops. These FACs worked closely with the general, dining with him and exchanging Intelligence gleaned by the *Ravens* and the general's roadwatch teams. A coordination meeting took place each evening at 2030.

Raven operations were a little different in other areas. In MR I, the *Ravens* were controlling USAF/RLAF strikes against enemy insurgents moving toward the Plain of Jars. In MR III, the controllers and FAGs supported the Lao Army, using TAC air support as an extension of artillery. MR IV *Ravens* handled mostly interdiction, after receiving their instructions from close air support and USAF Intelligence sources. Only the chief *Raven* at Vien-

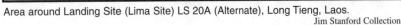

Area around Landing Site (Lima Site) LS 20A (Alternate), Long Tieng, Laos.
Jim Stanford Collection

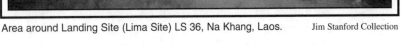

Area around Landing Site (Lima Site) LS 36, Na Khang, Laos.   Jim Stanford Collection

tiane operated in MR V, the activity there being more political than military.

Karl Polifka (*Raven* 45) flew FAC missions in the U-17 and T-28:

THE U-17 WAS a Military Assistance Program (MAP) airplane sent to several countries. It was a C-185 [*Cessna Skywagon*] with a 300 hp engine, seven hours of gas, and eight rockets *à la* the O-1. The C-185, as any bush pilot will tell you, is a damn good airplane for its intended use. Its only benefit as a FAC bird is endurance. It's hard to see out of, has side-by-side seating, and picks up speed very quickly in the dive. Like the O-2, another design intended for something else, it was a bit marginal for FAC use.

A USAF F-105F Thunderchief, armed with AGM-45 Shrike missiles, bombs a surface-to-air missile (SAM) site in North Vietnam, 1967.   USAF

Nonetheless, we had one for a time. I flew a total of 7 missions in it, totaling 42 hours. Mostly, it hauled groceries from NKP.

On 12 June 1969 I took a U-17 north to site 185 (Phou Tia), not far south of the NVN-Lao border and southeast of Dien Bien Phu. My backseater, speaking not a word of English, was a ground commander who'd finally lost his nerve and was given the "easy" task of flying with us. He died when an inept *Raven* crashed on his first unsupervised mission.

"Rainbow" at LS 185 was lonely and wanted some air to stir things up. The weather darted in and out and I was able to work four ships, two "Marlin" (Thuds) [*F-105 Thunderchiefs*] and two "Locust" (F4Es), expending all eight rockets in the process. Southbound, my backseater talked sign language to me, and I hooked with "Kingpin" at LS198, Houei Hok. This site, with a 900-foot strip, was northwest of LS185, damn near in North Vietnam, and truly at the ends of the earth. This whole area is the worst terrain northern Laos has to offer, sawtooth ridge after sawtooth ridge.

Kingpin had his troops (which couldn't be many) out on an operation, had 1,500 refugees milling around his site, and had a squad in contact with a company of NVA about two kilometers to the east. "Could I help?" Rats! I'm out of rockets, how can I work fighters? On the other hand, we know without saying that if I don't intervene, the NVA will kill the squad and then butcher 1,500 women, children, and old men. Not this time.

"*Cricket*, *Raven* Four-five, I have troops in contact. I need air now, and good air, rendezvous zero-one-zero at ninety." This is an approximation, we don't have TACAN and Channel 98 doesn't work this far north anyway. "Roger, Four-five, Machete, four Fox-Four-Echoes your way, come up two-three-six-decimal-six." *Cricket* gave me their approximate current position and asked for them to push it up.

The call sign and the fact that they were F-4Es made me confident. Recently introduced, they were flown by very experienced crews, bombed very well, and were very reliable. Only much later did I learn that their idea of sport was randomly strafing Hmong villages.

I made a pass on the beleaguered squad at the apex of an open ridge of three fingers. There were seven men, two of whom jumped up waving as I passed by at 20 feet. Tufts of earth and foliage tripped up around them from streams of AK fire. Wonderful!

The weather improved. It was clear with a high gray overcast at about fourteen grand AGL, perfect for working fighters. Machete checked in and I briefed the dismal situation. The grabber was that we would work roll-in timing so that I was the target, when I rolled my U-17 violently. This meant I had to be on the treetops right on top of the bad guys. I first flew an ID pass over the friendlies as a reference.

Then I began making passes over each concentration of NVA , rocking the wings and rolling off into a valley as the inbound fighter called a release.

My backseater, having done his job in pointing out the situation, hunkered in the back seat, eyes closed, waiting to die I guess. I'm sure he didn't find this a cushy job at this point.

The official minimum safe distance for CBU-24 is 1,000 meters. We worked it up to 100 meters of the friendlies. We worked Mk-82 slicks [*low-drag bombs*] closer. Nineteen minutes, perhaps two dozen low passes later, the bad guys were gone. Kingpin said later that there were 60 bodies, many parts, and numerous blood trails. I was touched when the flight came down to cover me as I tried to do a BDA, strafing the shit out of the AK fire I encountered.

I was really low on fuel when I landed at Moung Soui on the way home — not at all amused to find that there was no fuel since, I learned later, the attaché's office had stopped supply since the place was "in imminent danger of capture." They had failed to pass that on to us. I turned drums on their sides and poured enough into an empty oil can to get a few gallons in the tanks, landing home near sundown.

Polifka continued with his flying experiences in a T-28 Trojan:

THE T-28 WAS, of course, a trainer — the "A" with 850 hp for the Air Force, and the "B" and "C" with 1,425 hp for the Navy. In 1961, the Navy gave up some 250 Bs and Cs to Project JUNGLE JIM. These were remanufactured as the "D" with six wing stations and two .50 cal. faired under the wings (625 rounds). It had TACAN, VOR, FM homer, FM, VHF, UHF. We're talking high tech. The Vietnamese got them, then they went to the RLAF and Thais, then, lastly, the Filipinos.

Although Dick Shubert flew a few sorties in the "Tango" [*T-28*] before he left (I was in the back seat on one), the real impetus came in the summer. I extended my tour three months and was checked out in late July. The *Ravens* didn't think much of the check-ride process. Follow-on *Ravens* got even in the check-out process by slowly moving the stick forward during a spin recovery, a maneuver that really accelerates the spin. The check pilot, I am told, barfed every time.

I flew 150 FAC missions in the T-28, almost all of them in the D-5 model, some in Bs and Cs. The T-28 was not a good FAC airplane. The low wing made VR difficult, and three hours of gas was it, period!!! But, it was great fun and, given good Intel, VR work was not essential. On my first mission in the Tango, about 5.5 hours total time, I was working a pair of A-1s blowing up some buildings on the south PDJ. I rolled in after Two's last pass, called a hooch, announced a rocket through the door, and from a slant range of 2,500 feet, did it. Pure luck, of course, but it impressed the shit out of the A-1. "How much time you got in that?" "Bout five, maybe six hours." Real silence.

A great advantage for me with the T-28 was having 28 rockets (we could carry 42, but usually didn't, there being a shortage of LAU-7 pods — a shortage for us, of course. Not that we ever jettisoned the things). Most targets were, in reality, area targets, troops spread around (or would soon be spread around), supply dumps whose precise location was an area, whole villages ("fortified structure complexes"), and so forth. With the Tango, you could brief the target and mark four corners in one pass, instructing the fighters to "fill the box." It worked well.

We tended to think the Tango quite speedy after the O-1. It cruised at 135 mph with ordnance, 175 without, and was limited to 250 downhill with stores, although I did 325 with no problem. My normal routine was to roll into a 30-degree dive (at 45, the speed built too fast) from 5,000 feet AGL, release rockets between 2,000 to 1,500, recover by 1,000 feet, and go over the top at 5,000 feet, then circling down during the strike, crossing through the target area at 50-100 feet to get BDA, moving along at 180-200 KIAS.

Eight Hmong/Lao flying T-28s were also at 20A, using the call sign *Chaophakaow* (*Tchaophakaow*) which translates as "Lord White Buddha," a call sign as well as a prayer. The most famous was Ly Leu, the only pilot whose death brought tears to my eyes. The last of these eight was KIA in 1972, after 3,000+ sorties. (Ly Leu, who was Vang Pao's son-in-law, was killed by a 12.7mm antiaircraft gun as he flew low, down near the tree tops, as he often did. As he struggled for altitude, the enemy gunner followed him up. The Americans attended his funeral, observing the Buddhist customs.)

By the summer of 1970, there were 24 *Raven* controller spaces. This peaked to 27 the following year, and then the number dwindled. Inexperienced volunteers came along, as it was hard to get seasoned O-1 FACs after the aircraft was withdrawn from the USAF inventory. A RLAF Forward Air Controller training program started to fill in as the USAF program was folding up.

Craig William Duehring, *Raven* 27, had been flying as *Allen* 17 at Duc Hoa, Ha Nghia Province, III Corps, with the 25th ARVN Division, from August 1969 to April 1970. As the war quieted down in 1969, he was looking for something more interesting. By April 1970, he was "sheep-dipped" and heading for Vientiane, Laos. Duehring related his late-war experiences:

THE NEXT DAY one of the guys flew in to pick me up and take me to Vientiane. There I met the finest leader I have ever worked for in the United States Air Force, Bob Foster. He was the Chief *Raven* and had more leadership in his little finger than most people will ever assimilate in their bodies in their entire life. I remember sitting in his office. By this time I picked up on what was happening. I knew there were five regions, and the hottest one was MR II. Usually guys spent three months up there, and if they survived, three months in an easier place like Savannakhet, and then they went home. Or it could be vice versa, you spent three months somewhere and then went up to 20 Alternate.

Foster said, "I'm going to send you to Lima Site 20A. My only instructions to you are to work as hard as you can and do the best possible job you can. If along the way you piss somebody off, you send them to me, because part of my job is keeping people off your back so you can work." I had never heard anybody talk like this. At that point I worshiped the man. He was a wonderful officer and we all respected and admired him.

So, I went downtown. At that time Long Tieng (20A) was under attack so the FACs had been moved to Vientiane. They did this at various times. Usually during the dry season we would get pushed back, and during the rainy season we would go forward. When it was wet, they couldn't resupply their troops. This was the dry season. A bunch of the guys were there, Harry Aderholt, Jeff Thompson, Hal Mesaris, and others. We worked out of a house in Silver City, a compound in Vientiane, and commuted to Long Tieng (20A).

The next day Tom Palmer flew me up to 20 Alternate in the backseat of a T-28. That was my first day in the war. We flew around and put in an airstrike some place. I was totally lost. There were mountains all around. We landed and he said this is going to be your home. "Now, let's get in an O-1 and I'll ride in the backseat." (I had flown the O-1 in Vietnam). I asked for a checklist and was told, we don't have checklists. "You do know how to fly, don't you? If you really need one, we can order it, but it will take a couple of months." So, I said never mind.

My first mission was the backseat of a T-28. The second mission was the front seat, with Palmer looking over my shoulder and helping me out — we put in some airstrikes and landed for lunch. Then Palmer said, "Now, this afternoon go out — I just want you to get some experience. I'll put the most experienced interpreter, Yang Be, in your backseat." He said, "Don't put any airstrikes in, you're too new. Just take these maps and get to know the lay of the land and where places are."

So we took off and Yang Be was chattering away on the radio and he says, "OK, now you go to Lima Site 26." Where's that? He said, "Up that valley," so we went there. He said, "Many enemy attack, big fight, troops in contact." I said, "I'm not supposed to put in any airstrikes." He said, "You must, there's no one else." OK. So the first flight of A-1s came up. I was very nervous. I was flying very high, afraid I would screw this up putting strikes in. A second set of A-1s came in. Six A-1s all together. Vang Be said, "Oh, very good, enemy fall back now." I didn't see much quite frankly. I could see the friendlies, but I was not low at all. We went home and later on I got a DFC for my first day. We had over 200 enemy killed during that action. I said, "Wow!"

Looking back, I think that given the mission at the time, we were as effective as anybody was in the war, man for man, because of the amount of work we did, and the fact that we were given the opportunity to use some judgment. Actually some folks did better than others. If you came up a little short in the judgment area, you were kind of escorted out of the country.

I was discouraged by the effects of fatigue on the men. Fatigue makes things seem worse than they are. I had an incident once with my backseater. . . . We were excited about going out and accomplishing something. I don't recall if it was taking a hill, or taking back some territory. I said, "Let's go, we can do it." He said, "Calm down, relax, you know, there will

Arrowhead Lake, a prominent landmark in the PDJ.
Byron Tetrick Collection

always be another day, another battle, another time we can take that hill. Remember, in another six months you'll be home. In six months to a year, if I'm still alive, I'll still be here trying to take that hill." What he was really saying in his own broken English was that if you intend to take that hill, and keep that hill, then I'll go and risk my life and do that, but if you're going to take it and then give it up the next dry season, when I saw my brother and my cousin and everybody killed going up this hill, then why should I do it?

This had a big effect on me. I became a lot more critical — and in fact quite critical — toward the end of my tour. I said to the guys, if you have a goal here, you want to go take the country back and give it to the good guys, fine. But if all you're doing is just marking time, staying in one place, everybody is dying for nothing.

During 1970-1971 there were ten *Ravens* at Long Tieng where the USAF had an operations center. In late 1971, the NVA, showing tremendous military strength, began a major dry season offensive. The *Raven* emphasis shifted from Long Tieng to Pakse on the banks of the Mekong River and the edge of the

Bolovens Plateau, which controlled the gateway to the south.

After four months at Long Tieng, Frank Kricker, *Raven* 40, went to Pakse where he was chief *Raven*:

WE FLEW AT elevations from 1,500 to 4,500 feet. The ridges were often obscured by low-hanging clouds. The PDJ had a large lake called Arrowhead Lake. On a routine day there was sporadic gunfire. It was hard to find the enemy. They were good at hiding. When you got them to come out, it was a good day. There were no dull days. It was always a different situation. We flew single-engine aircraft so we didn't operate after dark. Our aircraft couldn't survive a high threat. The constant firing of 14.5mm and 23mm guns was not a good thing for small aircraft.

We weren't exempt from the ROE but had almost *carte blanche* about what to attack. You'd know pretty much what was going on. Usually we had a native for a backseater. One day five monks were coming down a road in saffron robes. They didn't look out of place to me, but my backseater was going crazy. He said they are not monks, not our people. He knew something was wrong, so we fired off a salvo of rockets and the fighters (Laotian T-28s) checked in right behind us. The monks took off their robes, and out came their automatic weapons.

Our best air, the most accurate, came from the Laotian Air Force. They flew lower and slower. Anything you could hang on that airplane (T-28), they could put within 50 feet on the ground, regardless of the wind. However, they didn't have the response time, or ammo loads of the faster aircraft.

One day, the wind was blowing 50 knots. We just pointed our Bird Dogs into the wind and they took off. When we came back, we landed on the taxiway, into the wind, with a three-foot landing roll. There was no control tower. We just announced our intentions.

So we took off because it was important for us to get out there. We found a truck flooded and stuck in middle of a stream. It was in bad-guy territory. A perfect opportunity and we couldn't get any air. It was too windy for the fighters to take off. Since the USAF wasn't flying, we called up the Laos and said we need some T-28s. The Laotian pilots could care less about the high winds.

So here come three of them, all jabbering. They all had American names: *Hollywood*, *Cowboy*, and *Shit Hot*. They hear these words in English and that becomes their call sign. They tried to be very professional on the radio. One guy, his name was *Shit Hot*, checks in. "*Raven* 40, *Shit Hot* calling you." *Raven* 40, "Go ahead." *Shit Hot* said, "We have three airplanes, we are ready to bomb." *Raven* 40 said, "I have a target for you, a truck." "*Shit Hot* see truck, *Shit Hot* in, can do with one hand." (This was what they said when very cocky.) *Shit Hot* came around and rolled in; his bomb was way off. *Raven* 40 said, "*Shit Hot* that's ridiculous, you aren't even close." "Ah, yes," says *Shit Hot*. "It's very windy." So two comes in; he drops, and his aren't any better. Three comes in, and he's way off. They are correcting wrong.

So I said, "OK the wind is out of the north so here's what you do." *Shit Hot* makes noises with the mike of a pilot going back to basic bomb school. I told them how to aim. So, here he comes, wrestling with the problem. He drops the bomb and he releases too low and the bomb doesn't arm; but it goes through the cab of the truck and breaks the frame. The truck collapses. What a hit! He pulls off and I said, "Bull's eye, that is the best bomb I have ever seen." The second guy followed the same instructions and dropped at the right distance and it hit the stuff on the back of the truck blowing it up, and setting

Raven Frank Kricker loads rockets onto his O-1 in Laos, 1970.   Frank Kricker Collection

Pakse Air Base in March 1971. The *Ravens'* hooch is the large building in the center on the corner.

Frank Kricker Collection

Ravens flying toward Pakse Air Base in O-1 Bird Dogs in 1971.

Frank Kricker Collection

off *Shit Hot's* bomb which exploded. On a normal day they could strafe or bomb or hit any kind of a target, even a man running down the road. They were good. The T-28 was a perfect aircraft for that, bulletproof, and could take a lot of battle damage.

———————

In June 1971, Kricker was flying over the town of Paksong which was held by the enemy, looking for targets for three Navy A-7s that had just checked in with him. Usually the NVA guns were placed at the

edge of the town, but as Kricker went over Paksong at about 300 feet AGL, he was suddenly faced with a dual-mounted 12.7mm gun which was located by a building in the middle of town. Kricker said he could see the gunner's face.

The gun opened fire and Kricker felt his airplane coming apart as the shells ripped through it. His engine was hit, but even though losing oil pressure, Kricker managed to turn and pull off. The Navy jets were right behind him, spreading CBU and Rockeye (a thermite bomb) and they destroyed the gun.

Kricker crashed in a coffee plantation a few miles from town. The impact tore the wings off — the way you're supposed to make an emergency landing. Kricker saw blood and hoped it was his backseater who was bleeding, but it wasn't. Kricker's left toe was shot off, and a bullet had opened up his right hip. An Air America chopper showed up quickly and took him to a hospital in Udorn, where he had 40 stitches put in his leg. The episode changed Kricker's mind about them never getting him.

Kricker was awarded the Silver Star for flying a mission in support for two CIA men, each in an Air America Sikorsky H-34 Choctaw, who were putting a roadwatch team on Muong Mai, a mountaintop above where Route 7 entered the Bolovens. The main body of troops was being flown in by Air Force H-53s to land after their seven-man squads had secured the area. No one thought the enemy was there, but as the first chopper went in, it was hit by a remote-controlled rocket. The chopper was damaged and the copilot received a mortal wound. After the men had jumped out, Kricker escorted the H-53 to a safe emergency landing area.

The Air Force choppers, hearing all this, turned around and headed back to Udorn. But the

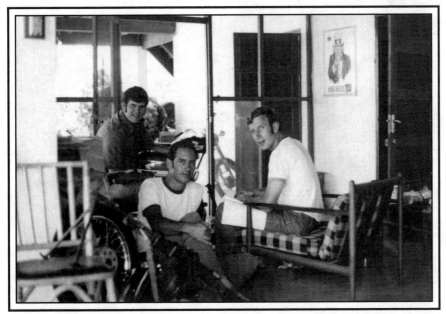

Living quarters at Pakse Air Base. L to r: Lloyd Duncan, Frank Kricker, and Jim Hix.

Frank Kricker Collection

Frank Kricker with Laotian Air Force pilots at *Raven* Headquarters at Pakse Air Ops Center.
Frank Kricker Collection

ground team in the landing area couldn't hold out without these troops. Kricker got on the radio and told the Air Force guys, "The mission's on. The guys are on the ground and nothing's changed." The choppers turned around and headed back to the mountain.

———— ✈ ————

Kricker flew his O-1 between them and the A-7s and T-28s he was directing for strikes. The second team landed under heavy fire. Even though Kricker said he wasn't worth a damn after being shot down, he still laid his life on the line in a desperate situation:

FATIGUE COULD BE a problem. You just get burned out. Some months we flew 125 hours. When we got tired, we went on vacation. We had blanket temporary duty orders and [*special*] black passports [*that allowed us to*] go where we wanted to, just get on an airplane and go, as long as we had things covered. They would buy us a ticket.

The hardest thing to deal with was the loss of life. It's tough when guys close to you get killed, and a lot of the guys in that program got killed. It wasn't a healthy deal. It was a nasty situation. The single toughest part of the job was the death of people close to you. It got so bad that, if a new guy came in, you would try not to get close to him. You couldn't afford to.

It was a crime what we did to the people of Laos. We told them we were going to do all this stuff and then we left. It was tough, you feel kind of guilty personally, like you let somebody down, and we really did. But, individually it wasn't our fault, but our country really left those people in the lurch. It was a brutal thing to do to those people. We threw them to the wolves.

———— ✈ ————

A "secret invasion," Lam Song 719, was launched by Vietnamese troops (Congress had prohibited the

Joe Scheimer, *Raven* 42, in Pakse, Laos, in 1971 with one of the *Raven* O-1 Bird Dogs. Transportation around the base was done primarily by motorcycle.
Joe Scheimer Collection

use of American ground troops in Laos) on 8 February 1971 in lousy weather. Its objective was to cut the Trail and seize the Laotian city of Tchepone, a supply hub that was situated strategically at a critical Trail junction. O-2s and OV-10s provided air support. English-speaking Vietnamese flew with the FACs to provide communication with the Vietnamese ground forces. USAF FACs, gunships, and flareships provided night support. However, this invasion failed miserably.

During 1971-1972, there was a new enemy offensive. The clandestine B-52 bombing of Laos, code name "Good Look" (the same name used to bomb Cambodia), failed to stop the enemy offensive. As the bombing escalated, so did the size of the Trail. By March 1972, the NVA had seven divisions in Laos, including tanks and 130mm artillery pieces, moving toward Vientiane.

Darrel D. Whitcomb, *Raven* 25 and *Nail* 25, was one of the last Forward Air Controllers to fly as a *Raven*, and then the last FAC to land when the cease-fire took effect in Cambodia. He began flying Forward Air Control at Nakhon Phanom, 23rd Tactical Air Support Squadron, in late February 1972. He FAC'd with them over the Ho Chi Minh Trail, and then back to Da Nang during the Easter Offensive until September 1972. Then Whitcomb transferred to Project 404, the Steve Canyon program, as a *Raven* FAC:

BY THEN knowledge of the *Ravens* was rather common. But, there's another twist to it as far as getting into the program. At the time there were quite a few applicants and only a few slots open. That program, like all the rest, was winding down. H. Ownby and I knew the guy who was doing the detailing for

Battle damage on a *Raven* O-1, May 1971. Frank Kricker Collection

Frank Kricker at a landing site up on top of a hill from Saravane on the Bolovens Plateau, with Khanti interpreter and First Lieutenant Thing (middle), B.G. 42 (battalion), in front of Air America fuel truck, 1970. Frank Kricker Collection

that, Jocko Hayden. He was a year or two ahead of us at the Air Force Academy. We ran into him one night and said, hey, we really want to do this, so he put our applications at the top of the pile. We both went to the *Ravens* in September 1972.

We FAC'd as *Ravens* for General Vang Pao up over the PDJ until the last day, 23 February 1973. We both flew that day and then came back and sat around for a week or so. Then I went back to the 23rd TASS as a *Nail* flying OV-10s. Initially when I was a

Nail, my call sign was *Nail* 70. When I went to the *Ravens* I was *Raven* 25. Then when I went back to the *Nails*, I became *Nail* 25. At that time the *Nail* FACs were flying in Cambodia. We flew combat over Cambodia until 15 August 1973. That was the last day. Since I had been there the longest, the squadron commander let me be the last guy to land. My last mission was south of Phnom Penh that day, and as I flew over the city on my back, I turned on my smoke generator and did a bunch of loops and aileron rolls. They reported that in *Newsweek* magazine. That was the end of our combat role.

The other FAC squadrons deactivated, so we ended up as the only FAC squadron in SEA, so if anything happened anywhere, we went. . . . We saw a tremendous amount of combat that way. I flew from the northern stretches of Laos, the Ho Chi Minh Trail, the northern part of South Vietnam, the southern part of North Vietnam several times (illegally), and all over Cambodia. I ended up seeing a tremendous amount of the war as a young lieutenant and captain just because of what the FACs did. We were ubiquitous to the war. The FACs were everywhere doing all sorts of missions. I developed a tremendous amount of aviation sense about what air power could do.

───────── ◦ψ◦ ─────────

Colonel Whitcomb was awarded the Silver Star — American's third highest medal for bravery in action — for his aerial skill and devotion to duty in a mission where he was shot and had an engine failure:

ON 10 DECEMBER 1972, I took off alone from 20A. I flew this mission as an O-1 *Raven* FAC working with the Hmong Forces of General Vang Pao near the Plain of Jars in northern Laos. I was directing airstrikes against trucks on the Plain when ABCCC (*Cricket*) called me and reported that a friendly unit was being overrun and needed my assistance. I proceeded over to the unit's last known position and contacted their Forward Air Guide, call sign *Pressure*. He reported that his unit had been hit by a superior NVA unit and had to abandon their position. He requested that I cover his unit as they retreated.

He did not have a map, but through the use of smoke and mirrors, I was able to locate the unit near Ban Sorn. They were moving to the west. Searching to the east, I detected a large NVA Force in hot pursuit. I requested two flights of fighters with napalm

from *Cricket* but was told that no ordnance was presently available. So, I began directing artillery fire at the pursuing NVA. This stopped their pursuit and burdened them with casualties.

I then flew ahead of the column and observed what appeared to be an ambush being set up approximately 800 yards ahead of the column. A quick radio check to *Lumberjack*, the SKY [*a Hmong term for American CIA advisors*] advisor, confirmed that there were no friendlies in that area so I moved my artillery fire into the ambush. As soon as the NVA realized what I was doing, they began firing at me, and I began taking hits. I was flying at about 1,500 feet AGL.

Again, I requested air support, but none was available. So I called in two sets of Laotian T-28s with Mk-81 bombs. I advised the unit of the ambush and they immediately turned south. As the unit turned, the NVA realized that I had foiled their plan, so they really opened up on me and my T-28s. As I pulled off a rocket pass, I felt something hit my aircraft. I saw no superficial damage, so I continued my airstrikes. Then I realized that I had taken a hit in the engine and was losing all of my oil. Another bullet had come through the right door and through the back seat, chest high. If there had been a backseater with me, he would have been killed.

My first reaction was to leave the area. But with the fighters overhead, I realized that I was in a position to really help my friendlies. So I continued the airstrikes and completely disrupted the NVA operation. I then departed the area just as my engine failed. Fortunately, I had enough altitude to glide to the edge of 20A. Later, I met the ground commander and the guys involved. He thanked me and stated that had his unit stumbled into the ambush, they might not have been able to escape to friendly lines without taking heavy losses. That was great because most *Ravens* never get the opportunity to meet the guys on the ground that they have helped.

I stayed in the squadron until March 1974. We had a training program for the new guys, and we still were ready for combat missions. We watched what the Communists were doing in Vietnam and along the Ho Chi Minh Trail. We practiced for the EAGLE PULL operation, which was the evacuation of Phnom Penh, Cambodia, and also a variant for Saigon.

I think the *Ravens* were generally effective because we worked closer to the fight than those in South Vietnam. We were very close and personal with the Hmong. Tactically, we were very effective in their particular battles. Strategically, I don't think we had much of an impact on the war. Since the war, it has become obvious that the whole thing up in Laos with the northern *Ravens* working for General Vang Pao, that all we were really doing was staving off the inevitable of the much more powerful North Vietnamese against the Laotians and Hmong in that area. When the North Vietnamese wanted to draw off air power from the Trail or South Vietnam, they would increase their level of activity in northern Laos and we would send more airplanes up there instead of using them elsewhere.

Tactics don't win wars, and our whole strategy was flawed. The *Ravens* were very dedicated and sincere in what they were doing, but ultimately it was all waste because it had no overall positive impact on the war. It was very sad. We led the Hmong people on to where they could not survive without our help. Ultimately, we just abandoned them, as we did the South Vietnamese and Cambodians. We declared victory and went home. After that the North Vietnamese swept through and took it all. A tragic waste.

H. Ownby, *Raven* 26, summed up the effectiveness of the *Ravens*:

THE *RAVENS* were the single most effective use of manpower and machinery that I have ever seen. With very limited cost involved, as far as machinery and the necessary support and ordnance expended, we covered more of an area and stood more as a block to the North Vietnamese Army moving into Laos, than all of the standing armies in South Vietnam. The Air Force didn't learn any lessons from that except that explicitly, they never wanted to do it again.

The people who do a good job in the field, in a war, normally don't have the skills that get you to the top of the corporate structure. And the kind of skills that get you to the top of the corporate structure are pretty worthless when it comes to combat. Fear gets you to the top. The Air Force doesn't want young officers to use initiative because then the commanders would lose control. The *Ravens* had no supervision. The people who volunteered for the *Ravens* were so highly motivated they didn't need a boss. They did suffer from extreme fatigue and being overworked.

The name of the game was plausible deniability. We had losses because we were in a high-risk environment, not because we didn't have supervision. We were stressed to the maximum. But, it was the best job that ever existed.

Darrel Whitcomb had another close call:

I WAS WORKING in northern Laos one day by myself a long way from Long Tieng, up around Lima Site 32. One of the Hmong pilots was up there, call sign *Nockateng* 502; his name was Xiong Ly Tou. (In Hmong, *Nockateng* means "swooping bird.") A 37mm gun opened up on me and just kept on hosing me. In an O-1 you don't move very fast. I tried to move away from the gun and he just kept hosing me. I called *Cricket* on the radio and asked if there was any ordnance available. "I've got a gun really hosing me that won't let go." *Cricket* didn't have any available ordnance, but *Nockateng* 502 was also on the frequency and he asked, "25, where are you?" I told him, and he came flying over. The gun is still shooting and even though I'm jinking, the shells are coming mighty close. I can feel them and hear the whosh, whosh. A pretty naked feeling.

So, 502 says, "25, I'm going to get that gun for you." He rolled in and fired two rockets and hit the gun. The problem was, I couldn't roll in on the gun because then there wouldn't be any tracking problem with me going straight at the gun. I think 502, flying a U-17 (a U-17 is like a bigger O-1, a Cessna 185), disabled the gun and killed the crew. Xiong Ly Tou saved my life. A few days later I had a chance to thank him. All he said was, "Hey, no sweat *Raven* 25." The guy saved my ass. I'll always remember that.

Some of my most effective missions as a FAC I flew as a *Raven*. We got better Intel. Generally we flew lower, and we could see things. One day I was working northeast of the PDJ with a Hmong in the backseat to interpret with the ground teams. All of a sudden I saw a long column of troops wearing pith helmets and green jackets. I had my backseater check to see if they were friendlies. He called on the radio and then told me, "No friendlies around here." It was a column of North Vietnamese soldiers coming into the area.

I called *Cricket* and said, "Have you got any air for me?" He said, "We have two Marine F-4s inbound with Mk-83 daisy cutters (1,000-pound bomb with daisy-cutter fuze extender on the nose)." This was perfect for blowing up people. So, I had the fighters check in on my frequency. I told Lead, "Get here as quick as possible, I've got troops in the open." He said, "Give me a hold-down," so he could steer right to me.

I told him, "I want you to make a wide orbit when you get near here, because as soon as I put down my mark, these troops are going to scatter." So I said, "I want you to orbit around to the north. When I tell you to roll in, I want you to roll in on me, and when I see you roll in I'm going to fire a mark and pull off to the side. I'm going to give you a correction and I want you to lay your bombs in there."

So, we're ready to roll. The columns haven't scattered yet. They're not paying much attention to me. So, we rolled in and I fired my rocket. I'll never forget the radio call. He said, "25, I've got you, I've got the mark, I've got the bad guys, get the f . . . out of the way." I broke, and he came right over the top of me and started plastering these guys. Lead and his wingman worked their bombs back and forth, taking out the column. That's the kind of work we did as *Ravens*. It was brutal.

Conversely, of all the *Ravens* who were shot down, none were ever recovered. One of the guys who was shot down was our commander, John Carroll. He was shot down by triple-A on my day off. The guys tried to get in and rescue him. His engine had been hit and he went down on the southern part of the PDJ not too far from an enemy bivouac area. Within minutes they had surrounded him. They were shooting. A couple of *Ravens* responded and got some helicopters in to rescue him. Steve Neal ran in some fighters and worked the area to get helicopters in. Carroll had landed the airplane on the side of a little knoll, and then got underneath the airplane to fight the bad guys off. One of the choppers actually managed to hover next to the airplane's wingtip. The door gunner told me later, "I could see the guy laying there — his body was in pieces. I wasn't going to run in just to grab body parts. It was obvious the guy was dead."

That night we got some hard Intel by intercepts when they had identified the pilot by name, so we knew he was dead. The next morning (this was November 1972) I was the first FAC up. As I came over the ridge, I knew just where his wreckage was. Using my binoculars, I could see enemy all around the airplane. I called *Cricket* and asked if they had any ord-

nance available. They had LGBs (Laser-Guided Bombs). I said, get them over here, and I had them put a 2,000-pound LGB right on the wreckage. It destroyed the wreckage and Carroll's body too (I assume).

I became very adept at finding and destroying the North Vietnamese 130mm long-range guns. The enemy was very clever at camouflaging them, but they would not cover their tracks. All you had to do was follow the tracks to find the guns. The guns were very dangerous to the little people, so when we were up we would always monitor a common radio frequency. As soon as anybody started taking fire from these guns, they would come on and give the position, and tell us taking incoming from a certain direction. We could look up at the PDJ and see the muzzle blasts 20 miles away. You could put your eyes on it and fly right to it. We would put in airstrikes to blow off the cover, after which we would get a laser-guided bomb to destroy the gun. I got ten or fifteen of those guns. General Vang Pao heard about that and thanked me personally.

After the Treaty was signed, and the agreements to end the war, we had a big meeting, like a war council, one night. General Vang Pao was very glum. He didn't think he could do anything without his air power. He talked about the enemy and how tricky they were. They will sit down at the table and discuss and make treaties, but underneath the table they are always kicking you. That last day I was north of the PDJ putting in strikes. But, when I left I still heard voices saying, "*Raven, Raven,* we need airstrike!" It was terribly sad. We all felt terrible.

Then I went to Cambodia and flew down there in support of the Khmer government until 15 August 1973 when the law said we had to be out of Cambodia. It was anti-climactic. We read the Intel reports and could see what the enemy was doing.

The Paris Agreement on Vietnam was signed 27 January 1973. Laos was excluded from the talks, along with South Vietnam and Cambodia. In the Vientiane Agreement of February 21, 1973, peace was restored in Laos and a cease-fire took effect. The last day of the war in Laos, officially, was 22 February 1973. U.S. bombing was halted and, with it, the activities of the *Raven* FACs and Laos-based Water Pump personnel. The U.S. ended nine years of air combat operations over Laos. However, there were

River crossings
near Tchepone,
Laos, 1966.
James F. McMurray
Collection

B-52 attacks in February and April 1973 to strike Communist forces on the Bolovens Plateau in southern Laos and on the Plain of Jars.

The *Ravens* were sent home. Sadly, General Vang Pao had to be extracted by the CIA, as the enemy encircled Long Tieng. He would never return to Laos; eventually he settled in the U.S. Laos was abandoned by its U.S. allies, and suffered a bitter fate.

Chapter 9

The Fast FACs in Southeast Asia

THE FIRST LARGE-SCALE use of jets as tactical airborne controller aircraft — or FACs — occurred during the Vietnam War. Pilots in the jet fighter-bombers from Ubon, Udorn, Korat, Takhli, and Da Nang, as well as U.S. Navy pilots flying the Ho Chi Minh Trail, didn't have enough fuel to fly around looking for targets. In addition, the enemy's air defenses presented too great a threat to the slow FACs in certain areas. The Fast FAC program was initiated to correct this, replacing the O-1, O-2, and OV-10 in high-threat regions.

*The TF-9J Cougar (a two-seat swept-wing version of the Korean War-vintage Panther jet fighter) was the first jet FAC/TAC aircraft and used the call sign **Condole**. It flew low-level road recce-type sorties with a full load of 20mm (200 rounds) and eight five-inch Zuni rockets. The missions usually lasted about 45 minutes with in-flight refueling from a Marine KC-135A Boeing Stratotanker only on an emergency basis.*

A Marine Fast FAC F-4 Phantom.

The *New Jersey* came on line in 1965 for OPER-ATION SEA DRAGON when American land operations needed more heavy fire-support. A faster aircraft was needed that could fly into North Vietnam in the areas called Route Packages (RP) 1, 2, and 3, where the battleship was bombarding shore targets. O-1s were too slow, so the mission was assigned to the Marines with Grumman TF-9J Cougars, call sign *Tango*.

Early in 1966, the U.S. Marine Corps 1st Marine Air Wing (MAW) Fast FACs used jets because of the threat of 23mm, 37mm, and 57mm antiaircraft guns along the Ho Chi Minh Trail, the A Shau Valley, central Laos, and southwestern North Vietnam. The O-1s that had been used for these missions could not operate safely at low altitudes in these areas. By August 1967, the Marines were using the more sophisticated TA-4F. Detachment 1 of the 416th Tactical Fighter Wing was assigned the responsibility for Fast FACs in June 1967. They operated from Phu Cat Air Base as a unit of the 37th TFW until May 1969 when they transferred to the 31st TFW at Tuy Hoa Air Base. (Other jet operational fields in Vietnam in 1968 were Da Nang, Chu Lai, Cam Ranh Bay, Phan Rang, Bien Hoa, and Tan Son Nhut.)

In 1967, the Air Force formed the first truly Fast FAC dedicated unit using a highly experienced group of pilots flying two-seat F-100F Super Sabres using the call sign *Misty*. The *Misty's* primary mission was to assist in the interdiction of enemy supply routes in North Vietnam and Laos using visual reconnaissance and airstrike control. Secondary tasks included conducting combat air patrol over downed aircraft and personnel, suppressing enemy antiaircraft artillery defenses, and photo reconnaissance. Because of the high degree of risk, the *Mistys* were volunteers who flew this mission for only four months.

A typical *Misty* mission, flown by a single F-100F, usually would entail several aerial refuelings from a KC-135A. Between refuelings, the *Misty* would sweep its assigned area of operations at low altitude, almost always under intensive ground fire, looking for targets of opportunity. After locating several — barges, trains, vehicles, flak, or missile sites — the *Misty* FAC would call ABCCC to request strike fighters. The orbiting ABCCC (a C-130 on station 24 hours a day) would then divert airborne strike fighters to rendezvous with the *Misty* FAC. The rendezvous would be at a specific "Delta" point designated by the *Misty*. Delta points were selected to

An Air Force F-100 Super Sabre drops general-purpose bombs on Viet Cong fortifications in South Vietnam, 27 June 1967. The F-100 was flown as a Fast FAC aircraft by Major George E. "Bud" Day.

cover all areas controlled by the enemy. Each had a specific number, such as Delta 27. The strike fighter made visual contact with the FAC, who then marked the target with Willie Pete rockets and controlled the attack by radio.

Major George E. "Bud" Day

Major (later Colonel) Bud Day described his job as the first commander of the *Misty* Fast FACs:

IT WAS THE luck of the draw. I got a call from Seventh Air Force to talk about it. By the time I got down there, it was already underway. They had made up their minds it was going to happen, regardless of what I had to say. I wasn't sure that flying the F-100 around at 500 knots you would see a tremendous

amount. I had been in the fighter-bomber-nuke business over in Europe from 1955 to 1959, and the same business in SAC with F-84s. Down low you spend an awful lot of time watching the ground, just making sure you don't run into it. So I wasn't sure it would really work out that well. We decided instead of flying really low level, we would stick to a 3,000- to 3,500-foot altitude. You lost a little bit of the surprise, but it kept you out of rifle fire. You could see well enough from 3,000 feet. Every time you did something it was a trade-off. You're better off to be at 100 feet if you want a good look at something, but you get an awful lot of distractions. . . .

We didn't fly in pairs. That was one of the problems of the light-plane FACs. They had been flying in pairs up there and that's how we found out about the SAM threat. The Fast FACs came into business because of this. In March 1967, two *Covey* FACs were coming out of North Vietnam, flying a real loose-spread formation, probably about 100 to 150 feet apart. A SAM was fired at them and one was shot down. The other guy just happened to look up to see this huge orange fireball and the disappearing aircraft. That brought about the demise of the slow FAC up there.

These guys who conceived the idea of a high-speed FAC had talked to Dale Sweat, Seventh Air Force DO [*Director of Operations*], and Skip Stanfield, assistant DO. They made up their minds to try the F-100. Initially, it was called project COMMANDO SABRE. The F-4 was less than an ideal FAC airplane. The F-105 was out of the question because it had such a big turn radius. The loss rate of the F-105 was so high that it was out of the question to get it for a speculative mission. So, the F-100 was chosen.

We got underway in late April. I didn't have a real high degree of confidence that it would work all that well, but much to my surprise it did. I wasn't quite certain that you could see at 500 knots. You had to be at that speed to make that thing survivable. The loss rate was terrible, even flying at a reasonable altitude.

Day tells about his most interesting mission:

BEFORE WE STARTED operating up there, basically the North Vietnamese brought about anything down the Trail they wanted. I found out one night about a week later, when I got shot down and captured, and went up on the north side of the river that ran from Mu Gia to Dong Hoi, that there was a lot of truck movement south. I saw more than 300 trucks on the roads. They had moved a lot of gear, not only into South Vietnam, but into Laos and Cambodia. This included SAM 2s and "beaucoup, beaucoup" guns, as well as a lot of fuel, ammo, and those things people need to wage war.

This mission, where we killed three SAMs, was mid-August, about a week before I got shot down (26 August 1967). I knew there were quite a few of them but these were up north of an east/west line coming out of Dong Hoi. There was water and ferries where you had to get across the river. I wasn't really sure they had moved SAMs down across the river. I had killed one on a trailer that had broken down. They had to leave it out in the open. It was south of the

east/west line out of Dong Hoi. I knew they were moving them, but the roads were poor, some were just trails, so I had trouble with the idea of moving a SAM. The SAM trailer was about 50 feet long, and the SAM about 37 feet long, which was roughly as long as an F-100.

I was coming on station when a guy who worked for me, Barney Dalton, called me and said, "I've got a target up here for you." We had killed a bulldozer that was working late one morning, which was highly atypical. It was a great marker. He said, "Up by the bulldozer on the north/south road, just to the east of there I think I saw some barrels of fuel laying in the open on the road." That was odd, because usually they are careful. So, I got up there and put the field glasses on it from 7,000 feet. They started shooting at us pretty good, so I figured it must be a decent target from the flak that we were taking. I departed the area, made a call, and got some F-4s out of Da Nang loaded down with rockets and high-drag bombs.

Then I came back and made a low-speed pass across this thing. It did look like barrels. I got a lot of flak from that pass. When the F-4s arrived, I pointed out the bulldozer, which was easy to see, and then I tossed a mark in there and told this F-4 to depart west to east. It was a north/south road and I wanted him to take a heading of about 130 [*degrees*] when he dropped. If he was a little short or long it would have a chance of impacting in the woods right beside the road. So, he came through and fired a pod of rockets. It was really a poor pass. His rockets were way short, probably 80 or 90 feet west of the road, but even so, there was a ball of fire. Obviously it was gas storage. So, I told him it was a great pass. He really got shot up. It was a miracle they didn't shoot him down with all the guns turned on him. Now, I knew there was something really good there.

Some camouflage was blown away on the east side of the road. You could see four or five trucks. There was netting all the way across the road. There were 20 trucks on the east side of the road. I had the F-4s go through some more. As long as they dropped in the vicinity of the road, something blew. We had smoke up to 8,000 or 9,000 feet and fires burning up to 250 feet in the air. We kept opening up this road, which took a 90-degree turn over to the east into a village. We were not supposed to bomb civilian targets at that time. I wasn't aware it was a village, but in retrospect, I would have burned it out anyway, just because of what was there. Near the village was a huge camouflaged area, crescent-shaped, which was a truck repair depot. I put about eight F-4s in until they ran out of ammo after getting 17 or 18 trucks, and jillions of gallons of gas. The last one through opened up this kind of semi-circle.

Then I got some F-105s and put them in. More of the camouflaged road was blown away and more trucks were destroyed. When the second F-105 came through, there were three bright orange explosions, which were the SAMs. When a SAM goes off, there is no other explosion that looks like that. The fourth F-105 came through and blew up another SAM, so apparently there were SAM trailers in the woods. We killed three SAMs and probably more than 30 trucks and jillions of gallons of gas. Then a jeep popped out of the conflagration and headed east. I chased him. There were a bunch of truck carcasses on the road and not much room for him to maneuver. I came around in a big sweeping turn from the east to the south and fired a Willie Pete, which went right through his windshield. It knocked the guys out of the jeep, which blew up. That was probably the best mission I had up there.

Some missions weren't that productive, but all did some good. I think we paid our way better than a lot of units that did anything up there. We got to know the area so well and what the targets looked like, even when covered up. We knew minor changes like the guy noticing those barrels. The operation went on until we ran out of F-100s. Then they cranked up the other Fast FACs, *Laredo*, *Stormy*, and the units developed their own FACs.

When I first started, they didn't want us rolling in on any targets and shooting them up. Those restrictions weren't really the right idea. You had to have flexibility in the job, so that changed. They began to let the FACs go ahead and strike targets. It's a mixed bag. You need to have people with good discipline about what they are doing. The idea really is for the FACs to find targets and put other people in on them. Just going in and strafing really increases your loss rate, but there were times when you just had to do it, if the target was moving. But the majority of times, it was not a fleeing target. You were far better off putting the F-105s and F-4s in and let them do the work because that was what they were up for that day. Then you would survive to work more flights on other targets. At the end, the FACs were very aggressive, going airplane to gun. I never was really big on that unless there was something pretty strategic about the position of the guns. A $4,000 gun wasn't worth losing an airplane worth about 200 grand. I

didn't mind striking guns when you had a lot of airplanes at one time, where you could really mix it up and give them trouble tracking multiple targets. Those were cases when things were pretty much in your favor. I didn't mind going against them, but one-on-one was a losing proposition.

Major Day was shot down 26 August 1967 on his 67th mission, while striking a missile site near the DMZ. He was doing about 500 knots as he started his pass with full fuel. His F-100 took a hit in the aft section. He started to go "feet wet" (out to sea) but the controls failed as the aircraft started to pitch over in an outside loop.

Day and the pilot in the front, who was getting his first ride, ejected. A Jolly Green rescue helicopter picked up that man and then headed for Day, who had fallen about a mile and half away. By the time the Jolly Green reached Day's location, it was too late. He had been captured by Viet Cong militia. His right arm was broken in three places and his left knee badly sprained. He was taken to prison camp, interrogated, and tortured. He escaped and evaded enemy patrols on his way toward South Vietnam, but was later captured again, sustaining more wounds. The latter part of the citation for his Medal of Honor reads:

> He was returned to the prison from which he had escaped and later moved to Hanoi after giving his captors false information to questions put before him. Physically, Col. Day was totally debilitated and unable to perform even the simplest task for himself. Despite his many injuries, he continued to offer maximum resistance. His personal bravery in the face of deadly enemy pressure was significant in saving the lives of fellow aviators who were still flying against the enemy. Col. Day's conspicuous gallantry and intrepidity at the risk of his life above and beyond the call of duty are in keeping with the highest traditions of the U.S. Air Force and reflect great credit upon himself and the U.S. Armed Forces.

These volunteer pilots who flew these challenging *Misty* missions were all highly qualified. During three years in Southeast Asia, 160 pilots flew more than 21,000 combat hours in the program. The suc-

Smoke rockets explode for airstrike near Tchepone, Laos, a major NVA road hub.
Jim Stanford Collection

cess of *Misty* led to the activation of several other high-speed FAC programs.

Primary control of all these aircraft was exercised by *Hillsboro*, the C-130 ABCCC, which got its authority directly from the Seventh Air Force. The out-country FACs provided raw Intelligence which was analyzed in real time through the ABCCC, resulting in immediate airstrikes when conditions permitted. But with the bombing halt of 1 November 1968, Marine Air Wing out-country activity concentrated on the interdiction of supply routes in Laos, especially STEEL TIGER South. This concentration of the air war on the Ho Chi Minh Trail was almost totally hidden by official secrecy.

The area around Tchepone straddled the turn-off point for the first major easterly road on which the enemy moved supplies into South Vietnam. The twisted web of jungle roads that made up the Ho Chi Minh Trail sneaked through the mountainous country of supposedly neutral Laos. To protect their routes, the NVA started using mobile, radar-controlled 57mm guns to travel along with their major shipments. Even heavier guns were used at choke points — and lighter 37mm were all over the place. One Marine unit and seven Air Force units flew the hostile environment of STEEL TIGER in Laos from one end to the other on a daily basis.

In August 1968, the *Stormy* FACs were formed at the 366th TFW in Da Nang. They were the first to fly the McDonnell Douglas F-4D Phantom in this role.

By the spring of 1969, the *Manual* FACs were routinely flying 200 sorties a month to provide continuous daylight coverage of the STEEL TIGER area in Laos. Several refueling cycles with a KC-130F Hercules tanker made this possible. The *Tiger* FACs, 388th TFW, flying F-4Es, operated from Korat AB, Thailand. FACs with call signs *Falcon*, *Laredo*, and *Owl* were also flying F-4s.

Ron Schuh, a *Falcon/Laredo* Fast FAC, related his experiences:

I WAS A FAST FAC flying F-4Ds. Our call sign *Falcon* was changed to *Laredo* in the summer of 1969. These were different names for the same organization out of the 432 TRFW at Udorn RTAFB. The *Falcon* program started in the spring of 1969 and worked airstrikes in Northern Laos [*for OPERATION*] BARREL ROLL. In the summer of 1969, the unit's name was changed . . . its mission was expanded to include central Laos (STEEL TIGER). Our F-4Ds had a SU-23 gun on the center line and Willie Pete rocket pods on the inboards.

Doing VR [*Visual Reconnaissance*], we flew as low as we could get. It depended on the defenses, what the target was that we were trying to see. I would go as low as 100 feet if I had to. You had to be smart about things. You obviously didn't want to run down the various routes. You didn't go by a target a multiple number of times if they were shooting at you. Then you stayed higher or did something different; but usually the first time through you got down quite low. Our airspeed was approximately 450 to 500 knots. You'd be surprised at how well you could see. It was just a matter of knowing what to look for. We would do a "butterfly" pattern. You would make a left turn, drop, and then roll to the right to look out the right side. Then climb up just a little bit and roll left and come back down. You're not keeping a constant altitude. You are varying it a hundred or so feet, up and down. It varies with the terrain. It's not that difficult if you know what you are looking for, like trucks, tanks, storage areas. Obviously there was a lot of stuff that we missed.

We had the advantage of having a tactical reconnaissance fighter wing with quite a few squadrons of reconnaissance RF-4Cs. They assigned an RF-4 to us, call sign *Bullwhip*, so we could direct photo reconnaissance of certain areas. We could look at the photographs ourselves as soon as they were developed. We had photo Intelligence that other people didn't have. If we saw something of interest when doing our reconnaissance, we could give *Bullwhip* the coordinates and he would go and run a strip of photos. We had photo Intelligence guys dedicated to our operation. Also, if they found something interesting in the photos, they could quickly radio somebody who was flying and tell them about the target.

A lot of things you did were based on your knowledge of the area and its air defenses. We spent a lot of time flying very low looking for things, unless we had specific targets to work an airstrike on. Then you would be up higher to rendezvous with the fighters. You would mark it and stay high to direct the strike until it was time to go down and do some BDA.

The Fast FACs were good for what they did in the high-threat area. We were generated to work these areas. The *Nails* and other guys couldn't survive in the high-threat area.

U.S. Marine Corps *Playboys*

Early in June 1969, the call sign of the Marine Fast FAC unit was changed to *Playboy* by Lieutenant Colonel Richard Hebert, named after the F4-U Corsair crews that flew similar missions during the Korean War. By July, there was a change in the min-

imum altitude of 2,500 feet AGL. Previously, it was common to stretch this restriction. Now the aircrews were permitted to utilize whatever altitude was expedient and sensible for the situation. Actually, flying very low was prudent; pilots who knew the area and flew at 500 feet AGL or below were seldom fired on because they were in and out of a gunner's envelope almost before he could react. And in August 1969, the low-altitude maneuvering was made easier as Pratt & Whitney J-52-P-8 engines with an additional 700 pounds of thrust were added to the TA-4Fs.

The *Playboys* could adjust for Grumman A-6 Intruders using radar offset-aim point delivery tactics in low-ceiling (500 feet) conditions. The A-6s could orbit above the clouds while the *Playboys* would slip through a hole in the clouds and navigate at 200 to 500 feet to find and pinpoint targets.

The enemy used visual acquisition with its manually tracked antiaircraft guns, and therefore could not follow jets at speeds over 400 knots that were maneuvering in three dimensions pulling up to three Gs. These guns — considered a medium threat — had forced the slow FACs up to operating altitudes of 8,000 feet or more AGL.

In a high-threat environment, the enemy had radar-tracking and surface-to-air missiles. The greater the threat, the higher the speed the jets had to maintain. But higher-rate turns and vertical and directional changes would impose higher Gs on the aircraft.

Laser-guided ordnance thus was one of the major breakthroughs in FAC operations and enabled FACs to accurately set up interdiction points. The "Pave Knife" early model designators were perched on the left cockpit rail of the F-4s. The disadvantage was that this blocked the backseater's vision out of that side of the aircraft.

To eliminate that problem, the next generation, the "Pave Spike," was located in the left forward missile well. The later "Pave Nail" program provided excellent data for the laser-guided bomb system that became so successful in OPERATION DESERT STORM.

USMC pilot Lieutenant Colonel Richard Hebert commanded the *Playboy* Fast FACs from 1969 to 1970 during STEEL TIGER, and planned, directed, and supervised the deployment of his squadron's Skyhawk and Phantom jets for combat missions out-country. His crews controlled strikes along the Ho

Chi Minh Trail, destroying trucks, road-building vehicles, and heavily defended targets including anti-aircraft weapons.

Colonel Hebert described the *Playboy* Fast FAC mission:

I WAS *PLAYBOY* One in Vietnam. My people were hand selected. They had to have a minimum of six months left to go on their tour in Vietnam and 100 jet combat missions. They had to pass my screening. They had to volunteer and go through an intensive training program, which included five airborne hops, three in the back seat and two in the front seat. If they passed muster, we designated them a TAC(A) [*Tactical Air Coordinator Airborne*] and they were assigned a *Playboy* call sign with a numerical digit (some kids used the year they graduated). After they flew 200 missions, I retired their call sign permanently so no one could ever use it again.

We had quite a roster of *Playboys*. Included was the number-one aviator in the Marine Corps, a three-star general, Keith Smith. He had just taken over as the Deputy Chief of Staff for Air.

Our *Playboy* name and bunny started back in World War II. *Playboy* magazine was going to bring suit against the Marine Corps for using the name *Playboy* as well as the bunny logo. We told them it was kind of asinine to bring suit, particularly during wartime in a combat situation. There was an out-of-court agreement that we would alter the profile of the bunny and they would allow us to continue using it. We did and the bunny on our aircraft has one ear sort of cocked, so that really didn't infringe on their trademark. We had a big party in Da Nang and we asked *Playboy* to send napkins and all the favors and things, which they graciously did in a big care package.

The airborne FAC mission refined itself and developed into Fast-mover FACs and slow-mover FACs because of the difference in the degree of hostility in a particular environment. Initially, it started out with O-1s for observation, naval gunfire spotting, artillery spotting and target marking, and strike control, which was splendid in-country in South Vietnam because all you had to contend with was small arms. Then when you got out on the Trail and over in Laos you were getting the 23s, 37s, 57s, and 85s and that's when they upgraded from the O-1 to the O-2. The O-2s flew an awful lot of out-country hops until they started taking intense fire and the damage rate was really getting up there, especially the *Coveys* and

Nails. Some went from O-1s to O-2 to OV-10s. The *Nails* were flying the OV-10s when I went out-country, but they had a base altitude of 7,500 feet.

We were operating down between 500 and 800 feet. We had the speed advantage, and I proved to my pilots that the incidence of hits decreased with an increase in speed. The average manually aimed AAA gun couldn't fire on a target moving in excess of 350 to 400 knots unless he was an expert gunner, so at that low altitude we just tried to maintain 400 knots on the Trail. We became very proficient in being able to spot targets in just a fraction of a second.

I established another criterion. A gunner on a manual AAA weapon, if he sees a target, or potential target, gets very tense and will be very alert for about ten minutes, but if there is nothing to satisfy that anxiety, he will relax. So, we never made successive passes unless ten minutes had expired between them. If you saw a potential target, you would mentally note where it was and then 10 or 20 minutes later come back for a second look.

The guys who didn't follow my rule, but pulled up and came back around for a second look, usually got shot at. One guy who was supposed to relieve me actually got killed, taking a round between the eyes. Keith Smith violated my rule and took a 37mm hit to the main landing gear so it was dangling and he had to divert into Ubon. The guys who went by the rules that we had determined were valid didn't have any problems. The ones who were out there doing their own thing had to answer for it, usually.

The A-6s with 500-pound bombs could operate in all kinds of weather. We would get down under the overcast at about 500 to 800 feet. The North Vietnamese thought no one would be flying because of the overcast, but we were down below it. We would spot the NVA and scramble the A-6s out of Da Nang. We'd send them to a specific TACAN/DME, pick them up, and put them over the area. Then we would let them set up their bombing track based on radar-significant navigational points. We would have them drop one bomb to mark and then we would tell them if it was left or right of target and they would adjust just like artillery. They were above the overcast and we flew underneath it. We could put them on target and it was very effective. It made the North Vietnamese be more surreptitious in their daytime activity regardless of the cloud ceiling and in-flight visibility.

I would do the same thing leading in flights of Air Force F-4s. I spotted a bulldozer working on a road at the end of a box canyon. The ceiling was about 600 feet, visibility three miles in drizzle. I told these guys, "If you want to follow me in, when I pull up, you pull up." They said, "We'll have a go at it." The two of them got behind me. I took them up the valley, and I fired a Zuni rocket (five-inch high-velocity rocket with a smoke head in it, very accurate, best for small targets) out far enough so they could visually acquire it and press in. They were about a mile up the Trail from me. When I put the rocket in, they went just below this ridge line where the dozer was working and saw it so I just had them open up. By that time I had pulled up, and they saw where I had started my pull. We popped out at about 3,500 feet AGL where it was clear on top. It demanded a lot of pilotage [*navigation by reference to checkpoints*] but it wasn't anything stretching yourself out to the end of the envelope, particularly with the jet.

To maintain the element of surprise, we would tell the ABCCC *Hillsboro* to go ahead and anchor the flight at angels [*altitude in feet*] 25,000 at some TACAN radial and DME. We would go up and rendezvous with them and give them a target briefing on a discrete frequency. When everyone had all the information they needed as far as target and safe bailout areas, direction and distance to nearest landing area or "feet wet" or whatever, we would start a big, lazy spiral down in trail and they would keep us in sight, leveling off at 14,000 feet, because that is about the limit of visual acuity for someone on the ground on an absolutely clear day. Other times in haze they could descend to 5,000 to 7,000 feet. So we'd get them down and then we would make one pass for our marking run. All they needed was a roll-in heading and a pull-out heading. It was very effective that way.

We did all the BDA for the ARC LIGHT B-52s. They were so high all they could see was jungle. Often when we were out on patrol, *Hillsboro* would say we had an ARC LIGHT at such and such coordinates. Would you go there and give us a BDA? We'd tell them how far off target they were. They were not effective. They were generating missions and sorties and firing off 750-pound bombs. The most effective bombing was FAC-controlled bombing against moving or stationary targets or troops in the open.

The fast-mover effort differed in the Marine Corps from the Air Force because of our artillery spotting and gunfire spotting capability, which the Air Force didn't have. In a pinch they could do it; anyone can spot artillery. But there were distinct differences in

the missions. The biggest boon to the overall effort was the Airborne Command and Control Center [*ABCCC*]. I sent my pilots to Udorn for an orientation flight out on the ABCCC so they could see how it worked — all the teletypes, gear, and how everything was coordinated. We started to use these in the 1968 battle of Khe Sanh because that required 24-hours overhead air for tactical air support, and also for aerial support like the C-130s and C-123s for re-supply, because the Marines were under siege, totally cut off. The only way the Marines at Khe Sanh persevered and survived was because of air support. You had to have a central command authority. The C-130 was ideal.

Whenever we were operating airborne, I had a dedicated C-130 *Playboy* tanker that had to be on-station orbiting about 25 to 50 miles off the coast at Hue. We would fly a double mission going back and forth, low level, for about 45 minutes. Then we would pop up to go out and tank and make successive tankings. If we had a real hot situation like a RESCAP [*Rescue Combat Air Patrol*] for a downed pilot where we had to remain on station longer, we would pull our tanker in closer. They didn't like that but we got them as close to the border as we could. That happened on many occasions.

The Air Force had probe refueling capability and we had the drogue. We tried to get them to equip one of their KC-135s that orbited over Thailand with a drogue, and occasionally they would do it. Sometimes guys got heavy wing hits with the fuel just pouring out, and it took the tanker just to get them back. The F-100F had a probe that could use our basket.

When a fighter was shot down, the Fast FAC with the most fuel would take charge of the RESCAP until a *Sandy* or A-1 *Hobo* aircraft arrived. Slow FACs, such as *Nails* or *Ravens*, might participate by operating at a higher altitude to observe and act as a radio relay while the strike aircraft delivered ordnance as necessary.

As a combined joint combat effort, the Fast-mover FAC program functioned extremely well. The ultimate command was Seventh Air Force out of Saigon, but direct command was exercised by the 313th out of Udorn that had control of the ABCCCs. It was Army, Navy, Air Force, and Marine Corps all participating to some degree. A tremendous number of daily sorties were dedicated to the out-country war. Aerial photos generated potential targets. The electronic sensor command at NKP had EW-121s [*Lock-*

Cargo for Marines at Khe Sanh is shoved off a USAF C-123 Provider of the 315th Air Commando Wing, as a Marine passenger, who has just emerged from the aircraft, dashes for a nearby bunker. The threat of mortar attacks at Khe Sanh kept everyone on the run during loading and off-loading operations during March 1968.   USAF

USAF pilots in a C-130 Hercules transport make a LAPES (Low Altitude Parachute Extraction System) drop of food and ammunition to U.S. Marines at Khe Sanh. The LAPES method allowed the crews to fly in, drop supplies without landing, and fly out, allowing more cargo to be moved into Khe Sanh in a shorter time. The LAPES method was used as a part of the air resupply efforts into the Marine position, 16 February 1968.   USAF heed Super Constellation] orbiting and picking up sensors to monitor trail activity. Infrared sensors detected body heat in addition to sensitive sound detectors. The Trail information was passed to NKP who relayed it to Saigon. It might be a day or two before it got to the operating commands, so I sent my Intelligence people to NKP, got with their working people, and set up code so we could call up at 4:30 a.m. and obtain the latest sensor activity for that night. Our Ops duty officer would go and plot it, so our first flight at 5 a.m. had Intel only 45 minutes old. We could fly to these areas and start putting strikes in. It was an extremely effective operation.

We assigned generic names to primary locations. Primarily references were called Delta Points — like Delta 12, which was also four corners because of the way the roads came in on the Ho Chi Minh Trail network. We used TACAN/DME off NKP. We had airborne TAC/DME so we could give the Air Force steers to our position. For example, George Washington's head was where the river came around like Washington's head profile. It was northwest of Delta 45. There was elephant's foot (a bend in the river), the parrot's beak, and near Khe Sanh an area up on a plateau called Sunnybrook Farm because it was like a huge pasture (it was elephant grass). You could say meet me at GW's head and people knew just where to go.

The North Vietnamese were masters at camouflage and often fooled the FACs. The NVA could build a canopy over a 50-mile segment of road. You would see a road go into the jungle and disappear. It was hard to detect. The guys who flew there on a daily basis could tell if a stream had been crossed. There was wet soil on one side. Bridges were built below the surface of the water. Pilots knew every nook and cranny so if there was ever anything out of place, they perceived it. Visual recce really paid off. You didn't have to go through the routine of having an aerial photo and an interpreter who really didn't know what he was looking for. The Marines had their own photo lab. The backseater had a camera with a telephoto lens and used 1,000th of a second. The film was processed immediately after the plane landed.

They had a dedicated RF-4B which could, if we wanted it, go out and take detailed photos. We could scramble him as necessary. Our photo room was adjacent to the ready room in the briefing area. Quite often, with a hot target, we would read the photos wet, and by the time the guys went to the aircraft and

cranked up, we had dry photos they could take with them. It was a very smooth-running operation.

———————⊛———————

During September 1969, *Playboy* developed a night Deep Air Support (DAS) tactical mission. The enemy gunfire was most intense at dusk in areas where nightly road repair or movement of supplies was to occur. The enemy gunners would take advantage of VR aircraft when they were silhouetted against the sky while the ground had already darkened. It was hard to pinpoint the gunfire under these circumstances. The *Hammer* technique was developed. TA-4Fs were sent to an area of suspected activity at twilight. The *Playboy* would come through the target area at maximum speed at a very low altitude, using his knowledge of the terrain to achieve surprise. When gunfire erupted, he would drop flares and then execute a high G pull-up to a perch from which he could locate the target and quickly dive down to mark it with a smoke rocket.

Two F-4B strike aircraft, escorting the TA-4F at a higher altitude, would then roll in on the flare-marked target with gun-killing ordnance. The fourth aircraft in this *Hammer* flight was a photo RF-4B that would make a high-speed photo recce pass within a minute of when the ordnance exploded. This gave excellent BDA.

The first *Playboys* to be shot down were Captain James Buffington and Major Robert Miecznikowski in July 1969. A Jolly Green based in Thailand rescued them after they had spent six hours on the ground.

Some *Playboy* aircraft sustained hits. All but one returned safely to base. On 27 December 1969, Major Richard Lewis and 1st Lieutenant Paul Phillips were forced to eject in Central Laos, just south of Tchepone. Air Force Jolly Greens made a successful pick-up 23 hours later, after an intensive antiaircraft artillery suppression effort.

In nearly a year of continuous operation, the loss of Larry Robinson was the first. On 5 January 1970, Major Larry Robinson was killed in action escorting a *Playboy* TA-4F on a modified (daylight) *Hammer* mission. Flying an F-4B, he rolled in on an active gun position that had been marked by Lieutenant Bud Garske. Several 37mm guns in the area fired at him. One made a direct hit in the cockpit. Both pilot and backseater went in with the aircraft.

In early March 1970, while on a VR/TAC(A) mis-

Mark Berent's last mission as a *Wolf* FAC.   Mark Berent Collection

Wolf Forward Air Controllers

The *Wolf* FACs were daylight controllers flying F-4D/Es from Ubon AB, Thailand, to stop traffic on the Ho Chi Minh Trail. Racing at 400 to 500 mph while twisting and turning at low altitude, they would crisscross back and forth across the Trail and zoom around the peaked karst. In spite of their speed and quick turns, they could spot targets and notice any change in the landscape that would give them a clue as to enemy whereabouts. They would deliberately maneuver in front of enemy guns to make them come up and give away their positions.

One *Wolf* FAC would relieve another after a four-hour mission. If he had enough fuel, he would join up and show him new enemy hiding places. The *Wolf* FACs talked to each other on a common channel, so that even while one was heading home, they could provide information. There was always a *Wolf* on the Trail, which proved to be very effective in stopping daylight traffic.

"*Papa Wolf* III," Mark E. Berent, first wrote of his FAC experiences in a February 1971 *Air Force Magazine* article entitled, "A Group Called *Wolf*." He reiterates much of that story here:

IT'S BEEN NEARLY 30 years since I flew my last mission from a fighter base in up-country Thailand, yet the memories — some sweet, some bitter — are all so intense that I can recreate them at any given moment in my mind.

Combat makes indelible marks on a man's spirit. Your political philosophy undergoes a rethink, and then, eventually, comes the inner affirmation, more solid than you ever thought Stateside, when you know why you are there.

A pilot had to have at least 100 combat missions and be a volunteer, to be a part of the tightly-knit fraternity of FACs. Our call sign was *Wolf*, and we wore a simple "*Wolf* FAC" flash patch on the shoulder seam of our flight suits. I was called *Papa Wolf* on the ground and *Wolf-Oh-One* while airborne. Our F-4 combat units didn't exist on any organizational chart, and had no unit manning document. But we were supported by the four fighter squadrons of the famed 8th Tactical Fighter Wing, the Wolfpack, who supplied the aircraft, maintenance, and weapons people, as well as the carefully selected, full-

sion, Lieutenant Colonel George Ward was killed by a single enemy bullet that entered his cockpit. A pilot in the backseat, 1st Lieutenant Duncan Higgins, flew the aircraft home. Ward and Robinson were the only two *Playboy* pilots killed in action. Two others were wounded seriously while flying, Major Dorsie Page and Captain Donald Swaby.

Later *Playboy* activity shifted to South Vietnam where a third aircraft was lost. Captain R. T. Rasmussen and Lieutenant Chip Mills ejected from their TA-4F in the A Shau Valley in the summer of 1970. Their rescue was dramatic. For six hours there was a running gun battle between the enemy, the Sandy A-1 RESCAP aircraft, and the Jolly Green door gunners. The Jolly Green sustained 15 hits before picking up the *Playboy* crew.

The *Playboy* FAC program terminated in STEEL TIGER on 15 September 1970 following a successful period of operation. The *Playboys* counted their experiences hunting on the Trail in Laos as second to none.

Mark Berent Collection

Wolf FACs in the fall of 1968, when Mark Berent was *Papa Wolf.*

time pilots and navigators who flew the *Wolf* mission.

They came from different squadrons, yet you couldn't have found a more closely knit fraternity of fighter pilots than these Fast FACs. They flew their jet fighters along the Ho Chi Minh Trail, in a role traditionally belonging to the slow-movers in the O-1s, O-2s, and OV-10s. But they're "slow" only relative to the ground speed of their aircraft as compared to that of an F-4 or an F-100.

If you ask any former Vietnam Green Beret about his "personal Air Order of Battle," chances are he'll respond with a somewhat irreverent sign and the words, "FAC, TAC, and Napalm." The men know who did the job in close air support.

As the interdiction war spread to North Vietnam and Laos, the plucky slow-movers did as well, operating at their normal low altitudes, where they could see things. Survival was pretty chancy for them. It was realized that something else was needed, to complement these slow-movers, something that could see down on the deck, yet maneuver fast enough to avoid the "severe myopia brought on by lead pollution!"

The Marines thus flew TA-4s as *Playboy* FACs, and in 1967, Colonel "Bud" Day became the first *Misty* FAC commander, using F-100s. *Stormy*, *Laredo*, and *Tiger* were also call signs of fast-movers from various fighter bases in Southeast Asia. Each of the units had more or less identical criteria for its members: must have 100 combat missions, must be top flight crews, must be unconditionally recommended by their squadrons, and must be volunteers.

Invariably, they were loners who liked to "mix it up," "get down in the weeds" to find the enemy, then challenge him to come out and fight. But, like the slow-moving FACs, they had to have the maturity to mix prudence with daring, to differentiate between courage and recklessness. They had to have a fast eye, a memory for detail, an ability to control several flights of fighters at once, and an intimate knowledge of every rock, bush, gun, bypass, truck park, and trail over hundreds of square miles. They had to know location and height of the black-rock karst, be intimately familiar with where the guns were and when they liked to shoot, and determine what positions looked promising for new sites.

These men had to be in excellent physical shape to withstand the four- and five-hour "trail-sniffing" missions where they twisted and turned, dived and zoomed, pulling Gs and jinking, with their heads constantly swiveling as they cut back and forth over the trails, around the karst, and through the passes at 400 to 500 knots. One *Wolf* saw a bush out of place on such a high-speed maneuver and chandelled up, rolled in to check it out, and found his gunsight square on a camouflaged command car. That kind of ability was common among all FACs, fast or slow.

The *Wolf* FACs were fairly representative of the fast-movers. Half were bachelors and all were top-rated officers, who most assuredly had minds of their own. *Papa Wolf* didn't have to lead this kind of pack; he sometimes had to move like hell to stay up with them.

There are memories of men lost in the *Wolf* mission — Jim, who spoke quietly while coolly directing hot firefights, and whose succinct last comment was, "Well, I guess we better get out," as his aircraft went uncontrollable from groundfire. Jim's backseater got picked up; but he's still there in the karst.

And Paul and Peter just never came back. Paul worked tirelessly as the *Wolf* Ops officer, and quiet, gentle Peter was on his first *Wolf* mission. Sturdy Grey, and Neal, the enthusiastic, laughing pilot we called Indian, got it one day while rooting out a bulldozer at the "Dog's Head" area. And Brad Sharp was the *Papa Wolf* who got blown out of the sky but was safely rescued with his backseater. Another, Rick, took a hit and was still having his skin glued back on after the war. His backseater was last heard from on the ground, over his survival radio, in a shoot-out with the enemy.

Kenny Boone, a direct descendent of Daniel, spent a night hanging in a tree while local Laos hacked all around the area looking for him, and Ray Battle, the founder and first *Papa Wolf*, once brought back his Phantom with the nose blown off and no landing gear. He walked away from that one. (Battle was Kenny's front seater.)

Despite their casualties, the *Wolves* spread more than their share of havoc. An array of enemy gunners could be seen rotting by their busted guns, and a number of enemy truck drivers had little more than a smoking steering wheel to show for their grand drive down the Ho Chi Minh Trail.

The *Wolf* Operations office was a folksy converted lounge, just off the main Intelligence room in wing headquarters, a favorite gathering spot for the strike pilots. To foil unfavorable reports from the Inspector General or other administrative teams that would

Ban Laboy interdiction point in the Ban Karai Pass at the bend of the river.

periodically inspect the base, the *Wolves* would merely flip over the "*Wolf* Ops" sign above the door. Its back side read "Lounge."

The *Wolves* didn't have much time for that sort of thing, though, as they had to be on the trails from before first light to dark. If a *Wolf* FAC had enough fuel after a four-hour stint, he would show the next man where new enemy matériel was hidden. Otherwise, they would switch to the *Wolf* common radio channel and talk each other in. They could procure air strikes for hot targets by calling the airborne command post, but mostly they had flights fragged to them the night before. They carried plenty of Willie Pete smoke rockets and a full load of 20mm — "mike mike" — and rarely returned with any of either.

The *Wolf* FACs, like the others, had huge areas assigned to them and would hum up and down their route structure looking for trucks and guns and trouble. They would make "bullfighter pirouettes" by suspected guns to make them give away their positions. They would look under karst overhangs and in caves for hiding trucks. To block traffic, they would destroy whole sections of the Trail where it wound around cliffs.

Except while controlling a strike, they were alone. Yet they successfully prevented daylight traffic flow and road repairs in their area, in addition to putting psychological strain on the enemy who always had to watch for someone on their trails. They provided real-time Intelligence on new trails being hacked out, foot and bicycle traffic prints, fuel pipelines, and revetted guns and truck parks, and they generally raised hell throughout their section of the Ho Chi Minh Trail. Shortly after the war, the units ceased to exist, except in the memories of the FACs and the strike pilots.

Little has been said about the courage and honor of the men in the field in Southeast Asia, the guys out doing the job, men like the *Wolf* FACs. Some came home alive, some are still there in the karst. Many spent years in the solitary hell of the "Hanoi Hilton." But the *Wolves* and *Tigers*, the *Playboys*, and the *Stormys*, *Mistys*, *Falcons*, and *Laredos* still live and fly in our memories. You just can't forget.

Chapter 10

FAC Support of Special Forces

*O*N SOUTHEAST ASIA, small Special Forces teams, often disguised as the enemy, were inserted into enemy territory to glean Intelligence for upcoming operations. As the war expanded, border surveillance camps were established to keep track of enemy movements in and out of South Vietnam. However, the Special Forces teams and camps lacked heavy firepower and needed the support of Army gunships and the USAF Forward Air Controller as a lifeline to tactical air power. The FACs working with the Special Forces had to have fighter-pilot experience, be extremely accurate, and have the ability to direct strike aircraft in support of recce teams nose-to-nose with the enemy. They had to be able to brave the worst weather conditions. The Army Recondo School, which trained commandos for long-range reconnaissance patrols in South Vietnam, briefed the new arrivals on Special Forces reconnaissance operations and related missions. Then, veteran controllers checked them out.

The Special Forces teams had arrived in South Vietnam in 1958 along with Military Assistance personnel. They worked with the local people in a counterinsurgency program because of increased enemy covert operations. New FACs joined Projects DELTA, SIGMA, or OMEGA, living at the Forward Operating Locations from which their teams worked. Project LEAPING LENA, set up in May 1964 and redesignated Project DELTA (Detachment 52 at Nha Trang with the 21st Tactical Air Support Squadron under the 504th Tactical Air Support Group) in December 1964, backed up this effort by sending special reconnaissance teams deep within Viet Cong territory to gather Intelligence. In October 1964, Military Assistance Command, Vietnam redesignated the U.S. Army Special Forces as the 5th Special Forces Group (SFG).

The 504th TASG furnished aircraft maintenance through its 21st Squadron. The FOL's ground maintenance men performed the minor repairs. If a plane broke down in an isolated area, a crew chief was flown out with parts to make the repairs. Ammunition — mainly rockets and rounds for hand-held weapons — came from the Army or Marines in I Corps.

Project DELTA involved U.S. Special Forces and indigenous forces conducting long-range reconnaissance and interdiction missions. They acted as hunter-killer teams in small search-and-destroy operations. OPERATION SHINING BRASS (which became PRAIRIE FIRE after 1 March 1967) was launched out of the camps in October 1965. DANIEL BOONE, its companion operation in Cambodia, carried no Americans on its teams.

Army helicopters dropped 12-man teams (each with three American Special Forces advisors) into the Laotian border regions where they set up road-watch listening posts — missions that could get very dangerous with immediate calls for help to the FACs. These South Vietnamese/American intrusions disrupted the enemy, enticing him to retaliate by attacking the lightly defended Special Forces camps. All the camps had for protection were light artillery, barbed wire, and various types of antipersonnel mines and explosive traps.

Forward Air Controllers assigned to ARVN units began to support the Special Forces camps beginning in 1965. By December, the Seventh Air Force had assigned FACs permanently to Project DELTA. (FACs in Laos were already working with SHINING BRASS.) The FACs developed a personal working relationship with the Army units. There was strong camaraderie with the Special Forces. The FACs would land at their camps, drink a cup of coffee, shoot the breeze, and possibly take the camp commander for a ride around the area. When a Special Forces camp needed a runway, usually a 1,000-foot dirt strip with a crown, the FACs would visit the nearest Army camp and borrow a bulldozer and crew. Sometimes the landing sites had to be blasted out with airstrikes.

Occasionally, the Special Forces FACs used a hand-held camera to aid in the selection of landing zones. They would photograph the potential LZ from some distance away so that they wouldn't arouse suspicion. The Army processed the film within hours.

The Army had FACs, also, flying L-19s, which were just like the O-1 but painted olive drab. The Army FACs also flew in and out of the Special Forces camps, but they couldn't put in airstrikes. Sometimes the pilots traded planes to confuse the enemy. The bad guys knew the olive-drab aircraft couldn't put in airstrikes, so they would shoot at them. But much to their surprise, they would receive immediate strikes.

David L. Shields was with the 21st TASS at Nha Trang when he volunteered for Project DELTA. He was sent to OPERATION McARTHUR in I Corps where he lived in a tent adjacent to the Tactical Operations Center. The Special Forces camp was a small triangle stuck in the middle of the jungle. Shields often flew with a Vietnamese in the back seat of the Bird Dog:

SOME OF THE teams were indigenous and of course they didn't speak English, so the man in the back had a separate radio system. He carried a portable in his lap. When there was trouble he would write a message on the window, using a "pointy-talkee," so we could communicate.

When we worked Navy guns, we had a naval fire observer in the back seat. We knew little about naval gunfire before going to Vietnam, but we picked it up very quickly. There was always a chopper available to fly out to a ship to pick up a fire observer.

When the DELTA teams were being inserted, the FACs flew 1,000 feet above them. There was a helicopter to carry the team and another for command

and control, plus from four to ten helicopter gunships. To keep from tipping its hand, the formation set a flight path that carried it right over the landing site. The in-flight helicopters matched the pitch of their rotor blades with the descending helicopter carrying the team so that the noise blended together. The team ship dropped like a stone, unloaded in seconds, then shot skyward to join the others who were only a little ways off. The FAC stayed above the operation, scanning the area for trouble, while the team members dug in and their commander made contact with him. If not detected, the team moved out, while the FAC lingered to monitor its progress.

The team contacted the FAC at dawn and dusk. Even though the FAC was not with the team during the day, he could respond instantly to calls for help. When the Special Forces had to break contact, they would call a FAC if it wasn't the prescribed airborne times of first and last light. The teams remained out for a week or less, and in many instances, things got too hot to even remain on the ground one day.

The Army gunships reacted the fastest, keeping the enemy off-balance until the TAC air arrived. To escape detection down in the jungle, the team spoke to the FAC in whispers, and when the enemy was too close for whispering, they used marking panels, signal mirrors, or released balloons. At night they used penguin-sized flare guns. The FACs preferred to point out the enemy position to the fighters without marking it, but generally they had to use Willie Petes. Most of the missions were real cliff hangers. The FACs had to pin the enemy down while the choppers plucked the team out. It demanded the utmost in FAC skill, with everyone on the ground in such close quarters. Sometimes the airstrikes were almost on top of the friendlies. Napalm was used, and often the friendlies were singed by it.

In December 1965, the first FACs to join the 5th SFG, Captains Kenneth L. Kerr and James N. Ahmann, were briefed on Project DELTA at Na Trang. They performed their first DELTA Forward Air Controller duty from 8 to 17 January 1966, during OPERATION MALLET, a U.S. Army 1st Infantry Division operation to clear the Highway 15 from Bien Hoa to Vung Tau. Helicopters dropped in nine DELTA teams to scout out the surrounding area and identify targets. Kerr and Ahmann took turns with a borrowed O-1 Bird Dog, controlling strikes in support of the DELTA teams. One day a team was ambushed by two Viet Cong platoons. Within 15 minutes, Captain Kerr had A-1 Skyraiders hammer-

ing the enemy as helicopters lifted out the team's survivors. During other skirmishes, the FACs had airstrikes within minutes of when the teams needed them. Later that same day, a DELTA team snuck up on a Viet Cong class in session. While the infiltrators ducked behind two giant ant hills, Kerr directed fighters in wiping out the students.

The 5th Special Force Group FACs found more action with OPERATION MASHER on 27 January. The 9th Marine Regiment from I Corps had spearheaded a 41-day drive, in support of the 1st Cavalry Division, against the Viet Cong in the An Lao Valley and Bong Son Plains area. Three DELTA teams pressed ahead of the troops looking for enemy units and positions. FACs covered the infiltrators during daylight hours. On 28 January, Team 1 called for help. With the team in extreme danger, the FAC flew in a blinding rain, found the team, and brought helicopters to extract it. The next day the enemy ambushed Team 2, killing two men and wounding four. A FAC directed artillery fire from the 1st Cavalry Division, making it possible for helicopters to pluck the survivors to safety. That same day Team 3 lost its radios during an ambush. The FAC detected the panel code (a prearranged code for visual communications) and called in helicopters for the extraction. The outstanding work of the Forward Air Controllers in OPERATION MALLET and MASHER underscored the value of having them accompany recce teams.

Major Richard L. Griffin served in Vietnam from September 1966 to August 1967 with the 21st TASS in Pleiku Province. He occasionally worked the 24th Special Zone, a combination of Pleiku and Kontum Provinces, assigned to the 5th SFG. Griffin described the mission:

OUR BASIC RESPONSIBILITY was to the Special Forces camps, most of which were camps with an "A" team in a pretty hostile area. We were not only tactical air support for them but we also did courier work, even beer runs. We were their only USAF contact. I went to four Special Forces camps in Pleiku Province: Plei Djereng, 25 miles west of Pleiku on the Cambodian border; Duc Co, south of Plei Djereng; Plei Mrong, six or seven miles northwest of Pleiku; and Plei Me in the south-central area.

Our operational guidance, in theory, came from corps headquarters. The Chief Sector FAC had other FACs working for him. Each FAC had a Special

Forces camp that was his. He monitored that camp's activity more than any other, but he kept up with other camps as well. My camp was Plei Djereng, so if it got hit, I would try to cover it. When you covered a specific camp you had detailed knowledge of it, such as where the concertina wire was laid out, mine fields, etc. The FAC would land at "his" camp several times a month to shoot the breeze and stay overnight on occasion. When more than one Special Forces team called for support, the FAC, who was simultaneously watching several teams, took care of the one in the most trouble. He would tell the others to "go groundhog."

I met with the COs and their teams to try and learn more about their operations. I was at the first camp only two days when the first major action I had to support took place. You didn't worry about what the Special Forces did. You just knew someone on the ground was in trouble. They would pull smoke to tell you where they were located, and that they need ordnance.

The first time you have TIC you're very careful not to put the ordnance too close to them. You talk it over with the guy on the ground. After the first couple of actions, you begin to think about tactical ground movement and other things. Putting in air, you've got almost the power of life and death given to you as a responsibility, and sometimes it was a heavy responsibility.

This action took place in the mountains east of Plei Djereng where a Special Forces-led group of CIDG [*Civilian Irregular Defense Group*], about a platoon size, ended up surrounded by about a regiment. The two American advisors and 30 CIDG ran into contact with the enemy late on the afternoon of 14 October 1966. Some of the wounded were removed by a "Dust-off" [*medical evacuation helicopter*].

The next afternoon there was enemy contact again. I put in three flights of A-1s and one flight of F-100s. One of the Americans was wounded. We got him out on a HH-43 Pedro helicopter [*the HH-43 Huskie*]. This was difficult because the guy had to hover on a 45-degree angle because of the steep hill.

That night *Spooky* [*an AC-47*] came out and kept the area well illuminated with flares. It was the first time I had put fighters in under flares with Willie Petes. The white phosphorus smokes everything up and it's beautiful going off at night. Our guys had pulled into a really tight perimeter. I was glad because it looked like we were really close to them, but

then at night everything looks closer. I had to fly back to Pleiku, but I took off again at first light the next day.

The team had run into a much larger unit and were now scattered in three little groups. I flew out to where their commander was in camp, about two or three miles down the hill from his team. As I landed, the commander came out and I left the O-1's engine running at idle. The wind was flipping him around and flipping the map I held. But that was real grass-roots war planning.

I suggested, "If those guys can all get together, they obviously can't go up the hill. But, have them come down the hill toward your camp. I'll put a strike down right in front of them over a rather broad area. Then we'll lift the strike and you have them clear through that area and get on the other side of it and set up another perimeter. We'll do the same thing again and we'll just keep doing it until we leapfrog them down." It worked. We put in a batch of strikes and got every one of them out of there without even taking any wounded.

Sometimes we had to put in airstrikes around the 360 degrees of a unit, just to keep the pressure off them. A lot of people were reluctant to use CBU, but in tight situations when you had to go in close, I found that CBU would do more to break an attack because you could scatter it out over a large area.

When we landed, we passed along most of our information in code. For example, "Broken Arrow" meant an American unit was in danger of being overrun. This would bring every available fighter/bomber to that spot. Some information was passed along to sectors by radio before we landed. We spent about 30 minutes with the corps Intelligence officer after we landed.

We wore the same clothing as the Special Forces — a tiger suit, which was sort of a status symbol. The Special Forces camp managers could get them for you. It made you feel like part of the operation and tended to disassociate you with the Air Force green-suit flying crowd. It was also better camouflage if you went down. The tiger suit had form-fitted shirts and the bottoms had nice little pockets, which were very handy for flying. By the time I got to Vietnam in 1966, General Momyer had just said no wearing of Aussie hats, or anything like that.

We also provided air cover for insertions on some occasions. However, most of these, when they did use the helicopter insertion routine, were quite "Sneaky Pete" operations, so they didn't want our cover. These guys would go in at dusk, night, or early light. They would insert into hot areas, sneaking around from tree to tree. We would talk to them, in code, of course. It was quite interesting because you'd hear these guys whispering on the radio. That's how hot an area they were in. And we would never fly over them. We did FAC some A-1s to help them locate the spot where they could insert a drop tank filled with whatever the guys needed, like ammo, supplies, or water. Instead of having a parachute to drop the things, the A-1 driver would come in there and punch off a tank.

Adjusting artillery was one of the fun parts of the job. Those guys had all kinds of ammunition and weren't afraid to fire it. On days when the weather was down and you couldn't get air, a FAC could fly his O-1 under the clouds and keep old "Charlie" on the move by dropping artillery in his lunch basket.

We tried some night VR with two people in the O-1 using Starlight Scopes. There was too much movement in the O-1 for this to work well. We had the same problem with binoculars, which we tried on a good moonlit night. It's really uncomfortable to fly along looking through binoculars. Dark night flying was hazardous. There was no horizon at night, especially at low altitude. And, there were no lights around on the ground for reference.

One of the beauties about being a FAC in Vietnam was that it was probably the most unstructured responsible area in the war. As a sector FAC you could pretty much do the job any way you thought was necessary. You had more latitude for different ways of doing things. We seldom had any interference from topside. Everybody had a healthy respect for the FAC. He was out there on the battlefield every day, and he knew what was going on.

Les Frazier had another "Pedro" tidbit:

AT PHAN RANG, the HH-43 Pedros were used to chase airplanes with landing emergencies. They would have a big fire bottle slung underneath and circle around near final approach. As the emergency Hun [*F-100F*] neared their position, they would haul ass toward the approach end of the runway, hoping to time their arrival with that of the emergency aircraft. All rescue chopper crews, Sandys, and Dust-offs drank free in our bar.

Ron Lamb, on the Internet, wrote that he had a 1.5-hour "combat mission" in the Pedro in 1972:

WE HAD ONE or two at Ubon. I had been on a night strike in RP-3 with a weakdick frontseater who jettisoned the centerline ordnance of four CBU-49s when he tried to dump wing fuel, when we had an emergency on takeoff. When we landed, he lied saying he had not touched the dump switch. We debriefed and went to bed. Couple of hours later someone is pounding on my door saying the Wing King wanted us airborne to find the CBU. Guess what — the Pedro! It had wooden rotor blades (not cleared for flight in rain), and flew at what appeared to be taxi speed all the time trying to shake itself to pieces. We flew all over western Laos looking for the CBU — never found them.

The clandestine nature of the DELTA operations permitted scant information to trickle out. The Special Forces FACs worked in relative isolation and were more self-directed than other FACs (except the *Ravens*). Sometimes the resulting decentralization hampered coordination of close air support.

Occasionally, the fighters' ordnance was too heavy for the situation. For example, if withholding 500-pound bombs spelled the loss of the team, the ground commander opted for the drop, and his men dug in. This happened on 15 August 1967 during an attack on a recce company near Base Camp 607, I Corps, along the Laotian border. Major Marvin C. Patton, 5th SFG Air Liaison Officer, and Captain Allan R. Groth rushed to the patrol's aid and called for fighters at the same time. The patrol was trapped on an H-shaped ridge at the end of a valley waiting for a helicopter to lift them out. Captain Groth, the first FAC on the scene, brought in airstrikes and directed helicopters down the valley where too much enemy fire obliged them to withdraw. Groth's plane ran low on fuel, so Major Patton took over, guiding napalm and 20mm cannon fire to within 30 feet of the team. When he ran out of rockets, he flew in low and dropped smoke rockets by hand. The enemy was driven back and the survivors were lifted out by sundown.

Major Groth was at Nha Trang with Detachment B-52 as a class "A" [*fighter qualified*] FAC:

WITH THE SPECIAL FORCES, we were always out in the field. The only time we went to Nha Trang, our home base, was for resupply, refit, and some training. Some of our A camps had bad runways, while others were excellent. If the Special Forces chose a location without an air strip, we would have to scrounge one. We would ask the nearest construction battalion to cut us out a runway near the Special Forces base. We would have to barter quite a bit to get these airfields built. They were only 1,000 feet of dirt with a crown on it made by a grader for water runoff. That would be enough for us to support the operation. To be effective, we had to be with the unit, make our own fields, and identify closely with the Special Forces.

The greatest part of our work was VR [*Visual Reconnaissance*]. We went to and from operations areas for several specific teams. They had to take a chance of being compromised to be effective. We utilized a special photo technique using a 200mm lens on a 35mm camera, black and white, to be developed in the field. We shot pictures from certain radiuses and angle of bank at certain rates. We would develop a stereo effect, which would identify the taller trees that would be a hazard to helicopters.

We also scouted trails. We flew low enough to see beneath the foliage. Finding a trail, we determined its width. We estimated what the trail could support logistically. We operated in all sorts of weather short of zero-zero.

In 1968, there was an important operations area from west of Hue Phu Bai to the A Shau Valley. The North Vietnamese were building a secret road so that they could re-occupy Hue. Because of the rainy season, there had been no flying over the mountains west of Hue since the previous October. There were no visual reconnaissance records. Project DELTA moved up to Hue Phu Bai. At the first breaks in the clouds and ceiling of 500 feet or so, FACs flew back in the mountains and found that road. FAC David L. Shields recounted how he found trucks on his second day of reconnaissance and destroyed them:

I FLEW THE O-2 for the first time when we found that road west of Hue. I had just been checked out in the aircraft the week before. Ceilings were low and visibility poor (less than two miles), so we flew a rush check-out in an unfamiliar machine in adverse

weather. VR was easier in the O-1. You could trim the aircraft and fly it with the rudders. If you were circling, you could trim the O-1 for 30 degrees of bank and then just fly with the rudders. It was more difficult in the O-2 because you always had to have one hand on the wheel to steer.

VR with fleeing targets, you learned to believe what you saw the first time. The technique was to focus on an area, try to see as much as possible, then look away to the next area, rather than just scanning. Your first impression may, or may not, have been valid, but it might be the only impression you would get of the situation.

Regular Special Forces A camps in-country were supported by USAF FACs assigned to the U.S. Army, but the Special Operations Group had its own FACs. One of the special operations was Project DELTA, Detachment B-52, a special Intelligence-gathering unit for General William C. Westmoreland. In 1972, it was supervised by Major Marvin Curtis Patton, who also supervised Project OMEGA and Project SIGMA. All three carried out long-range reconnaissance patrol operations. OMEGA's area of responsibility was along the Laotian border in I and II Corps. SIGMA patrolled border activities in III Corps and encompassed the Parrot's Beak Region.

Project DELTA functioned in-country, largely in enemy-controlled areas. Its basic objective was to insert small reconnaissance teams into these areas. Teams usually consisted of one or two Americans and four or five South Vietnamese operating clandestinely. Roadrunner teams composed of South Vietnamese, wearing North Vietnamese and VC uniforms and carrying enemy weapons, infiltrated NVN units in their own territory. The teams had no artillery support, so they had to rely on close air support for outside firepower.

During support of the Roadrunner operations, the American FACs flew with an interpreter in the back seat of the O-1s. The FAC and then the ground commander flew over the area to pick out a suitable site for a LZ, depending on the extent of the operation.

Once the LZ was chosen, the team and its support elements went out together with one FAC, a helicopter carrying the team, a command and control helicopter, and four to ten support gunships. A flight pattern was established over the LZ in a way that would arouse as little enemy suspicion as possible. The FAC flew cover about 1,000 feet above the operation. Flying in a circular pattern, the formation made one pass over the LZ. The team helicopter quickly dropped down and unloaded. The other helicopters adjusted the pitch of their blades in flight so that the noise of the descending helicopter blended in with the other helicopters. If the team was spotted, or fired on, it was extracted quickly.

The team made initial radio contact with the FAC, remembering to speak in whispers to preclude the possibility of being overheard. Once the team was safe, the helicopters returned to their base. The FAC loitered awhile, nearby, but not where he might give away the team's location. The team tried to stay in about a week, contacting the FAC at dawn and at dusk. Except for these contacts, the FACs remained on the ground, ready for a quick response to teams in trouble.

When the Blackjacks (long-range recce patrols like mobile guerrilla forces) were operating, the FACs would be in the air 24 hours a day, operating on the fringes of the AO. The FACs would relieve each other. They came from Task Force 777 at Plei Djereng, some from Tam Ky, and some from Nha Trang. The FAC held the job of traffic cop by directing prepping of the insertion zone and maintaining surveillance to see if there was any enemy reaction in the area. The FAC made sure the cycle of helicopters going in and dislodging their load stayed on a tight schedule. Should there be trouble, the FACs could get an airstrike in ten minutes.

Balloons used to mark the perimeter of the Blackjack guerrilla forces were inserted through the trees above the triple jungle canopy. They were easy to pick out from the air and difficult for the enemy to pick up from the ground, whereas they could see and smell smoke markers.

While teams were operating in an area, it was designated off-limits to all ground personnel and aircraft by the corps commander. No one could enter without prior permission. Other units, not aware of the situation, could mistake these special units for the enemy, with catastrophic consequences.

Projects DELTA, OMEGA, and SIGMA were given very high priority on airstrikes. Ninety percent of their requests resulted in immediate strikes, primarily to support the extraction of teams in trouble. Major Patton was directly responsible to the DASC/ALO, who frequently didn't know the ramifi-

cations of the operation because he was not always cleared for the information about the activities.

Night operations were tricky for the FACs flying the O-1s. With only limited avionics, they couldn't rely on TACAN or radio fixes, so the FAC would pass his coordinates to one DASC, via the TACP, and a TACAN fix would then be established for the strike aircraft to rendezvous on. The transition to the O-2 came when Project DELTA moved into the A Shau Valley in March 1968. Subsequently, several O-2As were received from the 20th TASS.

PRAIRIE FIRE — Top Secret Operation

PRAIRIE FIRE was an intensely secret operation during which FACs supported the Special Forces teams operating in highly sensitive cross-border areas, often under heavy fire. PRAIRIE FIRE was a joint-service Intelligence-gathering project conducted with small Long Range Reconnaissance Patrols (LRRPs). Under the Military Assistance Command, Studies and Observation Group (MACSOG), Green Berets inserted indigenous teams, usually with an American leader, into areas where U.S. ground forces were not allowed. The reconnaissance teams worked all cross-border operations from Chu Lai to the DMZ.

Covey FACs, flying OV-10s, were the airborne commanders responsible for getting the "package" — the name given to the helicopter and fixed-wing assets necessary for the operation — safely in and out. Four Huey UH-1 Iroquois "Slicks" carrying the team, two AH-1 Cobra helicopter gunships, two A-1 Skyraiders, and, when necessary, some F-4 Phantoms made up the "package." The FACs had to neutralize the landing zone for the insert, cover the team while it was on the ground, and run the extraction.

Some of the most exciting FAC missions were flown by the PRAIRIE FIRE *Coveys*. It was a real challenging adventure, fraught with danger, excitement, the satisfaction of a job well done, and sadness when someone paid the ultimate price. The mission was top secret, so the pilots could not discuss it with anyone whatsoever. They had their own private briefing room. Flying with them were experienced Special Forces NCOs known as "*Covey* riders." The *Covey* rider assisted with map reading and radios, talked to the team on the ground, and interpreted the tactical situation for his pilot as well as the Mobile Launch Team (MLT) on the ground at Quang Tri or Hue Phu Bai.

It was dangerous work. In later years, in his *Da*

The *Covey* flag being raised by Lieutenant Colonel Robert Blanton and an unknown *Covey* as Lieutenant Wes Cochran and Fred Clark look on. The flag was made by the wife of Lieutenant Rick Townsend.
                                                                                            Dale Kingsbury Collection

Nang Diary, Tom Yarborough, *Covey* 221, told of a mission with a *Covey* rider, Sergeant First Class Jim Parry. They were involved in a terrible battle. Yarborough remembers the frenzied call from the team's one-zero. "Cubby, Cubby. This is Papa *Delta*. Have very bad situation. Many VC. You bring big bomb right now!" Arriving at the scene, Yarborough found a solid cloud deck covering the area. In an earlier action he had calculated a bearing and distance from Quang Tri's TACAN, so in spite of the 3,000-foot peaks jutting around the valley, he entered the cloud deck. Luckily he got down under the clouds and broke out, at 300 feet, in the valley with steep cliffs all around. There was no way to get fighters down under the clouds, so *Covey* 221 went right to work making several passes as he fired at the enemy.

With each jink to miss a ridge coming up in front of him, a trio of 12.7mm machine-guns opened fire on him. The team's one-zero, showing concern, radioed, "Cubby, you be careful. Many VC shoot at you. Please be careful." *Covey* 221 shot off all his rounds of 7.62, and then his rockets. When he was "Winchester" [*out of ammunition*] he had to return to Quang Tri for fuel and ammo. Sergeant Parry climbed in with him, and as they went back to the battle, two Cobras and three Slicks joined in. When

they got to *Covey* 221's TACAN let-down point, he left the Slicks in a holding pattern and had the Cobras tuck in as close to his wing tips as possible. They were not trained instrument pilots, so their only reference was the wings of the OV-10, a ticklish situation indeed. They made it down through the "soup" successfully, ending up at the north side of the valley. Jim Parry called the team on the "Fox Mike" and analyzed the tactical situation with him. He then marked targets for the Cobras. Leaving them to go about their attacks, Yarborough climbed up through the 3,000-foot cloud deck to the orbiting Slicks. The warm sunlight greeted him and he dreaded going back down through the repulsive weather that cleverly hid the karst rock formations, the mountain peaks, and the enemy fire. Nonetheless, he left one Slick on top in reserve, and had the other two join up on each of the OV-1O's wings. The OV-10 had its gear and flaps down so that it could slow to a speed that matched the Slicks' speed.

When they arrived in the valley, there was no room under the extremely low ceiling for all the aircraft to maneuver. Yarborough sent the Slicks in for the extraction, and, to get out of the way, flew about one klick north, only to be harassed by two 23mm guns. He had to get the northern karst between himself and the guns. As these guns quieted down, he listened to the radio chatter, learning that Slick Lead was in a hover, about to pull the eight-man team. "Lead's off and heading north to your position, *Covey*."

The Slick needed the OV-10 to take it up through the thick overcast. Yarborough had to do something to get away from the 23mm guns and back to the Slicks. Sergeant Parry held his breath while Yarborough executed a chandelle up into the clouds. At the top of his sharp, turning pull-up, while the OV-1O's airspeed decreased, he kicked in some bottom rudder, crossed his fingers, and zoomed back down on a reciprocal heading. He reasoned that if they hit one

Kham Duc Special Forces Camp, 1966.   James F. McMurray Collection

of the karst in the steep dive, they'd never feel a thing.

As luck, or skill, would have it they broke out of the clouds at the same place where they entered them. A string of 23mm strung out behind them. Yarborough quickly advised the Hueys not to move north, toward the guns, telling them to remain in orbit where they were. With these large guns firing at them there was no time to lead two elements of helicopters up through the clouds, so he gave the Cobras a heading to climb out on while he joined up with the Slicks. Once again, with gear and flaps hanging, he led the Slicks up through the clouds. The weather had worsened, so they didn't break out until reaching 5,000 feet. The Cobras made it out and joined up with the Slick that was waiting on top. Yarborough remembers them talking. He chuckled when the Slick asked, "How was it down there?" One of the Cobras answered, "No sweat. This was an easy one." (Yarborough, pp. 235-244)

The Miracle at Kham Duc

Another hair-raising rescue took place at the Special Forces camp at Kham Duc in May 1968, in which FACs played an important role. Kham Duc Special Forces camp was south of Khe Sanh in I Corps in the northern section of Quang Tin province, about 75 miles west of Tam Ky, and only 10 miles from Laos. Approaching the air strip was like flying down into a green bowl. The steeply rising ter-

rain, composed of densely forested hills covered by a double and triple canopy jungle, rose in all directions around the 6,000-foot strip. After the fall of Lang Vei in February 1968 during the Tet offensive, Kham Duc was the only border surveillance camp remaining in I Corps.

Kham Duc was vulnerable to enemy attack from the surrounding hills. In early May, large enemy forces were reported in the camp's area, building roads to connect their trails in Laos with Route 14 south of Kham Duc. NVA attacked the camp, causing a successful evacuation after some bitter fighting and heroic deeds.

Hillsboro, the ABCCC, which usually worked over Laos, had been diverted to Kham Duc in mid-flight as the situation became critical. On 12 May, when Duty Controller Robert Gatewood, an F-100 fighter pilot, and Senior Controller Colonel Claude Turner were on *Hillsboro,* there was a communications breakdown. All day there were indications of a command and control breakdown, and not everyone knew that an evacuation had been ordered.

The FACs were the men responsible for directing the successful fighter attacks. The first Forward Air Controller to arrive at Kham Duc on 12 May was Captain Herbert J. Spier, an O-2 pilot working with the American Division at Chu Lai AB. He was there well before daybreak and more than three hours before the ABCCC. Spier's first sets of fighters worked under flares from a C-47 flareship. When the sun came up, so did the fog. By then, Spier was familiar enough to continue directing the fighters. He assigned altitudes and let the fighters line up on his aircraft. The Air Liaison Officer on the ground, Captain Willard C. Johnson, assisting the American Division and the Special Forces A team, could not see either the FAC or the fighters, but could hear the bombs impacting, and was able to direct Spier to bring the bombs closer to the camp's perimeter. Spier was relieved at 0730, but came back that afternoon for the final evacuation.

When the fog cleared, three FACs were flying over Kham Duc. Two flew at the same altitude, parallel to one another over opposite sides of the Kham Duc runway. Each controlled the fighters striking on his side of the runway. The third FAC flew below the ABCCC at an altitude above the two FACs working alongside the runway. He took the aircraft from *Hillsboro* and fed them to the FAC that needed them most at that time.

Captain Philip R. Smotherman was a FAC working the morning missions. He knew of the desperation of the defenders at Kham Duc, because he had been working the radios in the American Division Tactical Operations Center when the offensive was brewing. He took off from Chu Lai mid-morning and arrived over Kham Duc at 1030. Initially, he was the high-altitude FAC. After that, Smotherman took up a position on one side of the runway and put his first pair of F-100s on a .50-caliber gun position, which silenced those guns. He next controlled a pair of Marine A-4Ds. While directing the fighters, his O-2 was struck by enemy fire and his right wing tip was shot off. Smotherman lost control of the O-2's ailerons, and soon the elevators were jammed. All he had were engines and rudders for control. It seemed like he would have to bail out or crash-land outside the camp perimeter, but then he estimated he could make the strip if he was lucky. A departing C-123 almost ran over him, and dodging this traffic almost cost Smotherman his chance to make the air strip.

Fortunately, Smotherman was able to crash-land on the strip and move his O-2 off to the side of the runway so it wouldn't block evacuating aircraft. The enemy launched mortars at his O-2. Smotherman was picked up by a Special Forces sergeant. By then, Smotherman was the only Air Force officer on the scene, so he was ordered to serve as Air Liaison Officer by General Momyer. He was able to work in some fighters as ground FAC. In fact, he had one strike so close to his position that he could feel the heat of the napalm. During the afternoon, he was slightly wounded. It was a desperate scenario. Smotherman left Kham Duc on the last passenger-carrying C-130 along with the remainder of the Special Forces leaders and some CIDG troops.

The entire time Smotherman was in the air or on the ground, he was in contact with the American Division's Tactical Air Control Party at Chu Lai. He and the other FAC pilots passed information to the TACP about the types of ordnance needed and the status of Kham Duc. At times, the TACP lost contact with Kham Duc and thought the camp had been overrun. However, through Smotherman and the other FACs, General Samuel Koster's headquarters learned that the tactical fighters had been holding off the enemy while the helicopters and Air Force transports were evacuating troops.

The fighters, directed by the FACs, did outstanding work. At times they had to drop napalm on the friendly side of the perimeter fence to drive the enemy off of it. As the day wore on, and fewer defenders were left, the strikes had to be put in more rapidly to save the remaining men. At the very end, the ordnance was delivered as close as 25 meters to the last defenders. Earlier in the day, 140 tactical fighter sorties allowed the Marine and Army helicopters to save a large number of people. Later fighter support, also directed by the FACs, made it possible for the C-123s and C-130s to complete the extraction.

When the transports returned to Kham Duc that afternoon, the FACs controlled the fighters to suppress the gunfire along their routes. *Hillsboro* and the FACs tried to sequence the fighters in such a way that they were like an escort with their fire. Sometimes, the fighters made protective passes as close as 100 feet to the wing tips of the C-130s.

Hillsboro kept track of the arriving fighters and their ordnance and passed the information along to the high-altitude FAC, who then asked the two FACs working the runways what they needed. There was an abundance of fighters, and thus the FACs could choose what they needed. One of the early FACs on station, Lieutenant Colonel Richard P. Schuman, senior ALO for the American Division, was able to work a pair of fighters every 45 seconds. After flying four hours during the morning, he returned to Kham Duc in the afternoon for the final evacuation.

In the last hour, 1,400 people were evacuated by seven C-130s and two C-123s. This would have been impossible without the FACs and their fighters. There was intense ground fire at all times. Unfortunately one fully loaded C-130 was hit, causing it to crash and burn. Another C-130 crashed when its hydraulic system was shot up. The crew escaped and was picked up by a Marine CH-46 Sea Knight assault transport helicopter 20 minutes later. The fighters also destroyed aircraft left on the ground after the evacuation had ended.

Confusion caused a command and control breakdown. A C-130, under the command of Major Jay Van Cleeff, was ordered by General Burt W. McLaughlin, Commander of the 834th Air Division, to insert a three-man Combat Crew Team (CCT) of combat controllers — Freedman, and Lundie, and Major Gallagher. They didn't know that everyone had already been evacuated from Kham Duc. When they left their C-130, they discovered they were the only friendlies on the ground needing protection. The enemy was setting up machine-gun positions on either side of the runway, and ammunition dumps were blowing up all around them.

Several FACs sent to try and locate the CCT men were unsuccessful. Three C-123s were stacked overhead. Gatewood, the duty controller of the ABCCC, asked the first in the stack to land on the asphalt strip to see if the men would come out of hiding with an aircraft on the ground — if they were still alive. *Bookie* 750, commanded by Lieutenant Colonel Alfred J. Jeanotte, Jr., with his crew, nosed the C-123 over and headed down without hesitation. Fighters escorted him down to suppress the ground fire. *Bookie* 750 landed in a hail of fire, and rolled to the end, looking for the team. Not seeing the men, Jeanotte added power, and took off. As he banked his aircraft to the left, his engineer saw the three men running back to a ditch, while waving at the C-123. Jeanotte radioed Gatewood that he would go around and try again. Then, he discovered he didn't have enough fuel for another attempt.

Hillsboro called on the next aircraft in the stack to go in and rescue the team. They were briefed by Colonel Jeanotte. This C-123, call sign *Bookie* 771, had been diverted to Kham Duc for the emergency evacuation. The aircraft commander was Lieutenant Colonel Joe Jackson, with Major Jesse W. Campbell (a flight examiner and instructor pilot) flying copilot. Campbell had been giving Jackson a checkride.

They landed at the north end where the CCT was located, which gave them only 2,200 feet of runway to stop in. There were sharp fragments on the runway, and, luckily, the aircraft tires did not blow up. The C-123 touched down without reversing the engines (for braking), because this would have shut down the two small jet engines on the wing tips that were critical for the assault takeoff. Bullets were striking all around them. The CCT came out of the ditch and headed for the airplane. As the C-123 turned around, a 122mm rocket fired at them skidded to a stop a few feet in front of the nosewheel — the warhead had failed to explode. The C-123 carefully steered around the rocket, and with throttles fire-walled, it took off in 1,100 feet. *Bookie* 771 was on the ground less than a minute. Despite the fact that the enemy was firing at it the entire time, when the aircraft got back to Da Nang and the crew got out to

Harold Icke, *Bilk* FAC, in his room at Pleiku, December 1971.   Harold Icke Collection

count bullet holes, there were none. It was a miraculous escape thanks to the skill, tenacity, and courage of the aircrew.

For their actions at Kham Duc on 12 May, Major Jackson was awarded the Medal of Honor, Jeanotte the Air Force Cross, Trejo and Grubbs the Silver Star, and Campbell the Air Force Cross.

———————

Harold Icke, who arrived in Vietnam in August 1971, recalled his FAC missions:

AT PLEIKU, I first flew as *Covey* 525 (O-2) with most of my missions being Visual Recce in Cambodia. There was very little action and most of the time we put airstrikes on suspected locations and bunkers that we could see. We flew some in Laos and put strikes on the Ho Chi Minh Trail, but this was mainly left to the OV-10s. After a few months of gaining experience, I started to fly PRAIRIE FIRE missions as a *Mike* FAC with the Special Forces from Kontum. This was tremendously interesting as we were working with teams that were inserted into enemy territory. My call sign for these missions was *Mike* 525.

We all flew with the *Mike* call sign, even though we were *Coveys*. On a routine mission we flew to Kontum, north of Pleiku, and picked up a Special Forces guy, who worked with the indigenous (Vietnamese) team commander on the ground. Most of the Americans with the "indig" teams were U.S. advisors. One of the advisors flew with us in the right seat. Our missions were putting the teams in or pulling them out. The teams talked to the advisor after they got on the ground. These guys went into some unbelievable places. Sometimes the teams got in undetected, even with all the helicopters.

Other times they went in after a B-52 ARC LIGHT strike to see what bomb damage had been done. Sometimes we put in the guys who dropped those huge daisy cutters out of the back of the C-130s to make an LZ for the guys. Sometimes they went into Laos to watch traffic on the Trail up there. The Special Forces guys were a unique bunch of folks. They thought nothing of coming out of those expeditions, going to the hospital with wounds and healing up, and then going back out and do it again.

"X-Ray" Missions

According to Tom Yarborough, FACs were recruited for secret X-Ray missions flown out of Ubon, Thailand:

ROUGHLY ONCE EACH month, each of the four *Coveys* involved took turns staging out of Ubon, Thailand, for three days. The drill involved picking up a Laotian backseater known as "X-Ray." The X-Rays were villagers who had been recruited and trained by the CIA. Typical dress might be gray slacks, a short-sleeve white shirt, and jungle boots. Whenever they got wind of a lucrative target, they arranged to have Air America make a clandestine pick-up and take them to Ubon to fly with a *Covey* in an OV-10. Targets located by these flights had a high priority when the *Covey* pilot called *Hillsboro* saying he had a Statehouse-nominated, X-Ray validated target.

The *Coveys* were never privy to details, but just before our launch, the X-Ray showed up, ready to fly and eager to point out enemy troop concentrations, hidden supplies, and communication centers. They would go looking for targets in an Area of Operations that included the southern third of the Laotian panhandle, or Military Region IV. The Bolovens Plateau dominated this AO. It was a large area sloping up from the Medong River 75 miles east to the rugged cliffs overlooking the Xe Kong River near the Ho Chi Minh Trail, a series of strongholds and dirt strips known as PS sites situated throughout.

Mike Force in the Plantation

Karl Polifka, who worked with Special Forces units, described the Mobile Strike Force which translated to Mike Force:

THESE WERE roughly 500-man formations divided into three companies with four U.S. types in charge. They would come in a flurry of helicopters, sweep a potentially hot area for several days, and depart.

Several miles WNW of Duc Lap, running along the Cambodian border, was an overgrown tea plantation. This was the route of the NVA regimental assault on Duc Lap in August 1968 and an area that always seemed to have some activity in it. Nam Lyr mountain, some eight miles away in Cambodia, was said to contain a large NVA base camp and training area. Rumors had it that a huge tunnel system ran from Nam Lyr to the plantation. Certainly, the Cambodians were not in this part of their country.

On 17 December 1968, a Mike Force started a morning sweep through the plantation. Visibility was only a few feet in the thick secondary growth . . . under the cultivated trees. I was flying lazy circles overhead when the shooting started.

The three companies had become separated in the plantation undergrowth and, being unsure of the others' location, were hesitant to return fire when Vietnamese began popping up out of nowhere and firing. The force leader claimed that the Vietnamese were wearing SF tiger stripes but carried AK-47s. While this was probably a bit of license, the plantation quickly became a confused green sea of men shooting blindly. Several groups broke out of the plantation and ran through open areas and down roads before plunging back into the undergrowth. While I was sure they were NVA because of their behavior and terrain familiarity, the force leader wouldn't let me . . . use the CAR-15 carbine or rockets since he no longer knew where his force was.

The first order of business was to get the wounded to clearings where Dust-offs could get them. I had called for Dust-offs immediately and, since the troops didn't know where the clearings were, got down on the treetops and buzzed each group with wounded, directing them toward the nearest clearing that could take a Huey.

I was circling around at about 500 feet, a dangerous altitude for small arms, when an RPG [*Rocket-Propelled Grenade*] airburst, apparently directly in front of me. The cockpit filled with white smoke

Area 3261, looking toward Mu Gia Pass.

for an instant, there was a sense of overpressure, and the right front side window popped open (left already open). I glanced out on the right wing and saw that an inspection panel had been blown off. Don replaced me and I went back to Gia Nghia.

That afternoon I was back. It had taken hours to get the friendlies sorted out and moving as a group towards the west perimeter of the plantation. Just before they got to a north-south dirt road they started taking fire and I called for fighters.

F-100s, *Tide* 01, and his wingman, from the New Jersey Air National Guard arrived. One of their bombs hit too close to the friendlies. They weren't hit and the NVA stopped shooting and disappeared. The friendlies ran across the road and found that the Mk-82 had detonated square on the top of a vent shaft for the tunnel system from which they had been bedeviled all day. They dropped a Montagnard on a rope down 85 feet before the vent shaft was found to be collapsed — the main gallery being below that.

This sobering discovery caused the four U.S. types to have a brief conference and announce that they'd decided to get the hell out of there for the night and would I be so kind as to cover them? It was spooky to think about how extensive that tunnel system might have been.

Chapter 11

"That Others May Live"

Joint Search and Rescue

THE JOINT SEARCH AND RESCUE CENTER (JSRC), an integral part of the Seventh Air Force Combat operations center, with its command post at Tan Son Nhut Air Base, coordinated all USAF rescues in Southeast Asia. Rescue controllers were stationed at Song Tra, Republic of Vietnam, and Udorn, Thailand. Whenever a pilot was downed, all the resources of the Seventh/Thirteenth Air Force, the Army, Navy, and Marines were diverted to his rescue. The essential element was the A-1 **Sandy**, which gave fire-suppression support to the Army's Jolly Green Giant HH-53 helicopters. After 1970, the A-7 Corsair II supplanted the A-1 Skyraider.

Upon receipt of a Mayday, the entire search and rescue operation was activated. Often a FAC was nearby, and became the on-scene commander until the rescue team arrived. A-1 pilots would work the area to suppress enemy fire. Jets would arrive with the same objective. Many times a ring of fire had to be placed around the downed airman to keep the enemy away from him. There was a lot to do to make it safe for the rescue helicopters, and many times they went in for a pickup when the area was still hot. If a landing area wasn't available, they would use a Maguire rig, a special harness attached to a rope or cable to winch the pilot safely up into the rescue helicopter. It was a team effort in every respect. The airborne mission commander's duties would be passed like a baton from the FAC to *Crown* to *Sandy* to Jolly Green, as circumstances dictated.

The Rescue Coordinating Center was a modified C-130 Hercules that belonged to Air Rescue, using the call sign *King*. Until *King* arrived, the rescue crew coordinator was always a FAC. When a man was down in enemy territory in Laos, Cambodia, or even North Vietnam, the FAC located the downed airman, stayed over him, and tried to talk to him on 243, the emergency frequency. The *Sandys* (usually four A-1s) would come in with the Jolly Greens close behind (usually two of them), a high bird and a low bird. *Queen* was the call sign of the rescue center at Da Nang. *Joker* was the call sign of the JSRC at Tan Son Nhut.

Fred McNeil, who arrived in South Vietnam in late 1971, explained the training that pilots received in the event they were shot down:

A RESCUE OPERATION would have a slow or a Fast FAC. The procedures were standard as everybody was trained the same way. Now everybody went through the new water survival course at Homestead AFB, Florida (whether you had it in the past or not) so if you were shot down you could attempt to go "feet wet" over the water where the enemy had no control at all. If you were hit and shot down in-country, chances of being taken prisoner were high. Ideally you headed for the water the minute you were hit.

Rescues Remembered

Major Peter B. Lee was flying an A-1 on an interdiction mission on the Ho Chi Minh Trial in Laos in July 1970 when suddenly his aircraft took two 37mm hits. He was on his last pass against five cornered trucks when the tail of his aircraft was sawed off as it caught fire. He tried to tell his wingman, but his radios were knocked out, so he pulled the egress handle, which tossed him out. Soon his chute opened.

Lee hit the ground on the side of a hill about 1,500 feet above a river. He called his wingman on his survival radio. The wingman notified JSRC, and a massive rescue operation was launched. The downed pilot dug himself in. FACs were overhead talking to him every half-hour. Lee could hear voices on the radio saying in English, "American pilot, you're surrounded, surrender." Lee stayed well hidden and let the FACs know what he saw and heard on the ground. Since he flew A-1s on search and rescue missions himself, he knew the timing involved. He knew that one or more HH-53 Jolly Green Giant helicopters, escorted by several A-1s, would be launched, while FACs circled the area to put in airstrikes as needed to hamper the enemy. High above the scene, a C-130 Hercules would circle to provide aerial refueling for the Jolly Greens.

Launch times were planned so that strike aircraft would be available all day. The FACs established holding patterns for the jets and computed time-over-targets, to keep a steady stream of fire going to keep pressure on the enemy continuously and to prevent the enemy from closing in on the downed pilot.

There was a delay due to weather, but when it cleared, Major Lee assisted FAC Captain Jim Richmond (23rd TASS at Nakhon Phanom) from the ground, using his compass to get a bearing from his position to where the guns were. This enabled the FAC to take a fix from his position and guide ten jets against the enemy guns.

Later in the day, Captain Fred Parrott arrived in his OV-10 to relieve Richmond. He continued to mark gun positions for more strike aircraft.

By late afternoon, the on-scene commander, Major John C. Waresh, decided it was time to attempt the rescue. An HH-53 Jolly Green was ready as a half-dozen A-1 Skyraiders kept bombing and strafing the enemy gun positions. The F-4s and F-105s had done an excellent job of sanitizing the area, making it possible for the Jolly Green to drop down. Smoke screens were dropped around the pilot.

Major George C. Hitt was at the controls of the Jolly Green. As he started his approach to where the downed pilot was at the end of a valley between a high ridge and the river, there was hostile fire on both sides. Skyraiders accompanied the helicopter to suppress these guns, while other Skyraiders released

A USAF Douglas EB-66 Destroyer assigned to the 42nd Tactical Electronic Warfare Squadron, 355th Tactical Fighter Wing, on a mission over Southeast Asia, 6 March 1970.

smoke to screen the rescue ship. Major Hitt flew down the smoke tunnel, relying on the A-1s to keep the guns under control. The trapped pilot released a flare to mark his position as the Jolly Green got closer. The pick-up was successful. Eighteen hours after he was shot down, Major Lee was welcomed at Nakhon Phanom with a traditional hosing down.

Dutch Helms, *Bilk* 37, remembers a hilarious rescue in the A Shau Valley in the summer of 1970:

WE WERE PUTTING in strikes around Hamburger Hill, a flight of two F-100s. About the third pass, "Two" came through and just after he dropped his ordnance, he took some hits, probably from .51-cal. The whole aircraft burst into flames. He pulled up over the hill, and as he cleared the hill he bailed out. The ejection seat fired and boom, off he went into the air. At the same time there were two LOHs [*Light Observation Helicopters*] and about seven Cobras operating in the area. They saw him bail out. They were on the same frequency that I was so I called them up and said, "There he is." One responded, "Rog, I've got him."

The F-100 pilot got a good chute and started floating toward the ground. It was a windy day. He touched down in a clearing but bounced bad. The wind caught his chute and started dragging it 50 or 60 meters. In the meantime, a LOH had landed and the gunner had run out, and just as the Air Force pilot managed to free himself from his chute, still sitting on his ass on the ground, the gunner ran up behind him and grabbed him, dragged him into the helicopter, and quick, they were airborne.

I got a call from the LOH pilot and he said, "Hey, I think this guy's dead, he's pale and not responsive." To make a long story short, by the time we got him back to Camp Evans what had happened was that the F-100 pilot bailed out and knew there were enemy troops on the ground. So, when he hit, he bounced and lost his balance. He was being dragged and everything, thinking, "I've just got to get out of this parachute and get the hell out of here." Just as he unhooked his chute, he felt somebody grab him and knew for sure it was the bad guys and proceeded simultaneously to pass out, piss his pants, and shit his pants. He didn't wake up until he was in the helicopter heading back to Camp Evans. And, when he did wake up, he thought he was in a NVN helicopter until he recognized the American language. The poor guy just about had a heart attack being rescued.

If you go down, everybody's going to make the supreme effort to get you out. A peerless example took place in April 1972.

On Easter Sunday, 2 April, two Douglas Destroyer twin-engine EB-66s, *Bat* 21 and *Bat* 22, escorted by two F-105s for SAM suppression and two F-4s for MiG protection, took off from Thailand to escort a cell of three B-52s on a bombing mission just south of the DMZ. The enemy fired three SA-2s at *Bat* 21, getting a direct hit broadside with one of them, hitting the Electronic Countermeasures compartment. The aircraft disintegrated. Five American crew were lost, but one survival radio was activated. This happens automatically when an aviator bails out of his aircraft; an audible beep sends out a signal on emergency frequencies. Lieutenant Colonel Iceal E. Hambleton, the navigator, had ejected out of the aircraft. He was *Bat* 21 *Bravo*, so designated because he was not the pilot.

The first *King* bird to respond to the rescue moved its orbit to be right over the survivor, just south of the DMZ. It took three SA-2s. *Nail* 25, Darrel Whitcomb, recalled that fortunately the pilot saw them coming, and did a split S. But one of the missiles took out the number-four engine and the pneumatic system. These were "Brave 'doods' in a big airplane."

Several FACs took part in the rescue attempt. First Lieutenant Bill Jankowski (*Bilk* 34), flying an O-2 out of Da Nang AB, talked to *Bat* 21 *Bravo*, Colonel Hambleton, as he descended in his chute. Because of an overcast cloud layer, it was hard to get an exact position on the survivor, so Lieutenant Jankowski descended beneath the clouds and located Hambleton. *Bilk* 11, Harold Icke, recalled, "I saw him get shot down. I just happened to be headed up North that day when the SA-2 came up near the DMZ. I helped with the rescue. FACs talked to Hambleton continuously over the ten or eleven days he was down."

Luckily, an airborne SAR force was nearby, having been launched from Da Nang for an evacuation at Quang Tri that had been canceled. Two A-1s from that missions heard the calls. *Sandy* 07 and 08, heading north toward *Bat* 21 *Bravo's* position, had to fly under the low clouds hanging over the Cam Lo River valley, which made their job difficult. They talked to Hambleton and strafed enemy positions. He could see and hear enemy troops within 100 meters of his position.

Meanwhile, Lieutenant Jankowski flew south, looking for someone to rescue *Bat* 21 *Bravo*. Soon he

was on his way back to Hambleton with four U.S. Army helicopters, two AH-1 Cobra gunships, and two UH-1H Slicks. Hambleton was now hiding in the underbrush near the Cam Lo River. There was intense fire near him. The Army choppers made an attempt to close in for a rescue. Two were shot down. One Huey, *Blue Ghost* 39, was destroyed with one survivor who was captured. *Blue Ghost* 28, the Cobra gunship that was hit, was able to limp toward the coast where it crash-landed on the beach south of Quang Tri.

It so happened that the rescue was in the middle of a major enemy troop concentration which is what the B-52s were trying to hit. Colonel Hambleton was in the center of one of the invading NVA columns of troops. Within the no-fire zone established around Hambleton for his protection, the USAF controlled all airstrikes and artillery fire. While the intent of the no-fire zone was good, its creation caused many difficulties for the 3rd ARVN ground forces, giving the enemy an unprecedented opportunity to advance at will.

Nail 59, Captain Gary Ferentchak, on-scene to relieve some Da Nang FACs, was flying a Pave Nail-equipped OV-10 (with precision LORAN equipment, a light-intensification viewer, a laser designator, and a computer system). He was able to verify Hambleton's position (as fixed by Lieutenant Jankowski the night before) almost immediately, using a series of radio bearings off the survivor's radio correlated with the LORAN equipment. He was about 1,000 meters north of the town of Cam Lo on the north bank of the Mieu Giang River. FACs from Da Nang and Nakhon Phanom continued the all-night coverage. The weather was terrible. The LORAN fix was relayed to NKP where it was collated with recent photography. Computers printed out targets for bombers so that they could drop bombs through the clouds and haze. Hambleton was in a clump of trees in a large field, and thus the OV-10s put down area-denial ordnance around his position. *Covey* and *Bilk* FACs from Da Nang and *Nail* FACs from NKP maintained constant patrol over *Bat* 21 *Bravo*. The next morning two *Nails*, consisting of Captains Rock O. Smith and Richard M. Atchison, called in more airstrikes.

The following day, another OV-10, *Nail* 38, crewed by Captains William Henderson and Mark Clark, relieved Smith and Atchison. Coming on scene just east of Cam Lo, Red Crown, a Navy ship in the Gulf of Tonkin, called out an SA-2 warning, but *Nail* 38 was shot down by the missile. The crew bailed out. Henderson had bad luck and was taken prisoner, while Clark managed to escape and await rescue, only two kilometers from *Bat 21 Bravo*. FAC Harold Icke was the last one to talk to Henderson before he was captured. Icke didn't find out what really happened until after the war:

AT MIDNIGHT — and we were checking in with him every hour — it just so happened that Henderson had dug himself in to hide. The Vietnamese dug a .51-cal machine-gun pit right on top of him, and dug him out. They took him up North.

———— ⚬ ————

From 2 April to 13 April, 90 strike sorties a day were flown. Another OV-10, *Covey* 282, was shot down. The pilot was evading like Hambleton and Clark. The U.S. Marine backseater was not heard from. Two Army helicopters went down. On 6 April, the final attempt was made to pick up the two downed airmen. A USAF HH-53, *Jolly* 67, crossed the river safely, but missed hearing a warning on the radio from the *Sandys* circling overhead not to turn right over the village. Heavy machine-gun fire sieved the helicopter. Just as it made it back across the river, flames shot out below the main rotor. The chopper rolled 90 degrees and crashed and burned, killing all on board.

Despite the intensity of the USAF's efforts, they were no closer to rescuing the men. During these days, Harold Icke was on scene most of the time, only leaving to refuel. Once he launched under a rocket attack to get back over *Bat 21B*:

THIS GUY (Hambleton) was no spring chicken; he was 53 years old. He had nothing to eat but bananas and water. After we lost the Jolly Green, we were going to try and drop him some food. He had moved down toward the river. I was trying to locate him. I was flying over the general area asking him to . . . mark . . . a signal when I was overhead. Suddenly I saw him standing on the bank of the river waving something white. I said, "God, get back, get back, there are bad guys all around."

———— ⚬ ————

Captain William J. Begart was on-scene commander for part of the rescue operation flying an O-2A. Begart received a DFC when, "despite poor weather conditions and battle damage to his aircraft from intense ground fire, he directed tactical fighters onto the hostile troop concentrations, enabling the survivors to escape detection." (This O-2A, S/N 67-21395, was assigned to the 366th Tactical Fighter Wing (PACAF). In 1988, this same aircraft was acquired by the Dover (Delaware) AFB Historical Center. By coincidence, Colonel Bill Begart was Vice-Commander of the 436th Military Airlift Wing when this O-2A was delivered to the Museum at Dover AFB. He did not know he flew this particular airplane until he looked it up in his log book. Begart later became Wing Commander at Dover AFB. The USAF plans to display this O-2A as the centerpiece of its *BAT 21* exhibit at the Wright-Patterson AFB Museum.

The senior USAF officials decided not to try further aerial rescue attempts. The FACs relayed instructions to Clark and Hambleton to swim downriver away from the main concentration of enemy forces. Hambleton took longer to reach the river because he first had to work his way across a minefield.

Icke put in strikes and ended up with M-47 smoke bombs, which gave Lieutenant Thomas R. Norris, the U.S. Navy SEAL advisor, attempting the rescue along the river, cover. The rescue would never have worked without the strikes put in by the FACs on targets given to them by *BAT 21 Bravo* and Norris. When the A-1s arrived, they used Willie Petes for a smoke screen around the downed pilot. Harold Icke took pictures of the actual smoke screen that preceded the rescue.

Hambleton was rescued after a 12-day ordeal by Lieutenant Norris, who received his country's highest award, the Medal of Honor, for his part in the rescue. His citation reads:

Lt. Norris completed an unprecedented ground rescue of two downed pilots deep within heavily controlled enemy territory in Quang Tri Province. Lt. Norris, on the night of 10 April, led a five-man patrol through 2,000 meters of heavily controlled enemy territory, located one of the downed pilots at daybreak, and returned to the Forward Operating Base (FOB). On 11 April, after a devastating mortar and rocket attack on the small FOB, Lt. Norris led a three-man team on two unsuccessful rescue attempts for the second pilot. On the afternoon of the 12th, a forward air controller located the pilot and notified Lt. Norris. Dressed in fisherman

The river where FAC Harold Icke located *BAT* 21*B*. Lieutenant Thomas R. Norris received the Medal of Honor for his part in the rescue of *BAT* 21*B* in the area under the cloud in the picture, but on the river.   Harold Icke Collection

The rescue of *Bat* 21 *Bravo* was the largest-scale rescue attempt of the Vietnam War.

Captain Wilbanks, formerly an F-86 Sabre pilot, was a FAC in Vietnam, flying O-1s over the central highlands near Bao Lac and Di Linh, small cities 100 miles northeast of Saigon. Master Sergeant Robert W. Veigel, a ROMAD (Radio Operator/Maintenance/Driver) working with advisory air liaison teams assigned to the 4th Infantry Division, recalled the downing of Wilbanks:

THE DAY STARTED out as normal for the people at Gia Nghia, Advisory Team 37, but by the end of the day, the Air Force team would hear of the loss of a brother wearer of the blue. It was 24 February 1967. I sat monitoring the reports of the fighting in the next province at Di Linh. It was obvious that the fighting was intense. As I monitored the radio, I heard the head Air Liaison Officer for the 23rd ARVN Division at Ban Me Thout talking to a Forward Air Controller about the bad situation at Di Linh and asking for his assistance. I didn't learn the FAC's name until the next day. The ALO was informing him of the status of aircraft and forces in his area. Being quite familiar with the area, the FAC said he would go help out his friends.

disguises and using a sampan, Lt. Norris and one Vietnamese traveled throughout the night and found the injured pilot at dawn. Covering the pilot with bamboo and vegetation, they began the return journey, successfully evading a North Vietnamese patrol. Approaching the FOB, they came under heavy machine-gun fire. Lt. Norris called in an airstrike which provided suppression fire and a smokescreen, allowing the rescue party to reach the FOB. By his outstanding display of courage, and selfless dedication in the face of extreme danger, Lt. Norris enhanced the finest traditions of the U.S. Naval Service.

Richard L. Griffin (*Cagey* 12 and *Elliott* 22) remembered:

HILLIARD WILBANKS took off from Bar Duc, which wasn't even in his own sector. He had stopped in there to pick up a carburetor for another aircraft. As he took off, the 23rd South Vietnamese Ranger Battalion was being hit.

A small detachment of American advisors accompanied the Battalion. As evening approached, Captain Wilbanks, aloft on his 488th combat mission (at this point, Wilbanks had two months left in-country), contacted Army Captain R. J. Wooten, the senior American advisor with the 23rd Vietnamese Rangers. Captain Wilbanks was also in radio contact with two U.S. Army helicopter gunships hovering west of Di Linh. Searching the familiar terrain, Captain Wilbanks saw the enemy hidden in camouflaged foxholes on the hillsides. The Rangers were moving into an ambush. Captain Wooten's radio crackled with the FAC's warning just as the hillsides erupted with enemy fire. The VC opened up on the friendly forces and the two FAC airplanes above with mortars, machine-guns, automatic rifles, and countless shoulder weapons.

Wilbanks fired a marking rocket toward the center of the enemy fire, pinpointing the ambush site for the helicopter gunships to attack. One of the three choppers was hit, so Wilbanks advised the remaining pair of gunships to escort the crippled craft to friendly territory. A second FAC radioed that two flights of fighters were on the way.

The situation became desperate as the gunships had departed and the fighters were still far away. The VC departed their foxholes,

One of the A-1s that put in an airstrike on the mortar position at *Bilk* 11's direction with Lieutenant Norris came under attack after rescuing *BAT* 21*B*.   *Harold Icke Collection*

The actual airstrikes on the mortar positions. The A-1s were using "Willie Pete" (White Phosphorus) bombs that they used for smoke screens quite often. The airstrikes were on the north bank of the river and Lieutenant Norris and *BAT* 21*B* were on the south bank.   *Harold Icke Collection*

charging down the slope with bayonets and knives ready at the badly outnumbered Rangers. From overhead, Wilbanks fired a smoke rocket that exploded amidst the enemy force. The Viet Cong looked skyward and sent a hail of bullets toward the jinking Bird Dog. Wilbanks banked steeply and fired another smoke rocket. The Bird Dog had become the

hunter. Wilbanks made another low pass while intense gunfire followed his aircraft. Then he fired his last rocket. The Rangers knew it and the enemy knew it. The FAC had done it all, risking his life to inflict casualties on the enemy and to protect the Rangers. It was time for Wilbanks to pull off and wait for the fighters.

But, Hilliard Wilbanks was not finished. He still had his automatic rifle that he carried as a survival weapon. Pointing his O-1 at the enemy, he released the controls, and fired his rifle from the side window. The Bird Dog careened dangerously close to the treetops. Wilbanks grabbed the controls and jinked around so he could fire his rifle again. Now the Viet Cong were off balance and confused. The FAC reloaded another clip and attacked again. "Each pass was so close we could hear his plane being hit," said Captain Wooten. The second FAC tried to contact Captain Wilbanks, but there was no reply after the third rifle pass.

A Ranger advisor on the ground, Captain Gary F. Vote, pulled Wilbanks out of the wreckage of his plane which rested in no-man's land between the two forces:

HE WAS NO more than 100 feet off the ground and almost over his objective, firing his rifle. Then he began erratic moves, first up, then down, then banking west right over my position. I thought he was wounded and looking for a friendlier spot to land. I jumped up and waved my arms. But as he banked again, I could see that he was unconscious. His aircraft crashed about 100 meters away. Captain Wilbanks was alive when Captain Vote pulled him from the wreckage. Meanwhile, the two helicopter gunships that doubled as rescue birds returned. They fired their remaining ammunition into the enemy - positions and swooped down near the Bird Dog to pick up the FAC. They were driven off by enemy gunfire in four attempts. Under the direction of another FAC, two Phantom jet fighters raked the enemy with 20mm cannon fire. At last a helicopter, braving the withering gunfire, picked up Hilliard Wilbanks. He died in the chopper en route to the treatment center at Bao Lac. (*Air Force Heroes in Vietnam*, pp. 15-18)

Master Sergeant Veigel remembered: "Everyone on our radio net knew that a FAC had gone down and were silently saying a prayer for him when the radio operator at Bao Loc informed the ALO at Ban Me Thout that the FAC had died five minutes from medical assistance. The following year the Medal of Honor was presented to his wife."

Richard Griffin summed it up:

THERE WAS NO air around, and the ARVN Battalion was being hit. He kept shooting his rockets, M-16, and hand gun. The Army advisor could hear the bullets hitting his aircraft as it was flying very low to the ground. He was doing what the book said you weren't supposed to do. And, he kept shooting. The guys on the ground said if he hadn't done it, they would have lost the battalion.

According to Major Donald K. Schneider, the last part of Wilbanks's citation reads:

CAPTAIN WILBANKS' magnificent action saved numerous friendly personnel from certain injury or death. His unparalleled concern for his fellowman and his extraordinary heroism were in the highest traditions of the military service, and have reflected great credit upon himself and the United States Air Force.

On 29 June 1972, Captain Steven L. Bennett (in-country only three months) and his backseater, Marine Captain Mike Brown, who had volunteered for temporary duty in Vietnam to assist Air Force FACs in directing naval gunfire, took off from Da Nang Air Base in an OV-10 and headed northwest along the coast, arriving at Quang Tri in half an hour where they circled below a cloud deck. For the next two hours, the OV-10 crew adjusted naval artillery from the heavy cruiser *Newport News* and the destroyer *R. B. Anderson*, allowing the ships to pinpoint their fire against enemy positions near Quang Tri.

Darrel D. Whitcomb (*Nail* 25) recalled his rescue attempt of Captain Bennett (*Covey* 87):

I WILL ALWAYS remember 29 June 1972, just south of Quang Tri, when an American pilot, Steve Bennett, gave his life to save that of another. I spent two hours that day working strikes against targets in the Cam Lo area. As I reported my results to *Big Control*, I was told to contact *Covey* 87 working approximately 30 miles south along the My Chanh River. He had taken off about an hour after me with *Wolfman* 45 (Captain Mike Brown), a Marine artillery observer, in the back seat. They had planned to adjust artillery along the coast but were diverted to a ground commander who had critical troops-in-contact.

I rendezvoused with *Covey* 87. Since fighters were not available, he suggested I join him in strafing the enemy positions with our internal guns. Normally we didn't do this because of the SA-7 threat, but this was a critical situation. We set it up so that I would pull off to the south, and *Covey* 87 to the north. After my second pass I looked up and saw a large air-burst. *Covey* 87 had been hit by an SA-7 missile, although I didn't know that at the time. Almost immediately he made a Mayday call and headed east toward the Gulf of Tonkin. I quickly joined up next to him. I could see that the left engine was completely gone. There was a large hole in the wing, and the left landing gear (which is retracted in flight) was hanging down. Worst of all were the visible flames in the damaged areas.

His radios were damaged too. He could talk to me but not to *Big Control*. I switched over to the emergency frequency for him and repeated the initial Mayday call. A third OV-10, flown by Lieutenant Bob Temko of my squadron, joined up on the right side as we crossed the coastline.

A few minutes later *Covey* 87 told me he was going to eject once he was well out over the water. Almost immediately he called me again and said that his backseater's parachute had been damaged by the missile blast. This ruled out a safe ejection. The only way he could save his backseater was to make a crash-landing on the runway at Da Nang, where they could have a foamed runway.

Right after *Covey* 87 called me, we heard a voice on the radio say, "You had better ditch it, *Covey*." Ditching was considered extremely risky in the OV-10. It was not a strongly built aircraft. I saw a young OV-10 pilot drown after ditching his OV-10 in the bay near Chu Lai a few months earlier. Just as I reached down to push the transmit button and warn *Covey* 87 to disregard the specious call, *King* called me on the emergency frequency for an update on *Covey* 87's condition and intentions.

As I relayed the requested information, *Covey* 87 was continuously descending, a fact I neglected to notice, and in the middle of my transmission, *Covey* 87 bellied into the water about 200 yards off the beach northeast of Hue. I relayed this to *King* as the other OV-10 and I set up orbits over *Covey* 87. A-1s were on the way as well as a rescue helicopter from a Navy ship offshore. Several flights of fighters showed up and orbited overhead. When some civilians gathered on the beach and launched a boat, Bob Temko, not wanting to take any chances that they might be unfriendly, put down a line of strafe between the boat and the crash site. The civilians turned around with a nervous wave.

When *Covey* 87 hit the water, the dangling left landing gear caused the aircraft to partly cartwheel and break apart. It sank almost immediately. I made a low pass, saw a life raft, and only one survivor. Just as I pulled up, he called me with his survival radio using the emergency frequency, and identified himself as *Wolfman* 45, the backseater. We orbited his position until the rescue chopper arrived and pulled him from the water. Soon the A-1s arrived so we turned the rescue over to them in the vain hope that Steve would surface. Bob and I were by now low on fuel, so we headed back to Da Nang.

Later I met *Wolfman* 45, and we reconstructed the entire event starting with when I rendezvoused with *Covey* 87. He stated that Steve decided to ditch right after they heard the unidentified radio call stating that they had better do so. After that, he said, things really happened fast. The impact with the water was hard. The aircraft broke apart in front of *Wolfman* 45 which gave him an opening to get out of. He floated to the surface, expecting to see Steve. Instead all he saw of the aircraft was a little bit of the tail sticking out of the water. He pulled himself back down into the fuselage, trying to reach the cockpit and his pilot. He had to resurface for air. As he got ready to go down again, the aircraft sank. There was nothing more he could do.

Months later I learned that Vice President [*Gerald R.*] Ford had presented a posthumous Medal of Honor to Steve's wife and child in honor of his sacrifice. Although I never met Steve, his final act has always remained with me. I watched him die — you can't know a man any better than that.

———— ❧ ————

Steve Bennett's body was recovered the next day, 30 June, from the smashed cockpit of the submerged aircraft. He had had no chance to escape. His posthumous Medal of Honor citation reads:

As a forward air controller near Quang Tri, Republic of Vietnam, on June 29, 1972, Captain Bennett was the pilot of a light aircraft flying an artillery adjustment mission along a heavily defended segment of route structure. A large concentration of enemy troops was massing for an attack on a friendly unit. Captain Bennett requested tactical air support but was denied due to the close proximity of friendly troops to the target. Captain Bennett was determined to aid the endangered unit and elected to strafe the hostile positions. After four such passes, the enemy force began to retreat. Captain Bennett continued the attack, but, as he completed his fifth strafing pass, his aircraft was struck by a surface-to-air missile, which severely damaged the left engine and the left main landing gear. As fire spread in the left engine, Captain Bennett realized that recovery at a friendly airfield was impossible. He instructed his observer to prepare for ejection, but was informed by the observer that his parachute had been shredded by the force of the impacting missile. Although Captain Bennett had a good parachute, he knew that if he ejected, the observer would have no chance for survival. With complete disregard for his own life, Captain Bennett elected to ditch the aircraft into the Gulf of Tonkin, even though he realized that a pilot of this type aircraft had never survived a ditching. The ensuing impact upon the water caused the aircraft to cartwheel and severely damaged the front cockpit, making escape for Captain Bennett impossible. The observer successfully made his way out of the aircraft and was rescued. Captain Bennett's unparalleled concern for his companion, extraordinary heroism and intrepidity above and beyond the call of duty, at the cost of his life, were in keeping with the highest traditions of the military service and reflect great

credit upon himself and the United States Air Force. (Schneider, p. 69)

Medal of Honor to FACs

Only 12 Medals of Honor were awarded to Air Force pilots during the Vietnam War. Two of these went to Forward Air Controllers who lost their lives in the line of duty. Also, two were awarded to A-1 Skyraider pilots, Lieutenant Colonel William A. Jones, III, and Major Bernard F. Fisher, both having made daring rescues with complete disregard for their own safety.

Changes in Rescue Emphasis

The Pave Nail- and Pave Spot-equipped OV-10s helped the search and rescue forces change their reliance on the A-1/Jolly Green team that used firepower, tactics, and courage to a team of the A-7/Jolly Green that used more advanced technology. The *Pave Nail* OV-10s could locate survivors in bad weather or at night, because they were equipped with a night observation device that included a bore-sighted laser range designator called "Pave Spot" — a real asset to a rescue force because it could beam a laser to mark the slant range and heading of targets. By 1970, the faster OV-10s, carrying four 7.62 machine-guns as well as a rocket or gunpad, became more important in search and rescue than the slower, unarmed O-1s and O-2s — all working together to ensure "that others may live."

Epilogue

*I**T WAS NEVER THE** intention of the United States to defeat North Vietnam militarily. The U.S. goal was to give the South Vietnamese time to arm and defend themselves. In spite of all the U.S. training, and the huge supply of matériel and aircraft left behind, the South Vietnamese were overwhelmed when the North Vietnamese violated the agreements they had signed, by launching overwhelming attacks against South Vietnam in 1975. Not only was South Vietnam defeated, but Laos and Cambodia also fell to the increasing sphere of Communist domination.*

Unfortunately, the cost to the U.S. was devastating, not only because of the thousands of Americans killed or wounded, but also because of the money spent, and the divisiveness amongst the American public on the home front. For the U.S. Air Force alone, 2,118 personnel were killed, 3,460 were wounded, and 2,257 aircraft were destroyed. Of those men shot down, 586 were carried as

Missing-In-Action or captured, of whom only 368 were eventually returned to friendly hands. And 338 USAF Forward Air Controllers were lost in battle in the skies over Southeast Asia.

Beginning in 1975, Air Force Brigadier General Harry "Heinie" Aderholt began making arrangements to reclaim as many aircraft as possible from the Republic of Vietnam's Air Force, which had grown to be the fourth largest in the world with 2,276 aircraft in 1973. Many of the aircraft flew to Thailand, and eventually to other parts of the world. One of the O-1 Bird Dogs rescued was found in a rice paddy, stranded on a cart path with barely a foot clearance on each side of the main landing gear. Reports state that former FAC Briggs Dogood "paced off the length of the path, put some gas from a tanker into the plane. Then he got in and in a cloud of dust flew the O-1 off the cart path."

The conduct of war has always depended on technology, threat, tactics, and terrain. From the earliest days, man has always sought ways to have an eye in the sky. Technology in the 1990s provides near real-time images sent to ground commanders via uplinks to orbiting satellites. Troops can reconnoiter the countryside electronically. Ground commanders can see the whole battlefield, in real time, day or night. The Joint Chiefs of Staff call this "information dominance."

The laser-guided bomb technology of the Vietnam War days has become much more sophisticated. Computer technology aids the battle commanders in decision making. Leaders will make use of a mission-control room to disseminate information.

The Fast FAC program survived the Vietnam War as a key element in the employment of tactical air power in a conventional conflict. In the future, a data link between the missile and the FAC will provide the terminal guidance needed for the missile to hit the target precisely. A multitude of terminal guidance systems will be available to the FAC.

The most potent eye in the sky is "PowerScene," a 3-D terrain visualization simulator with a 32-gigabyte database. Using computer-enhanced composites of satellite imagery, maps, and photographs, PowerScene allows operators to "fly" over an entire country and see realistic details down to one-meter resolution. PowerScene can be used to map out routes and find defensible — and locate potential — ambush sites.

Another formidable element of information dominance is the E-8C converted Boeing 707 "Night Stalker," the most complex airborne system ever engineered. In the back of the aircraft, technicians at consoles can overlay maps or satellite photos on incoming radar data. Anything moving within a moving box 150 kilometers square can be identified.

But the ultimate effect of so much technology remains to be seen.

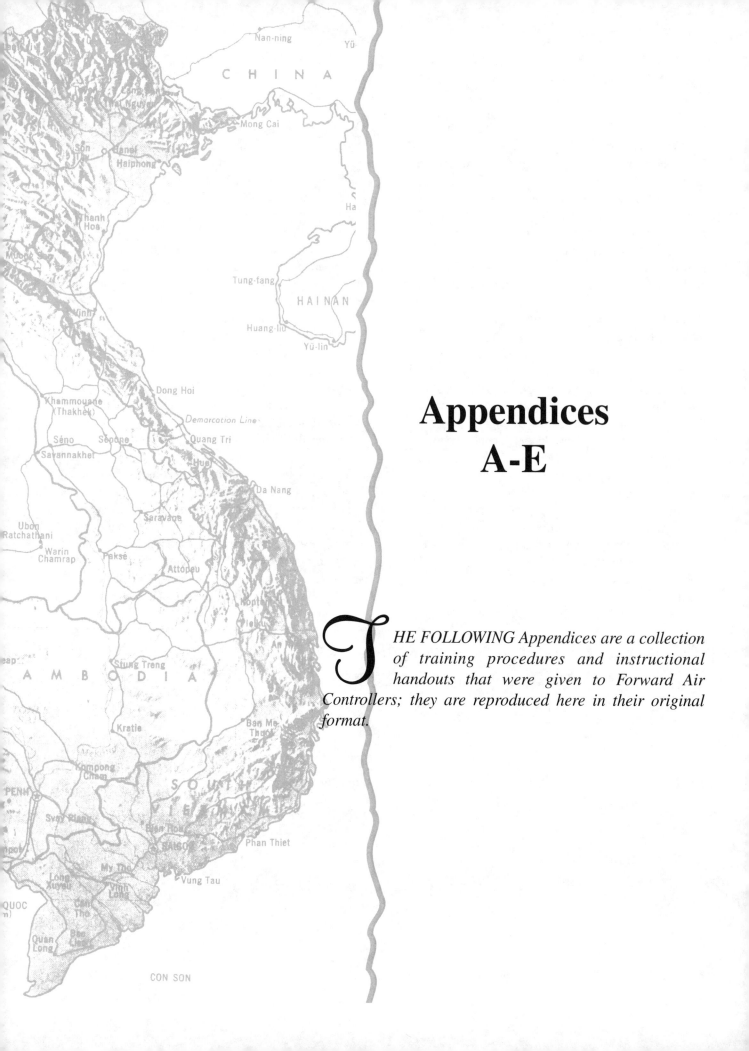

Appendices
A-E

THE FOLLOWING Appendices are a collection of training procedures and instructional handouts that were given to Forward Air Controllers; they are reproduced here in their original format.

Appendix A

Forward Air Control Procedures

FORWARD AIR CONTROL PROCEDURES

GENERAL:

a. It is of upmost importance that the FAC be thoroughly familiar with the Army command and control structure and know and understand their operational plans and maneuvers.

b. The effectiveness of airborne forward air control missions depends largely upon the knowledge and proficiency of the FAC flying in the control aircraft. In order to be effective in fulfilling his responsibilities in controlling air strikes, the FAC must know the strike aircraft capabilities, the effectiveness of the different types of ordnance and the ordnance delivery procedures utilized by the strike aircraft.

MISSION PREPARATION

The following sequence of events may vary but usually occur in the following order:

1. Planning the mission:

    a. Obtain and plot the target coordinates on your 1:50,000 scale map.

    b. Determine the location of friendly forces in the area closest to the target.

    c. Check with the Sector Intelligence Office for any additional information they may have in the area of your proposed strike.

    d. Locate the nearest "safe" area, if no friendly forces or civilians are nearby. Usually this is an area that is isolated, with few enemy troops around.

    e. Fill out your mission briefing card, with all required information.

2. Airborne:

Once airborne, the FAC should complete any last minute surveillance without giving away his intentions of striking the particular target. Utilize the element of surprise. Plan your strike in your own mind. Normally, you will know the type of fighters and their ordnance load. You can plan the direction of the attack and break, matching this to the terrain, nature of the target, and the battle situation. Note the weather in the target area, particularly the wind. Plan your attack so that the smoke from the ordnance will not obscure the remainder of the target. Note the friendly towns and outposts, and plan the best bail-out areas for use should your fighters have difficulty. Also consider anticipated enemy ground fire for both your observation position and for your recommended fighter pattern. Plan to be airborne at least 30 minutes prior to your scheduled fighter arrival time. Coordinate your pending air strike with applicable friendly activities in the area, such as the sub-sectors, to make certain that there are no friendly troops or operations in the proposed strike area. Give them the location and the scheduled time of the planned strike. Check your fuel and make note of the time you must depart the target in order to get to your airfield with a reasonable fuel reserve. Now you are ready to conduct the strike.

3. The Rendezvous:

After becoming airborne, make a radio call to your Sector Air Force radio station, to let them know that you are airborne. Advise them of your desired rendezvous location and working frequency, if these

have not already been assigned. Maintain a listening watch on this
frequency. The radio operator should be monitoring this frequency
and will be immediately available to you, to furnish any assistance
needed, such as making and coordinating a change in target coordinates,
or requesting additional flights of fighters as required. While operating in a hostile area, it is most important to keep the radio operator
or a ground station, advised of your location and intentions, so as to
be able to aid the rescue service, in the event you have an emergency
landing.

Proceed to the rendezvous point, taking time to make a last minute
check on the target situation, fixing in your mind the location or
points in the target area which you plan to place ordnance on.

The rendezvous portion of the airstrike is the simple act of the FAC
and the fighters meeting at a predetermined area on a predetermined
frequency.

Upon establishing radio contact with the fighters, direct them in to
the rendezvous by use of a TACAN and DME fix, UHF/DF or by describing
the physical aspects of the rendezvous. Topography will not appear
the same to the fighter pilot since he usually is flying at a much
higher altitude.

Use prominent landmarks, such as large canal intersections, cities,
bends in a highway or canal. Such a description will bring the fighters
to your area, where you can make visual contact. The usual method is
for the FAC to meet the fighters at the rendezvous, then proceed to the
target. Quite frequently, the target will be at some distance from the
rendezvous. Now, for example, if your target is 20 kilometers from the
rendezvous, it will probably take you almost 10 minutes to fly this
distance to the target. If your fighters are jets, they may only have
30 minutes total loiter and on-target time. Therefore, it will save on
time for you to hold near your target and talk your fighters in to you
from the rendezvous point. A word of caution - make certain that the
fighters are over the correct rendezvous point, before you start giving
them directions to find you. Once you have them in visual contact, you
must direct their eyes to find you. The best method to use is the
"clock" method; i.e., "I'm in your 2 o'clock position, low." This
sounds simple, but if you have a scattered cloud condition, the problem
becomes more difficult.

4. Target Description and Marking:

    a. Now, having established radio contact with your fighters and
while they are inbound, you should do two things. First, call your
radio operator and confirm the target coordinates with him, to be certain
you will be hitting the correct target. Second, have the fighters give
you the type and number of aircraft, the mission number, the ordnance
load and loiter and "Bingo" time. The amount of time the strike aircraft
can remain in the target area will determine the sequence of ordnance,

number of passes and time of expenditure. Diverted aircraft will normally have a minimum amount of time on target.

b.   Once you have established visual contact with the fighters,
make a note of this time, referred to as "talley" time. Then depart
the rendezvous point, with the fighters, for the target area. While
enroute, you can brief the fighters.

(1)   Describe the target to the fighters, such as "200 Victor
Charlie and base camp, with a Bl intelligence rating." Also describe
the terrain features, such as; i.e., "the target is located in heavy
foilage, or along a canal-running east to west, or structures in among
trees." Also give the target elevation and maximum height of obstacles,
such as trees. The weather conditions can be given, with the direction
and velocity of the wind, the altimeter setting and cloud bases if
known.

(2)   Next, the location of the nearest friendly positions,
given in a compass direction from the target, with the distance in
meters,(southeast 2000 meters).

(3)   Recommend bailout area and nearest friendly alternate
airport. Also advise them, if downed near the target area, to stay
away from trees and canals, or locations where the VC are suspected to
be located.

(4)   Advise them of any artillery being fired in the target
area or nearby, as well as known or suspected enemy ground fire. If
known, give location, type and intensity of the ground fire. If unknown, tell the fighters you will advise them if you encounter or
hear groundfire.

(5)   Recommend the attack heading and direction to break.
Factors to be considered in recommending the attack heading, direction
of break and sequence of ordnance to be dropped, will be the position
of friendly troops (making runs parallel to the friendly lines) or
settlements, ground fire, artillery, other aircraft or helicopters,
shape and alignment of the target, terrain, wind direction, position
of the sun and cloud cover.

(6)   Next, state where the FAC will hold and his altitude.
The FACs position will also be influenced by the type of fighter he
is directing. He may hold inside or outside the fighter's pattern,
using a figure eight or race track pattern. In some instances of low
level delivered ordnance, he may orbit over the target. He will always
inform the fighters of changes in his position and never place himself
on a direct line between the fighters and the target. Maintain visual
contact with the fighters, or, if unable to do so, make certain that
the fighter has visual contact with the FAC prior to clearing him in
on his attack. Maintain at least 1500 feet above the terrain, to
reduce the vulnerability to ground fire.

4

5. Conducting the Strike:

The FAC should remain clear of the target area as much as possible
until he is ready to begin the airstrike, to keep from alerting the
enemy. He should insure that the fighters have him in sight before
marking. The best procedure is, after briefing the fighters on the
target and related information, is to advise them that you are ready
to mark. When the fighters are in position and notify you to mark,
have the pilot of your aircraft place a marking rocket on the desired
part of the target, where you wish to start the strike. When the
fighters confirm the mark, the target, and have visual contact with
the FAC aircraft, they may be cleared in "wet" (to drop). The FAC
should not hesitate to direct the fighters to cease their attack and
pull off the target, if he is in doubt of any aspect of the attack.

The FAC will move to a position so that he can monitor the strike
and offer further guidance to effect the complete destruction of the
target. Normally, the FAC aircraft will move outside the flight
pattern of the strike aircraft while remaining close enough to observe
ordnance impacts. Make a notation of the time the first fighter
starts the airstrike. Brief information should be given as the strike
progresses, such as "on target," or "next bomb 100 meters north of
last hit," etc. Using the terms "long, short, left or right" can
meet some situations, however, using cardinal compass headings "north,
south, east or west," will reduce the possibility of confusion when
the fighters vary attack headings. Constant attention should be given
in making all communications short and as brief as possible. Also
keep an eye open for any ground fire, and if observed, advise the
fighters of the location. Adjust the pattern as necessary to reduce
the chance of the fighters being hit.

As each fighter nears his roll-in position, there are three bits of
information that you will need: (1) Who he is. (2) Where is he
coming from. (3) What ordnance is he going to drop; i.e., "Number
two inbound from the west, with a bomb." You should acknowledge his
call, then advise him where you want him to drop his ordnance, and if
he is in sight, clear him in wet; i.e, "Roger, number two, drop your
bomb 75 meters short last hit, on heavy tree area. Have you visual,
you are cleared in wet." This information must be given quickly, so
the inbound pilot will have time for a question if he does not see
the target. Do not clear the fighter in on a pass unless you have him
in sight and he has you in sight. The key to conducting a successful
strike with jet fighters is to keep track of the fighters and make
prompt corrections as needed.

The Bomb Damage Assessment Report (BDA)

When the fighters have expended their ordnance, the FAC should tell
the fighters to go "high and dry" for the BDA. (Make a note of the
time the fighters complete the strike). He should then confirm the
altitude that the fighters will be flying over the target area, to
insure adequate separation. Whenever possible, the BDA should be

accomplished from the same altitude from which the strike was controlled and with the fighters still in the area. The FAC should also attempt to keep a running BDA during the strike to reduce the exposure time (to enemy ground fire) required for the post-strike BDA. Give the BDA in its entirety to the fighter leader:

    a. Give him the target coordinates, with the area limits or radius in meters.

    b. Next, the time the fighters started the strike and time they completed the strike.

    c. Give the percent of ordnance on target. Normally it will be 100 percent.

    d. Give the percent of target coverage.

    e. Give the strike results; i.e., "seven structures destroyed, three damaged, two bunkers destroyed, one sampan damaged."

    f. State number of dud ordnance and type bomb, napalm, etc.

    g. Include any secondary explosions or fires observed.

Your radio operator will need to know the following:

1. What caused the secondary explosion or fire - napalm, bomb, rocket, CBU, etc.

2. Number of explosions or fires.

3. Color of smoke - gray, white, black, etc.

4. Height of smoke.

5. Density of smoke - thick, thin.

6. Where secondary occurred - open or wooded area, sampan, structure, etc.

7. Destructive effect - similar to 100# bomb, 250#, 500#, etc.

The fighter leader should read back the BDA for FAC confirmation. If correct, you may then clear him to depart the area. If the fighters did a good job for you, advise them so.

When the fighters have departed the area and you are leaving the area too, contact your radio operator and confirm that he copied the BDA. If not, repeat the BDA to him. Do not forget to tell him the "tally" time.

Upon reaching your destination airport, do not forget to close out with your radio operator and give him your landing time.

For a recap of primary ideas, the following items are outlined:

1. During an airstrike, the FAC is in command of the TARGET SITUATION.

2. Always be in immediate radio contact with the Direct Air Request Net.

3. The FAC is the eyes of the strike pilot.

4. The purpose of using a smoke-marking rocket is to keep distance between you and the target. Do not yield this advantage.

5. Keep the fighters in sight.

6. Keep the target in sight.

7. Do not clear the fighters on a pass unless you have them in sight and they have you in sight.

8. The FAC must plan the efficient distribution of ordnance.

9. The fighter strike can be no better than the direction received.

10. Close air support is the ultimate mission of the FAC.

Appendix B

Visual Reconnaissance

SECTION E -- VISUAL RECONNAISSANCE

20. The Visual Reconnaissance Program -- Next in importance to conducting airstrikes is the airborne FAC's responsibility for performing visual reconnaissance (VR). The insurgent enemy's survival is keyed to escaping detection to nullify the superior fire power of friendly forces. Any amount of sophisticated weaponry is useless without targets. Airborne FACs have an excellent opportunity to develop targets since they soon acquire detailed knowledge of the entire area of responsibility and can visually check this area on a daily basis. Recognizing this, 7AF developed a visual reconnaissance program for airborne FACs (7AFR 55-33). Continuing surveillance by the FAC not only discovers established targets for airstrikes, but also provides a source of bits and pieces of information to the Army Intelligence Section for correlation with data for other sources for target development.

21. <u>Recommendations for Conducting Visual Reconnaissance</u>:

    a. Work closely with the intelligence and operations sections of the ground unit to which attached. Prior to every flight, the FACs should know all reported and suspected locations of enemy activity and the exact boundaries of all specified strike zones; in addition, the FAC needs to have detailed information on all friendly units, including present position, planned movement, call signs, and frequencies.

    b. At all times while airborne, carefully examine the area below for signs of enemy activity, regardless of the type of mission being flown. When practicable, plan all flights to maximize VR coverage -- for example: Select a route proceeding to and from an airstrike target to overfly probable areas of enemy activity nearby.

    c. Establish a system to insure that all portions of your area receive periodic VR coverage, giving frequent attention to the more likely enemy locations; however, avoid following a set timetable which would allow the enemy to plan their activities around your coverage.

    d. On all flights, carry 1:50,000 scale maps of your entire area of responsibility. Carry similar maps of adjacent areas. You might need them in an emergency. Always keep track of your position on the appropriate maps, and immediately plot and annotate any significant sighting directly on your map.

    e. Study the appearance of the terrain and the general behavior patterns of the people throughout your area. Know what to expect to see, and be suspicious of any deviation from the normal -- the presence of these could well be the cause of the disruption.

29

        (1) Learn the eating, sleeping, working, travelling, and social routines of the people.

        (2) Know the normal harvesting processing, distribution, and storage procedures for all crops grown in your area.

        (3) Check villages and fields for the normal percentage of men, as compared to women and children.

        (4) Check dirt roads and trails for amount of usage, keeping in mind the reason for their existence. Remember that rain will wash away old wheel marks and the resulting mud will record travel since the rain; remember that the enemy operates primarily at night, so checking a trail at sunset and then again at the following sunrise could detect usage by the enemy.

        (5) Check roads for cuts and any sign of digging which could indicate mining; also, check along roads and waterways for possible ambush sites, indicated by trenches and foxholes.

        (6) Check shorelines and banks along waterways for marks in the mud and disturbed foliage which could indicate enemy activity. At dawn and when the tide is out are good times to cover these areas.

        (7) In the early morning and late afternoon, look for shadows in otherwise flat terrain -- they could be caused by enemy bunkers. Shadows are also useful in determining the height of an object, by comparison with the shadow produced by something of known height.

        (8) Remember that the enemy goes to great lengths to avoid detection from the air -- his facilities are small and well camouflaged, and often are completely underground in the form of caves and tunnels. In addition, people are very difficult to spot from the air unless they are in the open; consequently, stay alert for indications of human activity (i.e., smoke from campfires and disturbed flocks of birds) in suspect areas.

    f. Before making a general VR of your area, check specific points of interest obtained from the Army Intelligence and Operations Sections. Start scanning the area of the point of interest from as far out as possible -- as soon as the enemy realizes an aircraft is approaching, they will take steps to avoid discovery by dousing cooking fires, etc; a wisp of smoke may be the only indication you can find, so plot it immediately -- before it disappears.

g. When checking a specific point, start from the coordinates provided by the Army Intelligence Section. If you find nothing, imagine yourself as the enemy commander and check out any other likely points nearby.

h. At all times, avoid flying a straight line or a predictable flight path, such as staying directly above the river; frequently random turns makes your aircraft a more difficult target for ground fire. Also, analysis has proven that an altitude of 1500 feet above the ground is relatively safe for light aircraft subject to small arms ground fire.

i. To detect specific objects on the ground, stare at a point for a few seconds, then shift your stare to another point, continuing until you have covered the desired area by focusing on a succession of points. General area scanning (as used to spot other aircraft) is ineffective due to the lack of contrast between possible enemy targets and the surrounding terrain.

j. Check the area to the rear of the aircraft, as well as to the front and either side; personnel may feel safe to move about after the aircraft has passed.

k. If you spot a possible target, avoid a flight path which would indicate to the enemy that they have been discovered. If possible, continue your flight path as before the sighting and depart the area; draw a detailed mental picture of the target in your mind – when the target is no longer visible, make notes and sketches as needed. Always try to avoid making an immediate turn to overfly the target, and do not make repeated passes in the target vicinity. If the enemy is not alerted, the impending airstrike will be much more effective.

l. In some areas, heavy tree cover may completely obscure any view of the ground when flying at 1500 feet above the terrain. If mission accomplishment is keyed to checking an area of this type, you may elect to conduct VR at a lower altitude. If you decide to go below 1500 feet in heavily tree-covered areas, a few feet above the tree tops is the next safest altitude for protection from small arms ground fire/descend and climb out over known safe points.

(1) Before making a low level VR run, plan your descent, VR, and climb out so that all portions will be over heavily tree-covered areas. Select prominent checkpoints, which will be visible at both low and normal VR altitudes, to keep yourself oriented and to serve as a reference point for possible sightings. If no prominent checkpoints exist, be prepared to drop smoke grenades to help re-locate any sightings after the climb-out.

31

(2) During the low level run, as well as during the steep descent and climb-out, make random turns to make the aircraft a more difficult target for ground fire.

(3) For the best view of the ground from just above the tree tops, look at an angle of 45 degrees from the nose of the aircraft to the ground.

(4) Avoid flying over the same area twice, and stay alert for such objects as dead trees, which may project above the level of the surrounding.

m. The FAC should know the indicators that signify the enemy's presence or activity. Some of the indicators are as follows:

(1) Tracks -- human, animal and vehicle, indicating increased or recent travel. Water-soaked earth near a puddle or stream and tracks around new bomb craters indicate recent passage. Often direction of travel can be determined by noting the position of the damp ground in relation to the water.

(2) Movement of supplies or farming in isolated area -- farming may be indicated by drying grain or clothes, harvesting, or increased cattle population.

(3) Newly turned earth -- indicates foxholes, caves, tunneling.

(4) Camouflage -- evidence of something being hidden. Well camouflaged items may be hard to detect.

(5) The use of shadows is a key method of noting camouflage. At noon there are few shadows; optimum shadows occur early in the morning and late in the afternoon.

(6) Gun positions -- occupants may be hidden in the positions or nearby under foliage or in foxholes. If you find obvious positions; then closely VR the surrounding area to insure that they are not "sucker" positions causing you to miss nearby actual positions.

(7) Sampans -- unusual numbers, position or activity.

(8) People -- running and trying to hide or the complete lack of activity in an obviously occupied area.

n. What the enemy does when he thinks he has been spotted varies constantly and may be affected by terrain, training, situation, etc. The following are reactions to the presence of FACs in the past and some guidance

32

on where to look for the enemy.

      (1) Usually the enemy will stop and try to hide by blending into the background, especially near bunkers or camouflaged items. He may hide under cattle or try to imitate a bush, tree or dike.

      (2) If he thinks he is exposed, he will scurry for cover like a rat, running in short bursts from cover to cover. He moves when your aircraft is pointed away and freezes when you fly toward him. This necessitates watching to the rear as well as forward to spot enemy activity.

      (3) The enemy may change dress and hide his weapons to blend with the local population, or take off his hat and clothes, arrange them on the ground and escape the area while the FAC circles the decoy clothing.

      (4) Enemy base camps are often found near well-used trails and trail intersections, near cultivated areas along ridge lines or off of the main ridge line and near cleared areas under trees.

      o. Ground fire is usually heard rather than seen. If the source of ground fire is seen, the muzzle flash looks like a yellow strobe with a puff of smoke during the day and white strobe at night. Tracers leave a red streak but are usually used only by regular troops under attack. Snipers seldom use tracer unless they aren't worried about disclosing their position. The sound of ground fire has been described as follows:

      (1) Small arms -- click; snap; pop; muffled, dry stick snapping; cigarette lighter snapping shut; a whip cracking; popcorn popping; or a muffled, sharp engine backfire.

      (2) 50 cal -- a heavier, louder "woof," more decisive crack.

      (3) 20mm -- deeper, louder "pom," distinct, separated reports.

      (4) Rounds aimed at you crack more distinctly and a steady pattern indicates an automatic or belt-fed weapon.

      p. Light aircraft are not designed or equipped to combat ground fire; therefore, areas of known or suspected enemy ground fire should be avoided whenever possible, especially at low altitude. 1,500 feet has been calculated as being above the effective range of most small arms and low enough to conduct reasonable VR; however, your altitude should vary to meet the situation as hits have been reported above 1,500 feet and some targets require closer scrutiny than is possible at 1,500 feet. The FAC should always vary his maneuvers and patterns and never repeat in an area of suspected or known ground fire. In areas of jungle cover, the trees tend to give some protection, unless the FAC flies directly over the enemy or across an open area. To best combat ground fire once encountered, have a plan and react quickly to get away from the area. Immediate climbing or uncoordinated flight will cost airspeed and thus increase the amount of time required to get out of range. If there are trees, a good plan might be to dive to the deck, trying to get something between you and the gunner and picking up speed for getaway. A series of sharp turns will keep the gunner from getting a tail shot and may disrupt his lead. It is advisable to fly out of range before climbing. If you are above the effective range of the weapons, try to pinpoint their position for a strike, keeping to one side and out of range. Often dropping a smoke grenade may cause the enemy to cease fire in an effort to escape the airstrike which usually follows a FAC's mark. It is advisable to have armed fighters immediately available when marking a target, making a BDA or entering an area of suspected or known ground fire. To help decrease the effectiveness of ground fire, the FAC should fly into the area out of the sun and downwind. Attempt to stay over friendlies during strikes and avoid flying directly over the target or open areas, especially at low altitude.

q. The FAC must be alert at all times for other aircraft, realizing he is hard to see and has little chance for survival should a mid-air collision occur. The FAC shares the responsibility of avoiding a mid-air and must insure he has the fighters in sight and the fighters have visual contact with him before he clears them to make an ordnance delivery pass. It is also the FAC's responsibility to keep the fighters informed of other known aircraft in the area.

r. You may feel that your VR has produced a target worthwhile of an airstrike immediately. If so, then try to get it approved and get strike aircraft. In any case, report all sightings to the Army Intelligence Section as soon as possible after each flight.

s. Target approval authority varies in different areas and specific assignments. Therefore, no attempt will be made to delineate this responsibility. This approval authority is closely associated with the "Rules of Engagement." These rules also change. Be current and know these "rules" thoroughly.

34

Appendix C

Strike Diagrams

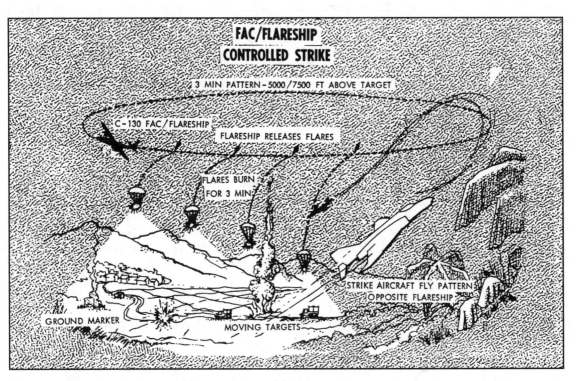

OVERHEAD HOLDING PATTERN

- ALWAYS BE IN A POSITION TO SEE THE STRIKE AIRCRAFT AND THE TARGET
- 2,000-3,000 FEET DIRECTLY OVER TARGET
- WORK STRIKE AIRCRAFT DIRECTLY UNDER YOU
- STRIKE AIRCRAFT CAN VARY ATTACK HEADING

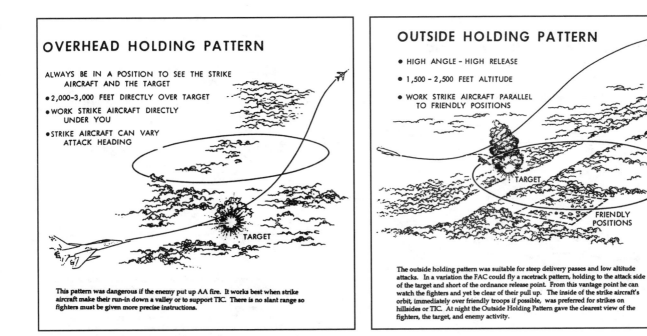

TARGET

This pattern was dangerous if the enemy put up AA fire. It works best when strike aircraft make their run-in down a valley or to support TIC. There is no slant range so fighters must be given more precise instructions.

OUTSIDE HOLDING PATTERN

- HIGH ANGLE - HIGH RELEASE
- 1,500 - 2,500 FEET ALTITUDE
- WORK STRIKE AIRCRAFT PARALLEL TO FRIENDLY POSITIONS

TARGET

FRIENDLY POSITIONS

The outside holding pattern was suitable for steep delivery passes and low altitude attacks. In a variation the FAC could fly a racetrack pattern, holding to the attack side of the target and short of the ordnance release point. From this vantage point he can watch the fighters and yet be clear of their pull up. The inside of the strike aircraft's orbit, immediately over friendly troops if possible, was preferred for strikes on hillsides or TIC. At night the Outside Holding Pattern gave the clearest view of the fighters, the target, and enemy activity.

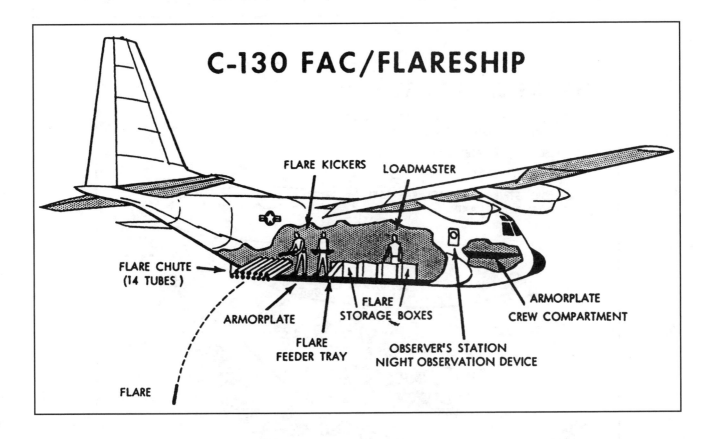

C-130 FAC/FLARESHIP

FLARE KICKERS

LOADMASTER

FLARE CHUTE
(14 TUBES)

ARMORPLATE

FLARE
STORAGE BOXES

FLARE
FEEDER TRAY

OBSERVER'S STATION
NIGHT OBSERVATION DEVICE

ARMORPLATE
CREW COMPARTMENT

FLARE

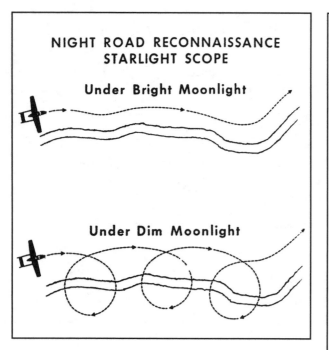

NIGHT ROAD RECONNAISSANCE STARLIGHT SCOPE

Under Bright Moonlight

Under Dim Moonlight

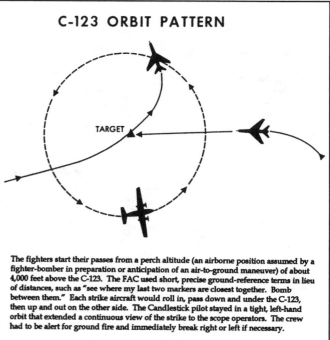

C-123 ORBIT PATTERN

TARGET

The fighters start their passes from a perch altitude (an airborne position assumed by a fighter-bomber in preparation or anticipation of an air-to-ground maneuver) of about 4,000 feet above the C-123. The FAC used short, precise ground-reference terms in lieu of distances, such as "see where my last two markers are closest together. Bomb between them." Each strike aircraft would roll in, pass down and under the C-123, then up and out on the other side. The Candlestick pilot stayed in a tight, left-hand orbit that extended a continuous view of the strike to the scope operators. The crew had to be alert for ground fire and immediately break right or left if necessary.

FIGURE EIGHT PATTERN

STRIKE AIRCRAFT AND TARGET CAN BE
KEPT IN SIGHT AT ALL TIMES

- 1,500 – 2,500 FEET ALTITUDE AGL
- 120 – 150 KNOTS
- WORK STRIKE AIRCRAFT PARALLEL
  TO LONG AXIS

TARGET

This pattern gave the FAC a wider view of the target area because he was more frequently pointed toward it.

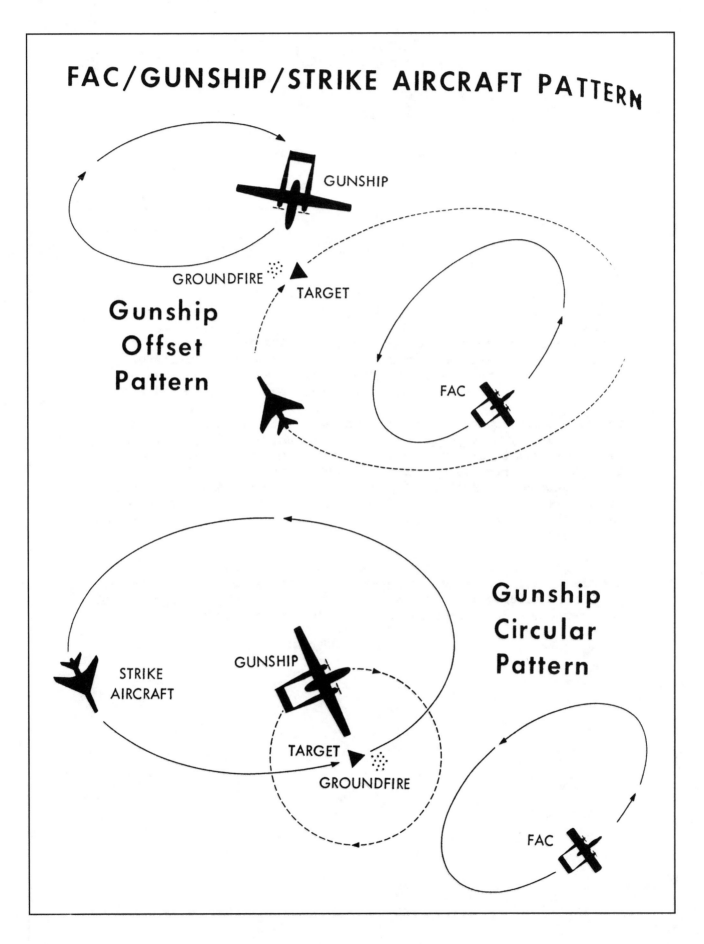

Appendix D

Munitions

MUNITIONS

The FAC must properly match the ordnance to the target, whenever possible. Plan carefully for the most efficient distribution of the ordnance. Know what the blast effects are, the effective area coverage of ordnance and the minimum safe distance for protected troops.

Normally when requesting ordnance for an airstrike, tell your radio operator what you <u>do not want</u>; i.e., "I do not want CBU," etc. Most fighter aircraft carry a standard load of bombs and napalm. Occasionally, you will receive aircraft with CBU or rockets, besides the regular bombs and napalm. If you specify certain ordnance, it will take extra time to unload and reload the fighter. This may cause the fighter to arrive too late to be used effectively on your immediate target.

If a fighter should arrive with some pieces of ordnance that are not applicable to your target; such as CBU and your target is located in a heavily foliaged area, do not waste it but have the fighter retain it. Perhaps a FAC somewhere else can use this particular ordnance.

ROCKET LOADING PROCEDURES AND DEMONSTRATION

1. Safety Precuations:

    a. Rocket arming switches - off.

    b. Trigger safety pin - installed.

    c. Rocket safety pins - installed.

2. Installing rocket into tubes:

    a. Motor head screwed in tight and tail grounding wire clip removed.

    b. Water tank and first aid equipment nearby.

    c. Grounding of rocket against launcher tube.

    d. Insertion of rocket with fins in horizontal and vertical planes.

When external ordnance has been loaded, preflight will insure that arming switches are off and safety pins are installed.

Arming will be accomplished in an area clear of other aircraft and with the aircraft pointing away from populated areas. Pilot's hands should be outside the cockpit.

O-1 INTERIOR CHECK:

1. Safety belt and shoulder harness.

2. Interphone control box switches and functions.

3. Control stick - how to install/remove.

4. Rudder pedals - how to raise/lower.

COMMUNICATIONS:

1. Radio discipline.

2. Mandatory calls:

    a. Report airborne to radio operator.

    b. Check on local Sector artillery fire.

    c. Check on U.S. artillery fire if near firing site.

    d. Confirm target coordinates to radio operator before conducting an airstrike.

    e. After an airstrike, confirm that radio operator has copied the BDA.

    f. Periodic position reports if on VR or escort mission.

    g. Close out with the radio operator before landing.

Appendix E

Forward Air Control Communications Systems

GENERAL STRIKE CHECKLIST

1. After takeoff, make radio contact with the Direct Air Request Net.

2. Coordinate rendezvous location and working frequency.

3. Find the target; note limits; note friendly positions; note safe bail-out area.

4. Plan the airstrike (inbound and breakaway restrictions).

5. Make radio contact with strike aircraft.

6. Give directions for rendezvous.

    a. Get information from strike aircraft.

        (1) Number and type aircraft

        (2) Frag order mission number

        (3) Ordnance load

        (4) Bingo time

        (5) Altitude and present position

    b. Give information to strike aircraft

        (1) Nature of target

        (2) Weather and winds

        (3) Height of terrain

        (4) Nearest friendly positions

        (5) Best bail-out position or heading

        (6) Anticipated ground fire

7. Complete visual rendezvous/enter target area.

8. Specific briefing on target (re-brief as necessary); restrictions on inbound-pass and breakaway.

9. Mark target

20

SECTION B - Atch 2
Pg 1 of 2

10. Direct airstrike

11. BDA

    a. Target coordinates

    b. Percent target coverage

    c. Itemize destruction

    d. Time on/off target

    e. Remarks

21

References and
Further Reading

Adcock, Al. *O-1 Bird Dog in Action*. Carrollton, TX: Squadron Signal Publications, 1988.

Air Facilities Data Laos. TX: K & S Militaria, n.d.

Anderson, William C. *BAT-21*. NJ: Prentice-Hall, 1980.

Andrade, Dale. *Trial By Fire*. New York: Hippocrene Books, 1995.

Bell, Dana. *Air War Over Vietnam. Volumes I, II, III, IV*. London: Arms and Armour Press, 1982, 1983, 1984.

Berent, Mark. *Rolling Thunder*. New York: G. P. Putnam's Sons, 1989.

_____. *Steel Tiger*. New York: G. P. Putnam's Sons, 1990.

_____. *Phantom Leader*. New York: G. P. Putnam's Sons, 1991.

_____. *Storm Flight*. New York: G. P. Putnam's Sons, 1993.

_____. *Eagle Station*. New York: G. P. Putnam's Sons, 1992.

Berry, F. Clifton. *The Illustrated History of the Vietnam War - Strike Aircraft*. Toronto, New York: Bantam Books, n.d.

Butler, Jimmie H. *A Certain Brotherhood*. Colorado Springs, CO: Cricket Press, 1996.

Castle, Timothy N. *At War in the Shadow of Vietnam: U. S. Military Aid to the Royal Lao Government 1955-1975*. New York: Columbia University Press, 1993.

Chinnery, Philip D. *Any Time, Any Place*. Annapolis, MD: Naval Institute Press, 1994.

Cleveland, W. M. *Mosquitos in Korea*. Portsmouth, NH: Peter E. Randall, 1991.

Conboy, Kenneth. *Shadow War, The CIA's Secret War in Laos.* Boulder, CO: Paladin Press, 1995.

_____. *War in Laos, 1954-1975.* Carrollton, TX: Squadron/Signal Publications, 1994.

Congressional Medal of Honor Library. *Vietnam, The Names, The Deeds.* New York: Dell Publishing Co., 1984.

Currey, Cecil B. *Victory at Any Cost.* Washington, D.C.: Brassey's, 1997.

Davidson, Lieutenant General Philip B. (USA, Ret.) *Vietnam at War.* Novato, CA: Presidio Press, 1988.

Davis, Larry. *Gunships.* Carrollton, TX: Squadron Signal Publications, 1982.

Dorr, Robert F. *Vietnam: The Air War.* London: Osprey Aerospace, 1991.

Drury, Richard S. *My Secret War.* Fallbrook, CA: Aero Publishers, 1979.

Fall, Bernard. *Street Without Joy.* Harrisburg, PA: Stackpole Co., 1961.

Flanagan, John F. *Vietnam Above the Treetops.* New York: Dell Publishing, 1992.

Francillon, Rene J. *Vietnam — The War in the Air.* New York: Arch Cape Press, 1987.

Futrell, Robert F. *The United States in Korea 1950-1953.* Washington, D.C.: 1983.

Gurney, Colonel Gene. *Vietnam The War in the Air.* New York: Crown Pub., 1985.

Hamilton-Merritt, Jane. *Tragic Mountains.* Bloomington: Indiana University Press, 1993.

Harrison, Marshall. *A Lonely Kind of War.* Novato, CA: Presidio Press, 1989.

_____. *The Delta.* Novato, CA: Presidio Press, 1992.

Karnow, Stanley. *Vietnam.* New York: Viking Press, 1983.

Kelly, Orr. *From A Dark Sky.* Novato, CA: Presidio Press, 1996.

Marshall, S. L. A. *West to Cambodia and The Fields of Bamboo.* New York: Doubleday, 1971.

Mesko, Jim. *VNAF South Vietnamese Air Force 1945-1975.* Carrollton, TX: Squadron Signal Publications, 1987.

Middleton, Drew. *Air War Vietnam.* New York: Arno Press, 1978.

Nalty, Bernard and Watson, George M., and Jacob Neufeld. *An Illustrated Guide to the Air War Over Vietnam.* New York: Arco Publishing, 1981.

Nichols, Commander John B. (USN, Ret.) *On Yankee Station.* Annapolis, MD: United States Naval Institute, 1987.

Norton, Bruce H. *Force Recon Diary, 1969.* New York: Ballantine Books, 1992.

Ohlrich, Walt and Ethell, Jeff. *The Incredible T-6, A Pilot Maker.* Osceola, WI: Specialty Press, 1983.

Parker, Jr., James E. *Codename Mule.* Annapolis, MD: United States Naval Institute, 1995.

Plaster, John L. *SOG The Secret Wars of America's Commandos in Vietnam.* New York: Simon & Schuster, 1997.

Politella, Dario. *Operation Grasshopper.* Wichita, KS: R. Longo Co., 1958.

Pratt, John Clark. *The Laotian Fragments.* New York: Avon Books, 1985.

_____. *Vietnam Voices.* New York: Penguin Books, 1984.

Reinberg, Linda. *IN THE FIELD: The Language of the Vietnam War.* New York: Facts on File, 1991.

Ridgway, Matthew B. *The Korean War.* New York: Da Capo Press, Inc., 1967, 1986.

Robbins, Christopher. *The Ravens.* New York: Crown Pub., 1987.

Robinson, Anthony, ed. *Weapons of the Vietnam War.* Greenwich, CT: Bison Books, 1983.

Sheehan, Neil. *A Bright Shining Lie.* New York: Random House, 1988.

Shiel, Walt. *Cessna Warbirds.* Iola, WI: Jones Pub. Co., 1995.

Simpson, Howard R. *Dien Bien Phu.* Washington, D.C.: Brassey's, 1994.

_____. *Tiger in the Barbed Wire.* Washington, D.C.: Brassey's, 1992.

Stanton, Shelby L. *The Rise and Fall of an American Agency.* Novato, CA: Presidio Press, 1985.

Stoffey, Bob. *Cleared Hot!* New York: St. Martin's Press, 1992.

Takeda, Masahiko, ed. *Airwar Over Vietnam.* Tokyo, Japan: Kesaharu Imai, 1984.

Tolson, John J., Lieutenant General. *Airmobility in Vietnam.* New York: Arno Press, 1981.

Tourison, Sedgwick. *Secret Army Secret War.* Annapolis, MD: United States Naval Institute, 1995.

Trotti, John, USMC. *Phantom Over Vietnam.* Novato, CA: Presidio Press, 1984.

Turley, Colonel G. H. (USMCR, Ret). *The Easter Offensive.* Novato, CA: Presidio Press, 1985.

Warner, Roger. *Back Fire.* New York: Simon & Schuster, 1995.

_____. *Out of Laos.* Ipswich, MA.

Wetterhahn, Ralph. "Escape to U. Taphao," *Air & Space*, Dec. 1996/Jan. 1997, p. 36-43.

Whitcomb, Colonel Darrel D. *The Rescue of BAT 21.* Fairfax, VA: Unpublished manuscript, 1996.

"World War 3.1, The Shape of Things to Come," *Forces ASAP*, Oct. 7, 1996.

Yarborough, Colonel Tom. *Da Nang Diary.* New York: St. Martin's Press, 1990.

U. S. Government Publications

Air-Ground Teamwork on the Western Front. Washington, D.C.: Headquarters, Army Air Forces, 1944.

Air Power in Three Wars (WWII, Korea, Vietnam), by

General William Momyer, USAF, Ret., 1978. Washington, D.C.: U.S. Government Printing Office, 1983.

Air Power and the Fight for Khe Sanh. Bernard C. Nalty, 1973. Maxwell AFB, AL, 1979.

Airpower and the Airlift Evacuation of Kham Duc, by Lieutenant Colonel Alan L. Gropman. Maxwell AFB, AL, 1979.

Air Force Heroes in Vietnam, compiled by Major Donald K. Schneider. Washington, D.C.: U.S. Government Printing Office, 1979.

Airpower and the 1972 Spring Invasion, compiled by Major A. J. C. Lavalle. Washington, D.C.: U.S. Government Printing Office. 1976.

Command and Control and Communications Structures in Southeast Asia, by Lieutenant Colonel John J. Lane, Jr., 1981.

The United States Air Force in Korea 1950-1953, rev. ed., Washington, D.C.: U.S. Government Printing Office, 1983.

USAF — Search and Rescue in Southeast Asia, 1961-1975.

USAF FAC Operations in Southeast Asia 1961-1965, by Major Ralph A. Rowley. 1972.

The United States Air Force in Southeast Asia — THE ADVISORY YEARS to 1965, by Robert F. Futrell, 1981.

The United States Air Force in Southeast Asia 1961-1973 — An Illustrated Account, ed. by Carl Berger. 1984.

The United States Air Force in Southeast Asia — DEVELOPMENT AND EMPLOYMENT OF FIXED-WING GUNSHIPS 1962-1972, by Jack S. Ballard, 1982.

USAF Manuals

Operational Training Course, O2/OV-10. Tactical Air Command Syllabus, 1982.

O-2 Operational Procedures. Tactical Air Command, 1974.

O-2 Pilot. Tactical Air Control, 1968.

Welcome to 20th TASS. Tactical Air Support Squadron, 1969.

The Airborne Forward Air Controller. Training Manual for the 4410th Combat Crew Training Squadron, Holley Field, FL, 1968.

Annotated Bibliography of the United States Marine Corps Concept of Close Air Support. Washington, D.C., 1968.

FAC Sheet, 22 Tactical Air Command Air Support Squadron, Aug. 1968, Sept. 1968.

Forward Air Controllers Training Prospectus. May 1969.

O-1 Phase Training Manual for the 4410th Combat Crew Training Wing, Apr. 1967.

Flight Manual — L-19A, L-19E, TL-19A, TL-19E, OE-1. USAF Series. Olmsted AFB, July 1959.

DOD Evasion Chart, EVC 500-1 (S.E.A.). Laos, Thailand, Vietnam. 2nd edition, March 1968.

DOD Evasion Chart, EVC 250-3 (S.E.A.). Laos, Vietnam. 2nd edition, February 1968.

Flight Manual, O-2A and O-2B, USAF Series, 1971.

Flight Manual, OV-10A, USAF Series, 1969.

Flight Manual, Performance Data, OV-10A, USAF Series, 1969.

Glossary

— A —

Aircraft Designations:

A = Attack.

AC = gunship and flareship.

B = Bomber.

C = Cargo.

E = Electronics.

F = Fighter.

HC = modified for in-flight helicopter refueling.

L = Liaison.

O = Observation.

P = Pursuit.

R = Reconnaissance.

A-1

Douglas Skyraider, single-engine reciprocating strike aircraft developed by Douglas at the close of WWII. Categorized as a slow mover, it had tremendous endurance, 8,000 pounds of external ordnance-carrying capability, and four forward-firing 20mm cannon.

A-4

McDonnell Douglas Skyhawk jet aircraft.

A-6

Grumman Intruder jet aircraft.

A-7

Vought Corsair II, single-engine, single-seat, all-weather, light attack aircraft.

A-26

Douglas Invader strike aircraft of the 56th SOW, Nakhon Phanom (designated as B-26 in Korean War).

A-37

Cessna Dragonfly jet aircraft developed from T-37 for counterinsurgency operations.

AC-47

Douglas C-47 transport converted into a gunship by adding the General Electric SUU-IIA minigun. The AC-47 had several nicknames: *Puff the Magic Dragon*, *Dragon Ship*, and *Spooky*.

AC-119G

Fairchild Flying Boxcar gunship with call sign *Shadow*.

AC-130

Gunship with call sign *Spectre*, modified with sensor equipment and armament.

AH-1

Bell Aircraft Company Cobra attack helicopter.

AA

Antiaircraft.

AAA

Antiaircraft Artillery.

AB

Air Base.

ABCCC

Airborne Command and Control Center (*also* Airborne Battlefield Command and Control Center). Usually a C-130 deployed in support of out-country air operations, it was an extension of Seventh Air Force Command Center. Pronounced AB triple C.

ACS

Air Commando Squadron.

ACW

Air Commando Wing.

ADF

Automatic Direction Finder that automatically and continuously measures the direction of arrival of the received signal, data usually displayed visually, not reliable in or around thunderstorms.

A FAC

Fighter Qualified Forward Air Controller.

AFB

Air Force Base.

AGL

Above Ground Level.

AGOS

Air-Ground Operations School.

AGCP

Air-Ground Control Party. (In WWII, Air-Ground Cooperation Party.)

Air

Fighter/bombers for an airstrike; air power.

Air Commando

An Air Force member engaged in counterinsurgency operations.

Air Force Cross

America's second-highest medal for bravery, awarded in the name of the President for extraordinary heroism while engaged in an action against the enemy.

ALPHA STRIKE

A preplanned ROLLING THUNDER mission against a specific target in North Vietnam.

Alleycat

The EC-130 ABCCC at night in the BARREL ROLL and northern STEEL TIGER areas, and the panhandle of North Vietnam. Also the OPERATION.

AK-47

Soviet Avtomat Kalashnikova 1947 automatic assault rifle, with 7.62mm bullets, used by the North Vietnamese.

ALO

Air Liaison Officer.

AO

Area of Operations.

AOB

Air Order of Battle.

AOC

Air Operations Center. Prior to 1961 known as Joint Operations Center. Subsequent to 1965 known as Tactical Air Control Center.

Angels

Feet of altitude.

APC

Armored Personnel Carrier.

ARC LIGHT

B-52 Operation begun in June 1965.

ARVN

Army of the Republic of Vietnam.

— B —

B-26

Douglas Invader strike aircraft used during the Korean War (designated as A-26 during the Vietnam War).

B-52

Boeing Stratofortress used by Strategic Air Command (designed to deliver nuclear bombs), with a range of 7,500 miles (unrefueled), used for tactical bombing.

B-57

Martin Canberra strike jet aircraft.

Backseater

Native Hmong officer who flew in backseat of O-1 to validate targets to the *Ravens*, and to authorize strikes. They were a trained corps in General Vang Pao's forces.

B FAC

Nonfighter qualified FAC.

BDA

Bomb Damage Assessment.

Bingo

Fuel or time to return to base, based on the amount of fuel required to return to base and alternate airfield.

Bird Dog

O-1 FAC aircraft.

Blackjacks

Long-range, mobile, guerrilla recce patrols.

Black Pony

Navy OV-10 aircraft patrolling canals and rivers in the Mekong Delta.

Black Passport

A passport allowing carrier to move freely through an area — similar to a diplomatic red passport.

Blindbat

Nickname of C-130 FAC/flareship aircraft operating in southern Laos, eventually BLINDBAT became name for all AC-130 flare missions. (See LAMPLIGHT.)

BLU

Bomb Live Unit. Refers to various ordnance, such as bomblets dropped from dispensers and special purpose bombs.

Blue Chip

Call sign of Seventh Air Force operations in Saigon.

Box Pattern

Fighter attack pattern on a target, with base and final legs always the same.

Break

A rapid roll maneuver.

Buy the farm

An expression indicating death, usually in a plane crash.

— C —

C-7

Canadian-built DeHavilland DHC-4 Caribou, a STOL twin-engine tactical transport, designated C-7 when transferred to USAF.

C-47

Douglas twin-engine aircraft. See AC-47.

C-119

Fairchild Flying Boxcar twin-boom transport.

C-121

Lockheed Super Constellation. EC-121 Warning Star was fitted with special electronics communications equipment.

C-123

Fairchild Provider cargo and transport aircraft.

C-130

Lockheed Hercules cargo transport aircraft.

C-131

Convair Samaritan used as an airborne hospital.

CH-34

Sikorsky Choctaw S-58 helicopter equipped with a four-blade main rotor and a tail stabilizer rotor. Also designated H-34.

CH-47

Boeing Chinook twin-turbine helicopter with two three-blade tandem rotors.

CH-53

Sikorsky large, twin-turbine helicopter with a single six-blade main rotor and a four-blade stabilizing tail rotor; Jolly Green Giant.

C and C

Command and Control.

CAR-15

Submachine-gun version of the M-16 rifle, with folding stock and shortened barrel.

Call Sign

Identifying words assigned to an aircraft, ship, unit, facility, etc., for radio communications.

Candlestick

Call sign for C-123 B/K Provider FAC/flareship aircraft in Laos.

CAS

Consolidated American Sources. Code name for the CIA in Laos; *also* close air support.

CASI

Continental Air Services, Inc., earlier called Bird & Sons. Code name for CIA airline.

CBU

Cluster Bomb Unit. Bombs composed of multiple smaller bombs in a single container. The smaller bomblets can be of many types, containing high explosives (HE) or white phosphorus (WP). They dribbled out of the tubes with little wing-like vanes helping them to float down. If released too high, they would drift away from the target. If released too low, they would not arm.

CCTC

Combat Crew Training Center.

CCTS

Combat Crew Training Squadron.

CIA

Central Intelligence Agency.

CIDG

Civilian Irregular Defense Group.

CINCPAC

Commander-in-Chief, Pacific Command.

"Cleared In Hot"

Fighter pilot could not drop bombs or fire his guns without first getting this clearance from the FAC.

CO

Commanding Officer.

COMMANDO HUNT

Air campaign for constant air umbrella over 2,000 square miles of the Ho Chi Minh Trail, including STEEL TIGER in the southern panhandle of Laos. Flown by Da Nang *Coveys*: O-2s at night, OV-10s by day.

COMMANDO SABRE

Operations begun in June 1967 to test jet aircraft in the FAC role. The F-100 was used to replace slower FAC aircraft in higher threat areas.

Continental Air Service

Privately owned air operation in Laos under contract to U.S. agencies, including CIA and USAID. See CASI.

Covey

Call sign of O-2 and OV-10 FACs, 20th Tactical Air Support Squadron, operating in North and South Vietnam and Laos.

Covey **Rider**

Experienced Special Forces member who flew with *Covey* FACs to help direct airstrikes and insert and extract Special Operations Group.

CRICKET

Operations in Laos of O-1E and AC-47 FAC aircraft and the C-130 ABCCC (*Cricket*) in northern Laos during the day (redesignated *Alleycat* at night).

— D —

Daisy Cutter

Mk-82 (500-pound HE) or Mk-84 (2,000-pound HE) bombs with fuze extenders, designed to explode at the surface to kill personnel, damage matériel, and to defoliate.

DANIEL BOONE

Special Operations Group code name for an Operation in Cambodia.

DASC

Direct Air Support Center (new name for ASOC subsequent to 1965).

DASH-1

A manual of operating procedures for a particular aircraft.

DFC

Distinguished Flying Cross.

DISUM

Daily Intelligence Summary.

DME

Distance Measuring Equipment.

DMZ

Demilitarized Zone.

DO

Director of Operations.

Drags

Drogue-retarded or parachute-dropped ordnance.

Dry Pass

An orientation pass with no ordnance drop.

Dust-off

Medical evacuation helicopter.

— E —

EB-66

Douglas Destroyer electronic-warfare aircraft.

E&E

Escape and Evasion.

ECM

Electronic Countermeasures.

Elephant FAC

Ground FAC team with English-speaking personnel; it could communicate both ground-to-air and ground-to-ground.

Extraction

Withdrawal of troops by air, usually helicopter.

Eyeball

Reconnaissance by sight rather than radar and reconnaissance sensors.

Eyeglass Scope

A Night Observation Device, also called Starlight Scope, that could compensate for motion of targets. Used on gunships, this direct-viewing scope detected targets by intensifying images through use of ambient (surrounding) moonlight or starlight.

— F —

F-4

McDonnell Douglas Phantom II strike aircraft. Also called Fox Fours. Several tons heavier than the F-100, it carried three times the ordnance. The F-4 had a backseater to call out altitude, airspeed, and dive angle. The F-4D had no built-in cannon. The F4-E had a Gatling-style gun slung underneath that fired 6,000 rounds per minute. With multiple ejection racks, the F-4 could carry up to 16 Mk-82 500-pound bombs.

F4U

Chance Vought Corsair fighter aircraft.

F-51

The designation for the North American P-51 Mustang during the Korean and Vietnam Wars.

F-80

Lockheed Shooting Star jet aircraft.

F-100

North American Super Sabre jet aircraft.

F-105

Republic Thunderchief. Single-seat jet fighter-bomber armed with 20mm Gatling gun and 6,000 pounds of bombs. *Also* known as the "Thud."

FAC

Forward Air Controller; Forward Air Control.

FAG

Forward Air Guide. Directs fighters onto the targets from the ground.

FARM GATE

Replaced JUNGLE JIM in December 1961 as covert USAF mission to train VNAF personnel, who in 1962 and 1963 flew T-28s with USAF markings. FARM GATE "advisors" flew combat missions in III and IV Corps. In July 1963 the secret designation was removed. Detachment 2 became the 1st Commando Squadron (Composite) of the 34th Tactical Group, still using FARM GATE name.

Fast FACs

Pilots flying FAC missions in jet aircraft.

Fast-Movers

Jet strike aircraft such as F-100s, F-105s, F-4s, etc.; Fast FACs.

Feet Wet

Fly or bail out over water.

Firefly

Call sign of A-1s used for other than search and rescue missions.

Fish Hook

The protrusion of Cambodia into Military Region III.

Flak

Bursting shells fired from AA guns.

Flaming Arrow (*Also* Fire Arrow)

Used by the Special Forces when radio contact was lost, to point at the heaviest enemy concentrations. F-100 pilots were trained to obliterate anything 100 meters beyond the camp in the direction of the Arrow. Could be made of many materials, metal gas cans filled with gasoline-soaked sand were often used, and ignited. Easy to see at night, hamlet defenders relayed to strike/flare aircraft the enemy's position with reference to Arrow.

Flechette

Small steel dart used in bombs.

FLIR

Forward-Looking Infrared Radar. A system giving a visual spectrum display from infrared radiation. Readout is in real time on a "TV screen."

FLR

Forward-Looking Radar.

Flying Boxcar

Fairchild C-119 twin-boom transport aircraft.

FM

Frequency Modulation. Radios for air-to-ground in FAC aircraft, AC-47s, A-1s, and Army helicopters. Known as "Fox Mike," these low-frequency radios were limited in range and power and subject to atmospheric disturbances. Not installed in fighter aircraft. Close air support of Troops-In-Contact with the enemy was only mission needing FM.

FOB

Forward Operating Base.

FOL

Forward Operating Location.

"Fox Mike"

See FM.

Free-Fire Zone

Designated area that was completely under enemy control, thus permitting unlimited use of firepower against anyone or anything in the zone.

Friendlies

The troops fighting against the North Vietnamese and Viet Cong.

FS

Fighter Squadron.

FTT

Field Training Team.

— G —

G

The measure or value of the gravitational pull of the earth of a force required to accelerate or decelerate any freely movable body at the rate of about 32.16 feet per second. To pull 3 Gs means to be subjected to the force of three Gs.

GCA

Ground-Controlled Approach for aircraft, using radar. The ground controller gives the pilot horizontal and vertical instructions, keeping the pilot on a straight line to the duty runway with the correct rate of descent for a safe touchdown.

Geneva Accords

Signed by the French and Vietminh on 21 July 1954 to mark the end of the French Indochina War. Vietnam divided at the 17th Parallel.

GRADS

Ground Radar Aerial Delivery System.

Guard

Special radio frequency used by pilots for emergency conditions.

Gunship

Armed helicopter, C-47, C-119, or C-130. A tactical innovation in the Vietnam War used extensively over the Ho Chi Minh Trail.

— H —

H-19

Sikorsky's all-metal, semi-monocque fuselage helicopter with one metal three-blade main rotor and an all-metal two-blade anti-torque tail rotor. The engine was mounted in front.

H-21

Piaseki's all-metal, semi-monocque helicopter, with two three-blade, all-metal rotors arranged in tandem that turned in opposite directions.

H-34

See CH-34.

H-46

Boeing Vertol Sea Knight, U.S. Marine Corps assault helicopter with water landing and takeoff capability.

H-47

See CH-47.

H-53

Sikorsky Sea Stallion helicopter nicknamed the Jolly Green Giant. See CH-53.

HC-130P

Lockheed C-130 Hercules cargo aircraft modified for in-flight refueling of helicopters.

HH-43

Kaman Aircraft Corporation's Huskie, a twin-rotor, single-engine helicopter. Rotors were inter-meshing, counter-rotating, each with two blades, mounted side-by-side. Nicknamed Pedro, used for local-base crash rescue.

HU-1

Bell Huey helicopter.

Hammer

Call sign of FACs, 23rd TASS (augmented), operating over the Lam Son operations area of Laos. The *Hammers* operated out of Quang Tri.

HE

High-Explosive (iron bomb).

Helio-Courier

Short Takeoff and Landing (STOL) aircraft used by CIA in Laos.

Hillsboro

The EC-130 ABCCC in southern STEEL TIGER area during daylight hour (designated *Moonbeam* at night).

Hobo

Call sign of the 56th SCW A-1 aircraft operating in Laos from Nakhon Phanom Royal Thai Air Force Base, Thailand.

Hooch

Traditionally a long, one-story wooden building on stilts in jungle country to discourage cobras, with open sides and screens. Your dwelling or bunk; it could be hut, tent, or poncho. Alternate spelling hootch.

Huey

See HU-1 Bell Huey.

— I —

IFF

Identification, Friend or Foe, a method for deter-

mining the friendly or unfriendly character of an aircraft, by other aircraft and by ground forces using electronic detection equipment and associated IFF units.

IFR

Instrument Flight Rules.

Igloo White

A surveillance system consisting of hand-implanted and air-delivered seismic sensors, relay aircraft, and an infiltration surveillance center. The signals were relayed to Task Force Alpha in a big concrete building at Nakhon Phanom Air Base where they were analyzed to locate truck parks. Igloo White was formerly called Muscle Shoals.

IMC

Instrument Meteorological Conditions.

In-Country

That part of the Southeast Asia conflict within South Vietnam.

"In Hot"

Fighter cleared in, ready to fire.

Insertion

Placement of soldiers in Area of Operation by helicopter.

Interdiction

To cut or destroy an enemy's advance by firepower.

IP

Initial Point — a well-defined point, easily distinguished visually and/or electronically. Used as a starting point for the bomb run to the target; *also* Instruction Pilot.

— J —

Jinking

An aircraft maneuver in which a series of rapid turn reversals and abrupt changes of roll and/or pitch attitude at random intervals prevents an enemy gunner from tracking the aircraft.

JOC

Joint Operations Center.

Jolly Green Giant

USAF Sikorsky HH-53 rescue helicopter with armor plating and 7.62mm rapid-firing miniguns. HH-53 has external fuel tanks and is air-refuelable for longer range. (See CH-53.)

JSRC

Joint Search and Rescue Center.

JUNGLE JIM

Original covert training and reconnaissance program. Detachment 2 Alpha, an element of the 4400th CCTS was dispatched to Vietnam under the code name JUNGLE JIM.

— K —

Karst

Sheer rock formations often rising 1,500 to 2,000 feet above the surrounding terrain. Rocks contain limestone with sinks and abrupt ridges, irregular protuberant rocks, caverns, and underground streams.

KB-18

An attack camera for the F-4 that mounts in the missile well.

KC-135A

Boeing Stratotanker used for refueling.

KBA

Killed by Air.

KIA

Killed in Action.

KIAS

Knots Indicated Airspeed.

King

Call sign for Search and Rescue (SAR) coordinator in a C-130 controlling majority of search and rescues over Laos; call sign for 3rd Aerospace Rescue and Recovery Group with several squadrons of HC-130s and HH-53 Jolly Green helicopters. Motto: "That Others May Live."

Klick

Short for kilometer.

KMT

Kuomingtang mercenaries in Laos.

Knot

A speed of one nautical mile per hour. A nautical mile equals 6,076.115 feet or 1,852 meters.

— L —

L-4

Army liaison version of Piper J-3 Cub.

L-5

Stinson Sentinel developed for liaison and communication missions during WWII and used in Southeast Asian conflict.

L-19

Army liaison designation for Cessna O-1 Bird Dog.

Lam Son 719

Army of the Republic of Vietnam invasion of Laos between January and April 1971, supported by U.S. air power.

Lao

Laotian.

LARA

Light Armed Reconnaissance Airplane.

Laser

Light amplification by stimulated emission of radiation. Laser-guided bombs detect the reflected laser beam and follow it to the target. Used in Laos to hit caves with enemy supplies or troops.

LAU

Launching mechanism.

LAU-3

A rocket pod containing 19 2.75" rockets.

LAU-32

A rocket pod containing seven 2.75" rockets.

LAU-59

A lightweight, cylindrical, seven-tube, expendable rocket launcher; tubes were reusable.

Leaping Lena

U.S. Special Forces and indigenous forces who conducted long-range reconnaissance/interdiction missions. They acted as hunter/killer teams to conduct small search-and-destroy operations, initially in I and IV Corps. Leaping Lena became Delta in 1964.

LGB

Laser-Guided Bomb.

Lima Site

Aircraft landing sites (dirt strips) in Laos used as resupply points.

LLLTV

Low-Light-Level Television.

LOH

Light Observation Helicopter.

Long Tieng

Also Long Cheng. 20 Alternate. CIA secret forward staging area in Military Region (MR) II in support of General Vang Pao's forces from 1963 to 1975.

LP

Listening Post.

LORAN

Long Range Radio Navigation System, a navigation aid operating from very low-frequency radio transmissions from master and slave stations using the time divergence of pulse-type transmissions from two or more fixed stations.

LRP

Long-Range Patrol.

LRRP

Long-Range Reconnaissance Patrol.

LTD

Laser Target Designator.

LS

Landing Sites known as Lima Sites.

LZ

Landing Zone.

Luang Prabang

Ancient royal capital of Laos.

LUCKY TIGER

Project to introduce A-26 Invader attack planes into Thailand.

— M —

MA-2A

Rocket launcher.

MAAG
Military Assistance Advisory Group.

MACSOG
Military Assistance Command, Studies and Observation Group.

MACV
Military Assistance Command, Vietnam.

MAP
Military Assistance Program.

MAW
Marine Air Wing.

Mayday
International distress signal used by aircraft and ships.

Menu
Collective code name for series of covert bombings of Cambodia between March 1969 and May 1970, such as Breakfast, Lunch, Dinner, Snack, Supper, and Dessert.

MGF
Mobile Guerrilla Force.

MIA
Missing In Action.

Mike Force
Mobile Strike Force: 500-men formations divided into three companies.

Misty
Call sign for F-100 FACs flying out of Phu Cat and Tuy Hoa Air Bases, Republic of Vietnam.

Misty **Bronco**
OV-10 Southeast Asia Test and Evaluation project.

Mk-24
Flares.

Mk-61
Flares.

Mk-82 Streamlined bombs with M904 fuze
Bomb set to detonate on contact or with several seconds' delay. Will penetrate concrete bunkers or bridges.

MLT
Mobile Launch Team.

Mm
Millimeter.

Monkey Mountain
A powerful communications and radar site northeast of Da Nang on a rocky, jungle-covered peninsula jutting into the South China Sea.

Moonbeam
The EC-130 ABCCC in Laos (STEEL TIGER at night). *Moonbeam*'s frequencies changed every day.

Mosquito
Call sign and nickname for North American T-6 FAC aircraft flown in Korean War.

MR
Military Region.

MSL
Mean Sea Level.

MSQ
Mobile Search Special.

MTI
Moving Target Indicator.

— N —

Na Khang
Lima Site 36, forward staging area for USAF SAR Operations for downed U.S. air crews.

Nail
Call sign for FACs, 23rd TASS, operating in Laos out of Nakhon Phanom Royal Thai Air Force Base.

Napalm
A petroleum jelly fire bomb. Usually released from 100 feet AGL in straight-and-level flight or from a dive at 450 KIAS.

Nape
Napalm.

NCO
Noncommissioned Officer.

NDB
Nondirectional Beacon.

Night Owl
Night combat operations in Southeast Asia. The delivery of ordnance by F-4s under their own flare illumination. Also call sign for Fast FACs of 497th TFS, Ubon Royal Thai AFB, Thailand.

Nimrod
Call sign for A-26 aircraft of the 56th SOW, Nakhon Phanom Royal Thai AFB, operating in Laos. The *Nimrod* pilots were qualified as FACs. Activated 11 June 1966 at Detachment 1 of the 603rd ACS (part of the 606th ACW).

NKP
Nakhon Phanom, a city and Royal Thai AFB in northeastern Thailand, nicknamed Naked Fanny.

NM
Nautical Mile.

NOD
Night Observation Device (Starlight Scope).

NVA
North Vietnamese Army.

NVN
North Vietnam.

— O —

O-1
FAC Cessna aircraft, named Bird Dog.

O-2A
FAC Cessna Super Skymaster aircraft nicknamed Duck, Oscar Duck, or Oscar Deuce.

O-2B

Cessna-built aircraft like O-2A but equipped for psychological warfare. Equipped to dispense leaflets and with loud-speaker system to talk to people on the ground.

OP-2E

Lockheed Neptune aircraft used for electronic observation.

OV-1

Grumman Mohawk.

OV-10

North American Rockwell Bronco, light combat aircraft used by FACs.

On-Station

Gunships or fast movers in position for mission or operation.

Ops

Operations.

Out-Country

That part of the Southeast Asia conflict outside South Vietnam, such as Laos, North Vietnam, and Cambodia.

— P —

P-63

Bell Aircraft King Cobra fighter-bomber.

PACAF

Pacific Air Forces.

Panel Code

A prearranged code for visual communication (most often air to ground) by use of marking panels on the ground (usually between friendly units).

Parrot's Beak

The tip of the Cambodian salient west of Saigon, South Vietnam.

Pathet Lao

The communist Lao guerrillas.

Pave Knife

First model of laser designator manufactured by Philco Ford. Went into service in the late 1960s.

Pave Low

Sikorsky MH-53HJ Project.

Pave Nail

Code name for night observation system using laser-guided bombs. Laser beams were pointed at the targets; the bombs locked onto the beams. Used in F-4s.

Pave Spike

Second-generation laser designator mounted in the left forward missile well of the F-4.

Pave Spot

Code name for a night observation device with bore-sighted laser target designator, used in OV-10.

Pave Way

The F-4 Phantom using various guidance devices:

Pave Way I (laser); Pave Way II (electro-optical); Pave Way III (infrared). Pave I was a 2,000-pound bomb, also known as "Papa Whiskey."

PCS

Permanent Change of Station.

PDJ

Plain of Jars, a critical military objective in northern Laos.

PEO

Program Evaluation Office.

Perch

An airborne position assumed by fighter-bomber aircraft in preparation for, or anticipation of, air-to-ground maneuvers.

Phou Pha Thi

Lime Site 85, an ultra-secret U.S. navigational site. Overrun in 1968 by NVN Army while guarded by the Hmong.

Pickle

Pilot releases ordnance (bomb load) by depressing the button on top of his control stick.

Pilatus Porter

Swiss-built STOL aircraft used by Air America and Continental Air Services.

PRAIRIE FIRE

MACV support reconnaissance commando (RE-CONDO) teams, normally organized to assess ground battle damage and locate lucrative targets for tactical airstrikes. They frequently worked behind enemy lines. Joint-service Intelligence-gathering project with small LRRPs. Indigenous troops (under MACSOG) were inserted by Special Forces teams. *Covey* pilots who flew this super-secret mission were not allowed to discuss it with anyone.

Press

To deliver below minimum safe altitudes or outside prescribed limits of speed, angle, etc.

PSP

Pierced-Steel Planking.

Puff the Magic Dragon

Built by Douglas, AC-47 with three 7.62mm guns that fire 6,000 rounds per minute. It carried 24,000 rounds of 7.62 ammo and 45 aerial flares of 200,000 candlepower. Also called *Spooky*. It first saw combat 15 December 1964 (day mission), first night mission 23-24 December 1964. The pilot used a sight on his side window to tilt the plane at the correct angle for guns to hit the target. See AC-47.

Pylon

A projection under the aircraft's wing from which to hang ordnance, fuel tanks, or ECM pods.

— R —

RB-57

General Dynamics-Martin reconnaissance bomber.

RB-66

Douglas Destroyer reconnaissance bomber.

RC-121

Lockheed Constellation. See C-121.

RF-4C

See F-4.

RF-101

McDonnell Voodoo fighter used for reconnaissance.

RAAF

Royal Australian Air Force.

RANCH HAND

Defoliation and herbicide operations of UC-123 aircraft. In January 1962, C-123 transport planes were modified into spray planes, flown by Air Commando crews at low level over parts of Laos, South Vietnam and the DMZ. They flew in four-ship formations to spray their Area of Operation.

R & R

Rest and Recuperation.

Raven

USAF FAC in Laos.

RCC

Rescue Coordinating Center.

Real Time

The absence of delay, except for the time required for the transmission by electromagnetic energy, between the occurrence of an event or reception of data at some other location.

Recce

Reconnaissance.

Reciprocal

Opposite in direction, said of a bearing, course, vector. A reciprocal bearing is the one taken, plus or minus 180 degrees.

Recon

Reconnaissance.

Red Crown

Code name for a U.S. Navy EC-130 for control with radar homing and warning equipment.

RESCAP

Rescue Combat Air Patrol.

Revetment

Pierced steel planking supporting walls of dirt; fortified area for aircraft protection.

RLAF

Royal Laotian Air Force.

Roadwatch

Roadwatch teams used hand-held truck counters (Hark 1), a survival radio redesigned with buttons for each type of military equipment, such as vehicle, artillery, or tank. Trail watchers pushed a button for each type seen. Data was relayed to aircraft overhead, which sent information to the 7/13th AF in Thailand.

Rockeye

A thermite bomb.

ROE

See Rules of Engagement.

ROLLING THUNDER

Bombing and interdiction campaign in North Vietnam to stop flow of supplies to South Vietnam. Off-again, on-again campaign was run from the White House. Targets chosen for political, not military, reasons. Conducted from 2 March 1965 to 31 October 1968.

ROMAD

Radio Operator/Maintenance/Driver.

Route Package (RP)

North Vietnam was divided into seven geographical areas to divide responsibility for operations between USAF, U.S. Army, and U.S. Navy; for example, RP-1.

RPG

Rocket-Propelled Grenade.

Rpm

Revolutions per minute.

RSU

Runway Supervising Unit.

RTAFB

Royal Thai Air Force Base.

RTB

Return to Base.

Rules of Engagement (ROE)

Directives issued by competent military authority delineating the circumstances under which U.S. forces will begin and/or continue combat engagement with other forces met. These were issued from 1965 on to all Vietnam-bound military personnel to minimize civilian casualties.

RVN

Republic of Vietnam.

RVNAF

Republic of Vietnam Armed Forces.

— S —

SAC

Strategic Air Command. Conducts long-range air operations in B-52 Stratofortress bombers against vital targets to destroy enemy's ability to wage war.

SAM

Surface-to-Air Missile.

Sandy

Call sign of the Douglas A-1 Skyraider search and rescue aircraft based at Nakhon Phanom.

SAR

Search and Rescue.

SCAR

Strike Control and Reconnaissance.

Scramble

To take off as quickly as possible (usually followed by course and altitude instructions).

Secondary

An explosion, after the main target has been hit, from unknown target.

SFG

Special Forces Group.

Shadow

Call sign of AC-119G Flying Boxcar gunship. First operational in December 1968.

SHINING BRASS

Cross-border reconnaissance into Laos and the DMZ in 1965; called PRAIRIE FIRE after 1 March 1967.

SIF

Selective Identification Feature.

Skycrane

Sikorsky S-64 helicopter used for military transport duties.

Skyraider

See A-1.

Slant Range

The line-of-sight distance between two points not at the same elevation.

SLAR

Side-Looking Airborne Radar.

Slick

A troop-carrying helicopter; also a low-drag weapon.

Slow-Movers

Relatively slow-moving strike aircraft (A-1, B-57, AC-119, AC-130).

SOG

Studies and Observations Group. A special covert warfare unit.

Sortie

One aircraft making one takeoff and landing to conduct a scheduled mission.

SOW

Special Operations Wing.

Special Forces

Military personnel called the Green Berets, with cross-training in basic military skills, organized into small multiple-purpose detachments. Mission is to train, organize, support indigenous forces in guerrilla warfare and counterinsurgency operations, and to conduct unconventional warfare operations.

Special Operations

Secondary or supporting operations which may be adjunct to various other operations, and for which no one service is assigned primary responsibility.

Spectre

Call sign of the AC-130 Hercules gunship, equipped with four 7.62mm miniguns, four 20mm cannons firing 2,500 HE incendiary shells per minute, Starlight Scope, FLIR, and SLAR. At first, O-2 pilots kept the gunships within the ROE while operating over Laos. In 1969, AC-130 pilots attended FAC school at Ubon; a crew was then designated as FAC-qualified.

Split-S

A maneuver combining a half-roll followed by an inverted half-loop, describing the lower half of the letter S. Used for rapid loss of altitude and reversal in direction of flight.

Spooky

Call sign of the AC-47 gunship (originally FC-47). Armed with three side-firing 7.62mm Gatling-style miniguns, and 45 flares of 200,000 candle-power.

Stall

A flight condition where the wings no longer generate enough lift to keep the airplane flying. Not an engine failure. Can be corrected with proper control inputs.

Starlight Scope

An image intensifier using reflected light from the stars or moon to identify targets.

STEEL TIGER

The geographic area in southern Laos designated by the Seventh Air Force to facilitate planning and operations. Term also refers to strikes in southern Laos against personnel and equipment coming from North Vietnam. Aerial interdiction in STEEL TIGER began 3 April 1965. No one could hit anything 200 meters from the Ho Chi Minh Trail without AIRA (Air Attaché to American Embassy, Vientiane, Laos) approval and FAC control. West of STEEL TIGER no one could hit anything without AIRA and *Nail* or *Raven* FAC.

Steve Canyon

Code word for covert FAC operations in Laos.

Street Without Joy

Highway 1.

STOL

Short Takeoff and Landing.

Sun Dog

23rd TASS flying over southern Cambodia.

Super Sabre

See F-100.

SUU-14A

Bomblet dispenser.

SVN

South Vietnam.

— T —

T-6

North American Texan two-seat aircraft used as a

WWII training plane and as an observation plane during the Korean and Southeast Asian Wars.

T-28

North American Trojan. Principal attack aircraft of Royal Laotian Air Force.

TF-9J

Grumman Cougar two-seat swept-wing version of Panther jet.

TAC

Tactical Air Command. Branch of USAF to coordinate air operations with ground forces against enemy combatants.

TAC(A)

Tactical Air Coordinator Airborne. A Marine/Navy term to describe the function of airborne strike control and FAC duties using a high-performance (Fast FAC) aircraft.

TAC air

A term used in Southeast Asia to encompass all aircraft sorties other than B-52 and strategic airlift.

TACAN

Tactical Air Navigation aid giving range and azimuth from the transmitter.

TACC

Tactical Air Control Center, joint USAF-VNAF center at Tan Son Nhut responsible for control of all air operations in South Vietnam and Seventh Air Force operations over North Vietnam and Laos.

TACP

Tactical Air Control Party.

TACS

Tactical Air Control System. The organization and equipment necessary to plan, direct, and control tactical air operations and to coordinate it with other services.

TALLY HO

Intensified interdiction campaign in southern Route Package 1 using O-2 FACs in the western mountains and F-100Fs in the eastern lowlands in 1966. TALLY HO also directed Navy gunfire against targets in North Vietnam with a Marine artillery spotter in the back seat. (Call sign *Tally Ho.*)

TASG

Tactical Air Support Group.

Task Force Alpha (TFA)

A filter point for sensitive information received under Igloo White/Commando Hunt, organized in 1967 at Nakhon Phanom, under Seventh Air Force.

TASS

Tactical Air Support Squadron.

TAWC

Tactical Air Warfare Center.

TDY

Temporary Duty.

Tet

The lunar holiday observed in Vietnam and other Asian countries.

TFW

Tactical Fighter Wing, consists of three tactical fighter squadrons.

Thud

See F-105.

TIC

Troops In Contact (with the enemy).

TIGER HOUND

Southern STEEL TIGER area south of 17° north latitude for FAC employment, 1965-1968. Redesignated STEEL TIGER South and its northern border moved southward.

TOC

Tactical Operations Center.

TOT

Time Over Target.

Tri-Border

Area west of Dak To, South Vietnam, at the convergence of Cambodia, Laos, and the South Vietnam borders.

TRW

Tactical Reconnaissance Wing.

— U —

U-6

DeHavilland Beaver later designated L-20, a large single-engine utility STOL aircraft.

U-17

Cessna 185 Skywagon with side-by-side seating. Greater range than O-1 but less useful as FAC aircraft.

UH-1

Bell Aircraft Iroquois helicopter, basically the same airframe as the HU-1 Huey.

UHF

Ultra High Frequency.

USAID

U.S. Agency for International Development.

— V —

VC

Viet Cong, Vietnamese Communists.

VFR

Visual Flight Rules.

VHF

Very High Frequency.

VMO

Marine Observation Squadron designation.

VNAF

Vietnamese Air Force.

VOR

VHF Omnirange for navigation.

VR

Visual Reconnaissance.

— W —

Water Pump

Air Commando Training Detachment 1, 56th SOG, Udorn, RTAFB, Thailand. Set up in March 1964 to train Laotian pilots to fly the AT-28 to support helicopter rescue operations. Also trained Hmong volunteer and Thai pilots.

Wheel Pattern

Fly in a circle around a target and roll in from random headings, in sequence.

Wingman

The pilot (and aircraft) who flies at the side and to the rear of the element leader.

Willie Pete

Nickname for white phosphorus smoke rockets.

Winchester

Out of ammunition.

Wind shear

A condition created by collision of winds from different directions.

Wolf

Call sign of daytime F-4 FACs assigned to the 8th TFW, Ubon Royal Thai AFB, Thailand. Flew day mission along Ho Chi Minh Trail.

WP

White Phosphorus; plasticized phosphorus munitions were used as marking rockets or bombs by FACs who directed airstrikes.

— Y —

Yak

A Russian-built fighter plane.

Yankee Station

Cruising area located 100 miles east of Da Nang in the South China Sea for Task Force 77 aircraft carriers flying ROLLING THUNDER missions against North Vietnam.

— Z —

ZPU

Twin or quad-barrel 23mm rapid-firing guns effective to 9,500 feet. A 37mm could shoot its clips of five to seven rounds up to a little over 13,000 feet. A good ZPU gun crew could track a fighter indicating 500 knots at a range of 1,000 meters.

Zorro

Call sign of the T-28 and A-1 aircraft assigned to the 56th SOW at Nakhon Phanom.

Index